In honor of
Dr. Thomas Bailey's
90th birthday 2007.

D1557147

Religious Diversity and the American Experience

Religious Diversity and the American Experience

A Theological Approach

by

TERRENCE W. TILLEY

and

LOUIS T. ALBARRAN

JOHN F. BIRCH

ERNEST W. DURBIN II

COLEMAN FANNIN

LORA M. ROBINSON

DANIEL E. MARTIN

MATTHEW G. MINIX

continuum

NEW YORK • LONDON

2007
The Continuum International Publishing Group Inc
80 Maiden Lane, New York, New York 10038

The Continuum International Publishing Group Ltd
The Tower Building, 11 York Road, London SE1 7NX

Continuum is a member of Green Press Initiative, a nonprofit program dedicated to supporting publishers in their efforts to reduce their use of fiber obtained from endangered forests. For more information, go to www.greenpressinitiative.org.
Printed in the United States of America

Library of Congress Cataloging-in-Publication Data

Religious diversity and the American experience : a theological
approach / Terrence W. Tilley ... [et al.].
    p. cm.
  Includes bibliographical references and index.
  ISBN-13: 978-0-8264-2794-6 (hardcover : alk. paper)
  ISBN-10: 0-8264-2794-4 (hardcover : alk. paper)
  ISBN-13: 978-0-8264-2795-3 (pbk. : alk. paper)
  ISBN-10: 0-8264-2795-2 (pbk. : alk. paper)
 1. United States—Religion—Congresses. 2. Religious pluralism—
United States—Congresses. I. Tilley, Terrence W. II. Title.

  BL2525.R4696 2007
  201'.5—dc22

                  2006036505

Contents

Acknowledgments

THIS BOOK IS THE JOINT PRODUCT OF A SEMINAR IN THE GRADUATE PROGRAM in theology at the University of Dayton, Winter Semester, 2006. The seminar members first of all acknowledge one another. We are thankful to one another for carefully reading the seminar's texts (all of which are discussed in this book), for creatively leading seminar sessions, for timely completion of writing assignments, and for thoughtful, good-spirited criticism of others' work. Without the camaraderie we developed as a seminar, this book would not have been possible.

Staff and graduate students at the Mater Dei Institute for Education, a college in the City University of Dublin, discussed and evaluated the ideas in chapters 2 and 3 in seminars with the seminar director in March 2006. We are grateful to Dermot Lane, rector, and Michael Drumm, dean, for facilitating those stimulating seminars. Professors Elizabeth A. Johnson and Maureen A. Tilley of Fordham University also graciously made helpful suggestions on some of the chapters.

Dr. Sandra Yocum Mize, chair of the Theology Department at the University of Dayton, and Marva Gray and Margaret McCrate, administrative assistants in the department, supported our work. They make it possible to do theology creatively at the University of Dayton.

We thank Dr. Tilley's graduate research assistant for the semester of the seminar, Timothy J. Furry, for his help with bibliography and other logistical support and his graduate assistant at Fordham, Maggie Meier, for help with proofreading. Matthew Minix toiled to bring together the references into a coherent list after the seminar's papers were submitted. We are especially grateful to our editor at Continuum, Frank Oveis, for his support, encouragement, and patience. It is a privilege to work with one of the best in the field.

As authors always are, we are deeply grateful to suffering relatives and supportive friends, far too many to list here. You know who you are. We couldn't have done it together had we not also been the beneficiaries of your love and patience.

A Note on Authorship

POSTMODERN DEBATES ON AUTHORSHIP SUGGEST THAT WE TRY TO BE CLEAR on the complex authorship of the book. The graduate student members of the seminar are responsible for the research, analysis, and initial writing of chapters 4 through 10. They have agreed to be recognized as coauthors of the chapters that bear their names and of the book. Terrence Tilley, an advanced student, is the lead author in that he directed the seminar, designed the research protocol, worked out the contract, assigned the chapters to the seminar members, was primary author of the first three chapters, and has cooperated in the rewriting and editing of chapters 4 through 10. All of the members of the seminar contributed material to and edited chapter 11; Tilley was the initial compiler. Some members of the seminar would not take one or two of the particular positions we take together or would formulate them differently were they working on an individually authored project, but all of the members of the seminar are in general agreement about the direction of the book.

Each seminar participant presented to the seminar at least one text for general discussion. Around midterm, Tilley submitted initial drafts of the first three chapters for the seminar to critique. The first three rules discussed in chapter 3 received their initial formulation from a presentation by Matthew Minix; the fourth rule emerged in discussion. The final formulation of the rules is Tilley's in light of the seminar's discussion of them.

In the final weeks of the seminar, initial drafts of chapters 4 through 10 were circulated for critical reading and discussion by all the seminar members. The participants then revised their essays and submitted them as their papers for the seminar; the director then rewrote them into chapters. The seminar met once more in the summer of 2006 to discuss and correct the penultimate version of the whole text. The director then revised the text in light of the discussion and submitted the final version to the publisher.

Texts with multiple authorship run the danger of being uneven. We have tried to address this problem by this extensive coauthorship process. We also note that unevenness in texts such as this may be a function of the terrain mapped as much as the map constructed. The practices of those who participate actively in multiple faith traditions are not similar to the theories of a classic inclusivist and cannot fairly be portrayed as if they were simply at different points on a line.

We have sought to be as careful and as accurate as possible. If we have erred in our discussion of any position, we apologize for those errors. We cannot hope we have written the perfect book, but we have sought to deepen one another's insights and correct one another's oversights. So we hope that our errors are minimal.

In our late capitalist, commodified culture, the real questions about authorship are, Who holds the copyright? and Who gets the royalties? To find the answer to the former, visit the copyright page. The answer to the latter is that the coauthors all agreed that whatever royalties this book generates are to be paid to the University of Dayton for the support of graduate students in theology.

Introduction

OVER THE LAST HALF CENTURY OR SO, THEOLOGIANS WORKING IN THE mainstream of Christian theology have transformed the landscape of Christian thinking about the diversity of religious traditions. The classic Christian view, that the maxim "outside the church, no salvation" entailed the damnation of all who did not accept Christian faith, was becoming increasingly untenable. Could God damn the six million Jews who died at the hands of the Nazis? Those victims did not have the traditional "exceptions" that were recognized in Catholic theology. As Europeans, they could not be said to be good people who God would save because they desired to do God's will despite the fact that they were invincibly ignorant of Christianity—the classic example of the isolated Chinese peasant who could know nothing of the Christian tradition did not seem to apply. Nor could they be construed as catechumens who desired to join the church but had died or been executed before they could. And they certainly did not fulfill a traditional Protestant demand that they accept Jesus Christ as their personal lord and savior.

The antithesis to such exclusivist attitudes is indifferentism, the belief that it doesn't really matter what one believes or which tradition shapes one's faith. The key thing is that one is a "good person." God then can save all, for religious affiliation doesn't matter. Yet such indifferentism is profoundly unsatisfactory to any who would take religious faith seriously. The emergence of such a view occurs as part of the eclipse of religious seriousness among the elite of Europe that began in earnest as a cultural phenomenon with the Enlightenment. For the religiously committed person, accepting indifferentism would be to deny the seriousness of religious commitment—something that seems "not compossible," that is, these are not a pair of attitudes that a person can coherently hold at the same time. One cannot coherently be both deeply committed to living in and living out a faith tradition and say that such commitment doesn't matter.

The Christian theologies of religions are not ordinarily construed as "post-Holocaust" theologies. Nonetheless, the increasing dissatisfaction with exclusivism *and* indifferentism emerges clearly only after World War II. For Roman Catholics, the promulgation of *Nostra Aetate* by the Second Vatican Council in 1965 is often reckoned as a watershed event in the treatment by Catholics of other faith traditions in general and Judaism in particular. But that declaration did not burst into being out of thin air. Decades of theological work, the action of Pope John XXIII in 1958 to revise the prayers of the Good Friday service that had rendered the Jews faithless traitors, and the increasing globalization of communication and culture are all part of the context for *Nostra Aetate*. But the cultural consciousness of the enormity of the *shoah* that began to emerge some fifteen years after the war is also part of the picture. We may not advert to that tragedy explicitly, but it is always at least implicitly present in Christian theological reflection—or should be.

The present book is not the first to trace the new patterns in Christian theology of religions. Alan Race (1983) and Paul Knitter (2002) offered two influential and useful surveys of the patterns. Race's threefold categorization has been widely criticized (see the survey by Perry Schmidt-Leukel [2005] that seeks to defend it from critics, but saves the triad only by making it so abstract as to be useless). Knitter grouped the variety of positions into four categories that portray the individual positions well but do not sufficiently acknowledge their diversity or account for crucial differences between foundationalist (typically liberal, philosophically grounded) and nonfoundationalist (postliberal, practice-centered) theologies. The present book offers a different, and, obviously, we think better approach that eschews simple categorizations.

Chapter 1 extends the work of Robert Schreiter (1985) and Tilley (2000). It is devoted to showing the significance of recognizing that all theology is constructed in particular locations. Influenced by a remark of our colleague William Portier, we use the term "sited theology." Chapters 2 and 3 respectively describe relevant factors in the cultural site and prescribe religious principles for constructing a mainstream Christian theology on this site. The principles in chapter 3 are derived from an analysis of historic and magisterial documents in the Roman Catholic tradition but represent what we see as an emerging consensus in mainstream Christianity. We are working in an explicitly Catholic context, but three of the eight coauthors live in and live out their faith in other strands of Christianity. We can and do work together in this Catholic context because the work is catholic as well as Catholic.

The central chapters of the book analyze what we see as an ongoing conversation among theologians about how we ought treat the problem and the promise of religious diversity.

Chapters 4 and 5 address "inclusivism," the view that the salvation wrought in and through Jesus Christ includes the salvation of those who are not explicitly Christian. Various forms of inclusivism are probably the "default position" for mainstream Christianity. The late Karl Rahner's classic position is often presented as if it were an ad hoc approach; we show how it is integral to his whole theology in chapter 4. Chapter 5 analyzes the more contemporary positions of the late Jacques Dupuis and of Gavin D'Costa; we show that these approaches, despite the reservations of some critics of Dupuis, fit the principles that Christians should recognize in accounting for religious diversity.

Chapter 6 discusses pluralist approaches. We glance at the work of Roger Haight but develop the thesis that a significant shift has occurred in Knitter's position. Although he is usually treated as a "pluralist" and continues to identify himself with this general approach (see Knitter, ed., 2005), his theology has evolved into a less foundationalist and more practice-centered approach, which he has dubbed "mutualism." This chapter details the differences between pluralism and mutualism and the difference this shift makes.

Chapters 7 and 8 detail the explicitly postliberal, nonfoundationalist approach that we call "particularism." Particularists focus on the issue of the opposing truth claims of diverse religious traditions, rather than the question of how God can save others. J. A. Di Noia and Paul Griffiths have developed particularist positions. Di Noia develops his position as an alternative to a foundationalist pluralism such as Rahner's. Griffiths has both inclusivists and pluralists in his sights. Sometimes castigated by their opponents as "exclusivists" of the worst sort (rarely, if ever, in print, of course), they have little in common, as chapter 7 shows, with the discarded exclusivism of the past. Chapter 8 presents Baptist theologian S. Mark Heim's developing form of radical particularism. Heim's work does not center on the issues of the truth of diverse traditions but asks how Christians could really affirm the particularity of each tradition. His answer is that we can think that God has provided diverse salvations for people shaped in the diverse traditions, rather than in some way denying the significance of the faith traditions by affirming that God grants all good people "Christian salvation."

Chapters 9 and 10 focus on two patterns that concern practice rather than theory, but do so in different ways. The comparative theology of scholars such as Jack Renard, Francis X. Clooney, and James Fredericks is the subject of chapter 9. Comparative theologians attempt to engage with, critically understand, and learn from other traditions. Comparative theologians eschew premature theorization in favor of discerning particular similarities and differences in practice and belief between traditions. Nonetheless, some more theoretically oriented scholars, for example Knitter and Griffiths, have made significant contributions to comparative theology. Chapter 10 deals with those who have internalized the conversations between traditions. If comparative theologians are "visitors to" or "resident aliens in" other religious traditions, others such as Raimundo Pannikar, Sallie King, and Roger Corless have "dual citizenship" in Christianity and in another tradition. This practice of multiple religious belonging is a radical and perhaps even dangerous undertaking. Multiple religious belonging may also seem to support the acceptability of the self-centered practice of "religious shopping" in a commodified culture (see pp. 38–41 below). Properly understood, however, it is an important, if esoteric, way for Christians to work with religious diversity much more as a promise than as a problem.

We are quite aware that our choice of exemplars is selective. Numerous others have contributed to these issues: Michael H. Barnes, Aloysius Pieris, Michael Amaladoss, Claude Geffré, Leonard Swidler, George Soares-Prabhu, and others make no significant appearance in these pages. We think that they have much to contribute to particular developments in the theology of religions, but time and space limit us in our choices. We have chosen those whose work has, for the most part, been widely discussed in the U.S. context. We think we have not omitted any significant issue or approach totally, but we recognize that our work might have been nuanced differently had we made other choices.

Most typologies of religious diversity have a key flaw. They implicitly treat the approaches to religious diversity as comparable and commensurable. That is, the positions can be compared to one another as a whole by measuring how well they treat the central issues of religious diversity. The problem is that the various approaches do not see the same issues and are concerned with different questions. Moreover, there is no umbrella category sufficiently detailed to be used as a standard of comparison for both foundationalist and nonfoundationalist theologies. Our view is that, finally, the approaches analyzed here are incommensurable. How, then, can we compare and evaluate them?

"Incommensurability" suggests that comparison and evaluation of these theologies is like the proverbial impossible attempts to compare apples and oranges or fruit flies and solar systems. To say that these positions are incommensurable simply means that there is no single umbrella concept to use in comparing them. However, one can always compare any *a* and any *b* with regard to a particular *x*. Specific apples and oranges can be compared and contrasted to each other *with regard to* their color, texture, sugar content, etc. As silly as it would be, we can compare and contrast solar systems and fruit flies *with regard to* their size, their water content, their life-span, etc. We can compare position *a* to an *x*, *b* to that *x*, *c* to that *x*, etc. We can then evaluate how each and all of them stand with regard to *x*.

We have chosen to compare each of these positions to two particular *x*'s. First, in each chapter, we have asked whether the positions fit the principles we derived in chapter 3. Do these positions fit the Christian tradition (explicitly in its Catholic form) reasonably well or are they in such tension with the tradition that they abandon one of the key principles? By engaging in this analysis, we can see how well or ill each works as a Christian theology. Second, in chapter 11 we ask how well each fits the actual site on which we construct a theology, the U.S. context, which we have discussed in chapter 2. Do these positions help overcome the deficiencies to which we are culturally prone? Would accepting them help deepen the strengths that we have as a religious community and as a culture? This is our second indirect comparison of the positions. If any or all of them are suitable as Christian theology (first question), then ought we advocate one or more of them as our theological stance here?

To say that we each emerged from the seminar with exactly the views that we held when we entered it would be false. Among other things, we have been delighted to find an unexpected convergence between the prescriptions of American sociologist Robert Wuthnow and the injunctions formulated by the Pontifical Council for Interreligious Dialogue in *Dialogue and Proclamation.* We have also come to appreciate positions we had not previously considered seriously. Finally, we have learned how the unrecognized divide between foundationalists and nonfoundationalists has impeded understanding and useful criticism.

Many modern philosophers and theologians are foundationalists. They presume that religious beliefs, to be rational, must have foundations in warranted philosophical positions, in premises that are so certain to be indefeasible (such as the Word of God for some theologians), or in irreducible experience. In dealing with religious diversity, foundationalists seek to construct a theory that provides "secure foundations" for interreligious dialogue.

Some recent philosophers and theologians have become nonfoundationalists. They presume that our practices need no foundation. One does not need a philosophical foundation for the view that there are other minds, for example, to show that other people we encounter are to be treated as subjects, rather than as objects. Nonfoundationalists find that the reasonableness or appropriateness of our practices is shown in and through engagement in those practices. No foundational argument is needed to show that practicing chemistry is reasonable and practicing phrenology is not. Rather, the work of chemists and phrenologists show the (un)reasonableness of the practices, and the practices of religious folk shows the significance and worth of the practices.

Nonfoundationalists in theology claim that religious beliefs are not foundations for, but constituents of, religious practice. One does not have to prove that God exists to engage in the practice of prayer reasonably and appropriately or that "lucky stars" exist to engage in the practice of thanking them. Nonfoundationalists do not try to show that there is common ground among religious traditions in order for interreligious dialogue to occur. One simply begins talking with others about something that is of concern to both, e.g., neighborhood crime. Both exploration of the meaning of practice and belief and criticism of practice and belief emerge from engaging in the practice.

Foundationalists assume that theory grounds practice/praxis and nonfoundationalists find that theory is an outgrowth of practice/praxis. Foundationalists fault nonfoundationalists for neglecting foundational issues. Nonfoundationalists point out that foundationalists are engaging in a practice of philosophical argument and ask how the interminable quest for foundations is not a waste of energy. But what they actually do is to construe the relationship of practice to theory differently. That a number of theologians of religious diversity have not attended to this difference has led to misunderstandings.

We have come to see how important it is to acknowledge these differences and to recognize that theologies of religious diversity work with different questions, engage in diverse practices, and seek different goals. We seek to portray that variety clearly in this book.

The work we have done together has at least nuanced our judgments. Some of us have found our opinions changed, even reversed, as a result of our shared investigations. We cannot promise (or threaten!) that the reader's views will undergo such shifts. But we do hope that our readers are open to that possibility as they explore with us the various approaches Christians have developed for understanding how God's grace and truth are or are not to be found in the diverse faith traditions of the world.

1

Siting Theology

Building Sites

THEOLOGICAL REFLECTIONS, LIKE CATHEDRALS AND PSYCHOLOGICAL theories, are constructed on particular sites for particular purposes. The lay of the land and the challenges of the site shape the possibilities for designing a theological construction. The most functional designs also travel well. Such adaptability applies to conceptual as well as architectural designs. Like plans for tract houses, libraries, and hospitals, theological patterns and designs can be exported from one particular cultural site and imported into other sites and adapted for use over and over again.

Edifices of stone and brick and wood are shaped by the materials available to the site. The Cathedral of Notre Dame in Paris, France, is built of the local beige stone. The gothic design is widely emulated, but the sandstone remains local. St. Peter's Basilica is constructed of the granite and marble of Italy. The domed basilica can be found throughout the Western world, shaped in stone, brick, and cast cement as well as granite and marble. The Cathedral of the Immaculate Conception in Burlington, Vermont, is shaped by green-glazed brick and topped by a copper roof. Its low horizontal windows do not lift the worshipers' eyes to the heavens as do Notre Dame's stained-glass windows or St. Peter's dome but bring their focus to the altar at the visual center of the semicircular space—a shape available for a Catholic worship space only after the liturgical reforms inaugurated by the Second Vatican Council (1962–65). The poured concrete and structural steel of the Cathedral of St. Mary of the Assumption in San Francisco takes a shape many compare to a washing machine agitator, blending the classic cruciform shape with a central focus on the altar topped by a multitiered sculpture of triangular aluminum rods that draws one's eyes on high. High on Cathedral Hill, its clear windows look out on the city named for St. Francis of Assisi, especially the golden dome of City Hall in the Hayes Valley—a fitting view for strongly, if informally, linked civic and ecclesial structures.

1

The central purpose for each of these churches is divine worship. They also may serve as meeting places or concert halls or art galleries. The art, music, and gatherings should serve the worshiping community, however indirectly. Each cathedral has distinctive adaptations of common elements from tabernacles to altars to organs. However different, each distinctive edifice on each particular cultural and topographical site is built to glorify God, to recall the divine majesty and presence for the people who gather within their fascinatingly different walls, and to send those same people into the world to spread the good news and love and serve their lord through serving their neighbors.

Great architectural designs and patterns do travel exceptionally well. They fit multiple sites. One can find churches, galleries, meeting spaces, museums, and concert halls around the world that adapt romanesque and gothic architecture, not to mention art deco, rococo, Bauhaus, Moorish, and various "colonial" patterns. While some patterns may fit ill with some sites, these styles can be found in widely scattered locales.

In a certain sense, these designs are incommensurable. One may find great gothic cathedrals and trashy imitations of them in some gothic revival buildings, but one does not evaluate colonial architecture by norms peculiar to gothic architecture. One may ask the same general evaluative questions about buildings of the same type. Does this church indeed bring worshipers to recall the divine majesty and worship God? Does this museum have the appropriate space to display the art it has collected? One may compare aspects of different types of architectural design by asking and answering questions such as How does each focus the space? What is it that those who enter typically notice? The norms, however, by which one does the actual evaluations of particular buildings are more particular to the type and the location than universally applicable to all kinds of buildings of all sorts of styles in every location—except at the most general and nondiscriminating level.

Psychological theories are also sited. Sigmund Freud's psychoanalytical theories were decisively shaped by his medical and psychoanalytic practice in late-nineteenth- and early-twentieth-century Vienna, a site productive of a remarkable number of distinctive theories in philosophy, psychology, and architecture. Eric Berne's transactional analysis began as a reaction against Freudian analysis and was shaped in the particular context of his medical practice in the comfortable consumerism and cultural diversity of the San Francisco Bay Area in the 1950s and '60s.[1] Both have a central place for childhood experiences in their patterns of analysis.

Freud's archeological therapy had the therapist listening to individual patients and seeking to get patients to uncover the hidden roots of their psychological problems deep in their childhood—and, in his rather speculative works such as *Totem and Taboo* and *Moses and Monotheism*, to uncover the social neuroses rooted in the "childhood" of Western culture. Berne's transactional analysis had the therapist/educator and clients working together to uncover the particular "games" the client played (among other things) so as to enable clients to change the bad interpersonal behavioral patterns into which they had fallen as they worked out the implicit script of their lives from childhood.

These two forms of analysis and therapy are profoundly different in theory and practice. Freud's is more a talk-centered therapy while Berne's is more behavior-centered. Each finds rather different keys to psychological ills in the sufferers' childhood. Freudian theory is pessimistic about human nature while Berne's therapy is relatively optimistic—influenced respectively by *fin-de-siècle* Vienna and California after World War II. Both find (rather different) keys in childhood. They have competing professional associations and journals. Yet both seek to enable the patient/client to live a psychologically healthy life.

Psychological theories can also travel well. Freudian concepts—neurosis, superego, id, ego, etc.—as well as Berne's concepts—"strokes," child-parent-adult ego states, "I'm OK, you're OK," etc.—have entered into common parlance. One can find therapists who practice these—and numerous other—psychotherapeutic techniques around the world. Both have had remarkable successes and failures—not to mention misunderstandings and parodies.

As with architectural designs, one can ask very general evaluative questions of varying psychological theories. Is the person undergoing therapy getting better? As with architecture, however, the specific evaluative criteria will differ depending on the way the theory constructs what is psychological health and the particular goals of the therapy. Moreover, psychological theories are notoriously resistant to theoretical or empirical evaluation as theories. One can compare them, of course, with regard to specific aspects or issues: How do the theories handle childhood? More practically, the success of therapies can be measured, perhaps, but "success" may well be due to the *practices* and the skills of the practitioners as much as or more than the theories as such. While theories may be comparable with regard to specific aspects, not only is it hard to see how such theories might be commensurable, but it is difficult to see how to measure the theories as theories.

Theological reflections are no less "sited" than cathedrals or psychological theories. They are constructed in particular contexts with particular materials for particular purposes. The best theological patterns also travel exceedingly well. In Christianity, the pervasive influence of Augustinian theology, the power of various forms of Thomism, and the insights of Latin American liberation theology are obvious examples of particular theologies that both reach for the universal from particular sites and provide patterns for theological constructions in sites far from their origins. Like good architectural patterns and psychological theories, good theologies are related in their purposes, comparable with regard to particular issues (e.g., How do these theologies construe human inclinations to do evil?), but are finally incommensurable in terms of evaluative norms beyond the most vague and general. In sum, the pattern for understanding, evaluating, and constructing theologies is analogous to the patterns for understanding, evaluating, and constructing cathedrals or psychologies.

The present work is constructed on a specific site that is informed by the religious and cultural components that we discuss in the next two chapters. Yet the present strongly contextual approach is not the only way that theologians construct their intellectual edifices today. Hence, showing how the present project differs from—and borrows from—other current theological designs will help situate its particular contribution.

Good Construction Plans in Theology

The present project, in brief, is a *constructivist* project that borrows from both *correlational* and *positivist* patterns typical of contemporary Christian theological work. There are almost as many particular approaches to theology as there are theologians. Any map of the territory can be misleading, especially if the reader asks more precision than the map has. The following is merely a broad-stroked sketch of the terrain.[2]

Correlational theologies typically focus on two variables roughly equally and seek to relate them constructively and critically. Typically, these foci are "past" (the tradition, the old creed, the Bible, etc.) and "present" (the contemporary situation, the new world, the modern interpretation, etc.). Given the present culture (variously described by various theologians), the key question is how can we relate our religious tradition to our contemporary culture. A correlationist theologian typically works with a specific contemporary philosophy, such as existentialism, process thought, or critical theory, or with dominant cultural "imaginaries," such as science, consumerism, oppression, or postmodernity. The point is to set up a mutually illuminating dialogue so that the tradition can be mobilized to criticize contemporary culture and cultural realities can be shown as illuminating or purifying the meaning of the tradition today.

Both Protestant and Catholic theologians use correlational theological patterns. Paul Tillich, Rudolf Bultmann, and Schubert Ogden provide examples from the Protestant side. Karl Rahner, David Tracy, and Gustavo Gutiérrez (at least in his earlier work) are Catholic correlationists. The key to correlationism is that neither "past" nor "present" is given unqualified primacy of place in theological work. Analyses of both the beliefs the tradition brings to the present culture and the culture that shapes the present members of the tradition are necessary components for correlational theology.

Some of the Catholic theologians who influenced the Second Vatican Council and who have interpreted it have focused on the motif of *aggiornamento*. The fathers of the council were to come to understand and respond creatively to "the signs of the times" through which God might even now be addressing humanity. The resulting documents and policies were "updating" the tradition to better fit the modern world. Although not usually categorized as such, theological *aggiornamento* can be understood as a type of correlational theology that contributed to the construction of the documents of Vatican II. Relating faith and culture is key for correlational theologies.

Positivist theologies typically focus on a variable and a constant. The constant, for example, the tradition, the old creed, the Bible, etc., is the focus of positivist theological construction. The primary question is not how to correlate "past" and "present" but how to live faithfully to the old creeds in this new situation. Situations change from time to time and place to place. Theologians need to recognize how various situations have affected both the living of the faith and the doing of theology in the past and the present, but these situations are not central. "The Gospel" is. Positive theologians may be in dialogue with the philosophies and cultural "imaginaries," but the point is not to be in dialogue but to proclaim the old creed in the new world. Fidelity to the tradition is the key to positivist theologies.

Catholic, Protestant, and Orthodox theologians can be found among the positivists. Orthodox theology seems inherently positivist; even theologians like convert Bishop Kallistos Ware who wrote sophisticatedly for a non-Orthodox audience sought more to proclaim the tradition faithfully than to correlate it. Protestant theologians Karl Barth, George Lindbeck, and Stanley Hauerwas are positivists in this sense as well. Their goal is to faithfully render the tradition not so much for those external to the tradition (the greater society or the university thinkers) as for those who seek to be faithful in and to the tradition in a culture that often works—whether wittingly or not—to undermine that tradition. Among Catholic theologians, neo-Thomist theologians such as Charles Journet and Augustinian theologians like Joseph Ratzinger (Benedict XVI) belong in this camp.

Some of the theologians who shaped Vatican II and its reception were and are theologians dedicated to *ressourcement*. Inspired especially by theologians who worked at or were allied with the French Dominican school at Le Saulchoir, for example, Yves Congar, they sought to retrieve resources from the history of the Christian tradition—especially the patristic period—to vivify the present belief and practice of the church. "Signs of the times" were seen not as an important source for theology but as indicating the context in which the updating work had to be done. *Ressourcement* is a fundamentally positivist approach to theology in that the key is fidelity to the tradition, rather than updating for a better fit with—including being a better challenge to—the modern world.

These two theological patterns are not clearly in fundamental conflict, except in the abstract description of them. Both *aggiornamento-* and *ressourcement-* oriented theologians made major contributions to Vatican II. Indeed, *aggiornamento* stands on the shoulders of *ressourcement*. Although theologians today may differ on the significance of the council and the meaning of its documents, their cooperation forty years ago was not merely tactical (see O'Malley 2006; Schloesser 2006). The theology or theologies of the council were and are the fruit of a cooperative venture in constructing Catholic theology on a site contoured by the social, political, and intellectual terrain of the modern world.

Depending on the time of writing and the precise problem under consideration, the same theologian can seemingly shift from camp to camp without fundamentally changing the theological approach. Edward Schillebeeckx, Avery Dulles, and Gustavo Gutiérrez sometimes write as if they fit in the correlationist box, and at other times as if they fit in the positivist box. The lessons are twofold: don't make a rough map into an ironclad box and do notice that each of these theologians constructs and reconstructs theological edifices differently as social, political, intellectual, and ecclesial site characteristics evolve.

The present constructivist approach differs in some ways from both correlational and positive theologies. Two texts are key in shaping this approach.

First, the approach Robert Schreiter took in *Constructing Local Theologies* (1985) is a major influence on the present work. Images of planting the seed of the gospel in the soil of the "new world" or of translating Christian concepts, texts, and images into "native" terms simply did not account for the best (or worst!) of indigenous theologies. Schreiter was dissatisfied with theories of acculturation, inculturation, adaptation, and conceptual translation as accounts of what Christian missionaries were doing when they established Christian communities far from their own homelands. He developed a rather elaborate theory to describe past and to guide future attempts to construct local theologies in the Christian tradition. In this theory, which some would see as correlational, Schreiter describes the process of creating theologies. Rather than implanting or translating the "old creed" for a "new world," Schreiter's work on local theology problematizes both concepts.

In contrast to correlational and positivist theologies, which tend to separate "religion" and "culture" or "tradition" from "contemporary context," or "message" from "audience," a theory of local theology finds these fundamentally inseparable. Every Christian theology was not a compromise between tradition and context or a proclamation of an essentially unchanging message, but a local theology, developed on a specific site with specific purposes to meet specific challenges, utilizing both cultural and religious resources from other times and places (the tradition) and cultural and religious resources in the particular time and places. What is happening in the missionary situation, for example, is not translation or adaptation of an established creed, but what has always happened in the history of Christianity: the creation of a local theology. Justin Martyr constructed a local theology, casting it in the form of a dialogue with the pagan Trypho. Pope Leo wrote a tome that sought to resolve confused arguments and to bring sense and coherence to belief in Jesus as human and divine. Augustine used the cultural and religious heritage from the Bible and the tradition to invent responses to the very local challenges from Manicheans, Donatists, Pelagians—not to mention from the sack of Rome in 410 c.e., which occasioned *The City of God.* Thomas Aquinas constructed a *Summa* to instruct young Dominican men who would become priests in a coherent understanding of the key tenets of the faith using the newly available philosophy of Aristotle melded with the neo-Platonic and Augustinian heritage that he had inherited in the emerging medieval university. Martin Luther invented a whole new theological approach out of the traditions of his Augustinian order and the background of medieval Franciscan sacramental theology in the context of the political and religious corruptions of the Renaissance churches and scholastic theology. Liberation theologies took the cultural, philosophical, and religious heritage of Catholic Europe and transformed it in the new location, which was characterized by Northern economic hegemony (with its local collaborators) and distinctive devotional practices to construct a theology captured in one of Gutiérrez's titles: *We Drink from Our Own Wells.* Each of these local theologies is just that: a local theology built on a local site, not a translation or adaptation of an old creed to a new world.

A key assumption of inculturation or translation theories important for correlational and positivist theologies is fundamentally flawed from this perspective. Even if "the faith" is the same no matter where it is lived in and lived out, there is no simple universal articulation of Christian theology to be "applied" in some way in a local context or "correlated" with a culture. Rather, Christian theologies form a communion of local theologies, diverse in origins, styles, and methods, but united in general goals as cathedrals are: to show people how to live and especially how to live and worship as followers of Jesus the Christ. Correlational theologies of course recognize that all theological constructs are culturally shaped. Correlationists assume, however, that the essence of the religious tradition can somehow be distilled from all those other local theologies and then infused into the new situation. The problem is that one can never really distill away the cultural "impurities" or isolate religious constants articulable in most, if not all, cultural contexts, except those of the most vague and formal—that is, practically and materially empty—formulas.

Schreiter, however, did not make clear what we claim here. He was concerned with the theologies of missions. Here we extend his explicit claim: *all* theologies are local. Some theologies constructed on particular sites have great power to travel exceedingly well. Some of their formulations, attitudes, and insights command attention throughout the Christian world. As noted in the last paragraph of the previous section, some theologies—for various reasons—become nigh unto universal, *de rigeur* understandings of the tradition to which many, if not all, other local theologies must relate by taking their claims into consideration. One simply cannot do any Christian theology today except the most esoteric if one does not ask the liberationists' question: What does this understanding do to the oppressed, for the oppressed, and to enable the oppressed—however they are oppressed—to do for themselves? One simply could not have done Catholic theology for the last hundred years if one did not consider how it was related to the theological work of that thirteenth-century European Dominican whose name denominates a set of movements: Thomisms. Yet none of these theologies are universal expressions of the tradition that simply need to be adapted, translated, inculturated. Rather, new theologies in new locales—and postmodernity is surely a new locale on this account—must be constructed in conversation with them. Privileging neither the "old creed" nor the "new world," Schreiter's approach is work in a different key from either the correlationists or the positivists.

Second, we also extend the approach that the lead author developed in *Inventing Catholic Tradition* (2000). Having accepted Schreiter's insights, Tilley transposed them into yet a different key. Whereas many theologians have focused on beliefs or creeds or doctrines as the center of theology, he argued for centering theological reflection as a *practice* that reflects both on (critically) and in (participatively) the multiple *practices* incarnated variously in the Christian tradition—including, but not limited to, the practice of believing. The key to the transposition is "practice," in this book a term of art. In brief, a practice "is a complex series of human actions involving definite practitioners who by these means and in accordance with these rules [of the practice] together seek the understood end" (McClendon 1994, 28; cf. Tilley 2000, 53–65).

The title of that book was a bilingual pun: the participle "inventing" is intended to evoke not merely the constructive task of theology but also the fact that constructions are the discovery and realization of possibilities that are present in the encounter of "old creed" and "new world," not translations or proclamations of the former in the latter. To make it explicit, *invenire* in Latin is properly transliterated as "to invent" but only properly translated insofar as it includes the fundamental sense of "to discover"! Some scientific inventions can't work because the conditions under which they could work don't exist; "cold fusion" provides an example. Some theological inventions can't work for an analogous reason; a Jewish theology of the ikon is at best a stretch for an aniconic tradition.

Some saw *Inventing Catholic Tradition* as aligned with the work of some positivists, specifically with postliberals such as George Lindbeck. Yet as *Constructing Local Theologies* transposed correlational theologies into a distinctive constructivist key, so *Inventing Catholic Tradition* sought to transpose both correlational and postliberal theologies into a constructivist key centered on practice/praxis (in the account, these terms are practically interchangeable, for good practice is praxis). Unlike some positivists, notably the recently developed pattern of radical orthodoxy (especially the early work of John Milbank), *Inventing Catholic Tradition* saw social theory and analysis as a useful handmaid rather than as a treacherous enemy. Influenced by the work of Gustavo Gutiérrez, Alasdair MacIntyre, and James Wm. McClendon, Jr., among others, it recognized believing as a form of practice, not a distinct way of holding truths and developing attitudes. Beliefs were construed not as a foundation for or a hard and fast rule for practice, but as a constituent in the practice of discipleship.

One problem with *Inventing Catholic Tradition*, as noted especially by Orlando Espín (2002), was its rather abstract and theoretical focus. In giving a theory of practice and recognizing numerous practices, it never really got to the "site" in which theology is practiced and religious traditions are lived in and lived out. This recognition is not a confession of acknowledged failure in the earlier work but the admission that the earlier work could not be complete because it was necessarily a general theory of tradition rather than a particular exploration. Its task was, in effect, a prolegomenon to sited theological work.

Constructing a Theology of Religious Diversity

The present text, then, can be seen as a particular exercise that is both a local theology and an invention of a tradition. Because it seeks to work through approaches to a specific issue on a specific site, it can overcome the shortcomings of the lead author's earlier work in the only way possible: to focus on particulars, rather than on the possibility of constructing theology in a particular context and construing traditions as carried by and carrying practices.

Chapter 2 portrays the "site" on which our theology is built. It describes the salient historic and contemporary characteristics of the United States as a site for building theology. We live in a nation populated by immigrants and their offspring that socially is religiously diverse and politically has a republican tradition not of disestablishment of religion but of nonestablishment of religion. These historical characteristics have promoted the development of powerful, nongovernmental civic associations that form the Christian denominations and other religious traditions. Of course, this is not to deny a tension between those who would find that this nation was founded on Christian principles and those who find that a distinctive Enlightenment tradition of democratic pluralism means that no religious tradition is to be culturally or politically privileged. Economically, we live in a society that is increasingly stratified and characterized by a form of comfortable (for many, but not all, by any means) capitalist consumerism. Consumerism powerfully shapes this site and those who inhabit it, even affecting the ways in which U.S. citizens of every religious persuasion are religiously committed. The commodification of religion may be a factor in the erosion of the deep social and democratic cooperation that is concern for the commonweal. This concern is still valorized in such slogans as "no child left behind" in educational opportunities or "equal justice and opportunity for all" regardless of creed, color, sex, or ethnicity—but which are all too often ignored in the rhetorical hegemony of a social Darwinism masked as rugged individualism that leaves many children from distressed families behind and dispenses different justice for poor and rich. Finally, globalization is a factor that cannot be ignored as our world has become a village; the squabbles between nations and religions have rooted themselves in our own neighborhood, and the potential for both profoundly increasing and somewhat leveling the differences between rich and poor peoples has exploded.

The third chapter then develops a "building code" developed from the Catholic tradition as a theological guide for constructing a theology of religious diversity appropriate to this site (and, which, of course, might be appropriately reconstructed on or imported into other cultural sites).

Each of the theories explored in chapters 4 through 10 creates at least as many problems as it solves or leaves key problems unsolved. Hence, chapter 11 proposes a "no necessary theory" account of religious diversity. The "no necessary theory" approach is somewhat analogous to the "no theory" position the lead author developed concerning the modern problem of evil in the past (Tilley 1991). Therein Tilley argued that to construct a theory of why God allowed evil in the world (a theodicy) was not to solve the problem but to contribute more evil to the evils already present in the world (Tilley 1991, 229–51). Here we argue that any theories of religious diversity that fit the theological principles developed in chapter 3, that fit the site described in chapter 2, and that do not get in the way of constructive interreligious practice or praxis are acceptable.[3]

More important is that these accounts of religious diversity fit within a way of faith that lives out our commitment to God and God's creatures by the praxis that transforms strangers and enemies into guests for our celebrations, friends in the struggle, and colleagues seeking understanding. We do not need a particular theory to discover and instantiate sociopolitical and religious practices of

- engaging in mutual respect, encouragement, and cooperation (not tolerance or indifference)

- practicing reconciliation among peoples of different traditions, including cooperation on particular issues of justice (not seeking *e pluribus unum*, but community of diversity)

- deepening of our own Christian commitments that show what it means to be devoted to a God who has become incarnate and is all-loving
- making a real effort to understand and support those others whom we believe God also loves and saves, though we know not how.

In short, we seek to defend and proclaim practices that affirm unremitting divine love and real actual diversity, even without a final theory to explain how these practices are consistent.

We seek, then, to identify which Christian theological constructs fit the site in which we live so as to make it a better place for Christians to dwell together happily with people of diverse religious commitments and for people of diverse religious commitment to live happily with the Christians in their midst.

2

Surveying the Construction Site

The Cultural Terrain

THE UNITED STATES OF AMERICA IS A DISTINCTIVE CULTURAL SITE FOR constructing a theology of religious diversity. The United States cannot be assimilated into a pan-Euro-American site called "the culture of modernity." Such a site would be an imaginative abstraction derived by reducing the variety of factors distinctive to local sites to a lowest common denominator, and then calling that abstraction the key for understanding "the culture of modernity." No such site exists. This is not to say that the cultural site of the United States can be viewed as essentially different from all other cultures or apart from other modern nations. Not only do immigrants from all over the world contribute to this site, but so do the heritages of European colonization and hegemony and the currents of global commerce. Moreover, because of unprecedentedly fast forms of communication, no cultural site is truly isolated. Hence, any radical forms of "American exceptionalism" that construe the United States completely different from other cultures and nations are untenable. "American distinctivism," however, remains legitimate.

What applies to culture applies to religion and theology as well. The United States is a distinctive theological and religious site, even if it is not theologically unique.[1] Analogues of the distinctive cultural and religious characteristics of the United States can be found in numerous other places. Many nations have both political freedom of speech and religion, for example. Many cultures also have undergone some form of secularization. Yet the fact that analogous characteristics are components in various cultures does not make the assemblage a "common culture."

For example, each modern nation has a military establishment, but the Swiss Army has a cultural place and impact quite different from the U.S. Army. Simply to assume that a cultural item such as "army" or "city" has the same "place" in every culture is unwarranted. Just as dots on a page can be connected by multiple lines, so can analogous cultural items be differently connected to one another in any culture. How the U.S. military establishment is connected to private industry, the range of its interests, and the cultural place it has in the nation differ from the connections, range, and cultural place of the armies of other nations. There is no reason to think that even if cultures have analogous cultural characteristics those characteristics are connected in the same way in every culture. How analogous cultural items fit in a culture, from ideals of freedom to practices of police maintaining internal order to expectations of virtue on the part of office holders to entertainment industries to linguistic patterns, differs from place to place.

Despite commonalities, each culture is shaped differently from that of any other. Even if there were a pan-European culture, French culture is different from English culture, which is different from Austrian culture. The actual shapes of actual cultures depend on what significance each characteristic has and how they are connected to form an always-evolving whole. Linguistic diversity differentiates cultures from one another in fundamental ways. As we shall discuss below, different cultures are religiously diverse in various ways. Religious diversity has a different cultural place in France or Italy from the place it has in the United States.

Politically speaking, for instance, the European nations have each had to resolve the issues associated with the historical establishment of religion whereas the United States has had a quite different history regarding religion, one of nonestablishment. As Pope Benedict XVI put it, "People came to realize that the American Revolution was offering a model of a modern state that differed from the theoretical model with radical tendencies that had emerged during the second phase of the French Revolution" (Benedict XVI 2006, 537). The political difference between violent disestablishment (the French pattern) and nonestablishment (the U.S. pattern) of religion is crucial. It means that "secularization" and "privatization of religion," both intimately connected with differing national polities regarding religion, take different forms on various cultural sites. The result is that "secularization" and "privatization" have a significantly different force in the cultures of France and Italy from the significance they have in U.S. culture.

Arguably, the nonestablishment of religion in the United States seems to be so distinctive as to be unique to this cultural site. This characteristic places living faith traditions in a different social and political location than they have in countries where the modern nation-states required the disestablishment of religion. Yet even the actual shape of disestablishment looks quite different from country to country or even within a country. In France, the state runs the schools; in Ireland, the state pays for the schools, but 85 percent of primary schools are explicitly Roman Catholic and run by the church. Even within France, Alsace and Lorraine have a different pattern of state support of religion from the rest of the nation, one derived from their German heritage.

In Europe, religious institutions lost economic support from the governments of the nations, but in the United States, religious institutions and communities never had national governmental support. Religious institutions had to develop ways to cope with not being supported. Religious institutions have to develop different strategies for coping with nonestablishment than with disestablishment, whether total or partial. For example, churches need to find ways to replace lost government revenues when they are disestablished. Yet churches that never received government money and consistently relied on pew rents, fundraisers, and voluntary contributions for their support face different economic challenges.

Our point is this: Even if there are characteristics common to or analogous in many cultures, this does not make a common culture. Such reduction to the common items, a reduction to the lowest common denominator, ignores the relationships between these characteristics on any specific site and misrepresents the thickness of each cultural site as if it were as evanescent as a light fog that might be found anywhere and on which nothing can be constructed.

What makes the United States a distinctive cultural site? Answering that question adequately would take many books, not a chapter in one book. Here we are concerned only with five key characteristics most important for constructing a theology of religious diversity: a nation of immigrants, religious diversity, political nonestablishment of religion, contemporary consumerism, and globalization. The next chapter focuses on the key rules of the Catholic Christian tradition for building a theology of religious diversity on this site. These are separate chapters not because we accept a form of correlationism that would essentialize two things that the theologian would then relate, the "cultural challenge" and the "religious response," for example. Rather, surveying the cultural site is like trying to portray a complex neighborhood where we own a building lot on one plat. We will necessarily sketch our neighborhood quickly.

Surveying the particular religious component is like examining the parameters for building a specific, distinctive house on the lot. Such parameters may—and typically do—include "off-site" components imported by the builders because they fit the site. These components contribute to the distinctiveness of the religious tradition that is simultaneously a part of the site and a contributor to the cultural diversity of the site. "Cultures" and "religions" are related not as questions and answers but as evolving wholes and shifting parts.[2]

Immigrants and Nativists

As the research summarized in *1491* shows (Mann 2005), the Americas were populated by people who were far from the "savages" European immigrants portrayed them to be. The various tribes were linked by extensive networks of commerce. A basic sustainable agriculture centered on a diet of maize, beans, and squash had spread, apparently from Mexico. The diet was supplemented or complemented with other foodstuffs, including meat obtained not from "the wild" but from a sustainable, nonintensive pattern of husbandry quite different from the patterns of the Old World—in part because the pre-Columbian Americans had no work animals larger than a dog. Agriculture had to be developed without the availability of beasts of burden. Yet the pre-Columbian Americans probably had a better diet than the peasants of Europe. The result was a populace much denser than previously thought and much better fed than the masses of Europe.

Nonetheless, the Americas in general and the United States in particular are countries populated by immigrants of the last five hundred years. Some 80 to 95 percent of the "native" population was wiped out rapidly by diseases, many of them introduced unintentionally by Europeans early in the first contact period near the end of the fifteenth century. The "original" populace in the Americas—who also had migrated, though much earlier, probably from northern Asia—had no resistance to these new diseases. By the time the English settlers arrived in the early seventeenth century, they encountered cultures that had been devastated in part by diseases introduced a century earlier by the Spanish, diseases that evidently spread rapidly over the far-flung trading network. Disease had brought about a dislocation that reduced flourishing cultures to a "savage" state, leaving a continent "empty" for European expansion and exploitation. That the flourishing cultures of the pre-contact period were no more savage than European cultures now seems obvious. That the continent, though not heavily populated at the time of the English settlements, was not empty now seems undeniable. Yet the United States became a nation of immigrants who supplanted the savages and filled the empty continent.

The history of immigration to the United States is an oft-told story. Immigrants flocked to the emptied land, made war against the native populations, increased rapidly, and elbowed the native survivors into reservations. English, the language of the dominant early immigrant settlements on the Atlantic seaboard, became the common tongue. Later immigrants were supported by extended families with a toehold in the United States or by cooperative societies that helped them set up farms or shops. They often learned a little English while keeping the language of "home" alive in domestic spaces. Yet their children and grandchildren learned to speak the dominant language in order to participate in the economy and the culture of the New World. Some of those children forgot the language of their heritage and became as "Anglo" as other American anglophones. Some of them would later see newer immigrants as poor and dirty, even crooks.

Freedom of religion is an important value for immigrants. Alan Wolfe described the conditions that make this freedom so valuable for them:

Once immigration takes place, religion can no longer serve as a source of identity the way it did in one's country of origin. To move is to choose; once a person opts to live in a society in which his or her faith is a minority faith, no amount of religious observation, no return to traditional practices, and no adherence to the letter of the law can ever equate one's faith in the new land with the way it was in the old country. Some immigrants recognize this by switching their faith when they switch their residence. Others try as hard as they can to hold on to the ways of their ancestors. But no one escapes the necessity for choice. Indeed, the reality of choice is even more true of the nonswitchers than the switchers. (2003, 242–43)

The combination of the diversity of faith traditions and nonestablishment— factors considered below—makes religious choice not merely a live option for immigrants but an unavoidable one. What is psychologically and socially necessary for immigrants is thus legally possible and becomes culturally expected of all. Immigration makes religion a matter of choice.

Yet immigrants provoke response from the settled population. A pattern of prejudice emerges and repeats itself. The newest immigrants are perceived by earlier immigrants as a threat. New immigrants work grueling jobs no one else wants for wages less than anyone else had taken. Recent immigrants and their children may then come to resent the very newest immigrants. This pattern of "nativist" prejudice repeats itself with every new immigrant group. "Nativism" is a profound hostility in attitude and behavior to immigrants (mostly) of a different nationality and religion than the "natives." In the United States, unlike European countries currently coping with immigrant populations, the nativists do not typically share the same ethnic or cultural background. This makes the patterns of nativism as distinctive as the patterns of immigration.

We are familiar with the nineteenth-century patterns of nativism in the United States. Signs in Boston shops proclaimed "Irish need not apply" for work. Respectable Philadelphians (and citizens in other cities) rioted against (immigrant) Catholics and burned convents and churches. Italians, Poles, Slavs, and others were herded into tenements in New York and company towns in Pennsylvania and Ohio, for example, in part to keep them away from and in subjection to the great-grandchildren of successful immigrants. Save for those exploited by the railroad barons and other entrepreneurs of the West Coast, oriental immigrants were kept out as being too different. After a century of almost untrammeled European immigration, symbolized by the inscription on the Statue of Liberty, the Immigration Act of 1924 dammed the flow.

Nativist attacks on Roman Catholic churches, convents, and schools occurred all too frequently in the nineteenth century. Similar attacks on Muslim centers and mosques have occurred more recently. Some of these attitudes and attacks seem to have been generated by economic fear. Cheap immigrant labor would take away jobs from those already settled in the United States. Religious belief may have been a peripheral matter in some nativist incidents. Prejudice against Irish immigrants in the nineteenth century and Central American immigrants in the twentieth, for example, seems to have developed out of economic concerns and ethnic prejudice as much as or more than religious ones. Some of these attitudes and attacks have been generated by the actions of tiny, often radical, minority groups within an immigrant community. Prejudice against Muslims, Buddhists, and Hindus in this country shows that nativism is not yet dead. The pattern of prejudice repeats itself (see Wuthnow 2005, 64–66). Diana Eck wrote of one instance:

> When Muslims in Edmond, the suburb of Oklahoma City where the University Central of Oklahoma is located, planned to build a mosque in 1992, a move was made to deny a building permit because, as a Pluralism Project researcher reported, "One of the minister's wives [sic] attended the first public meeting and vehemently opposed it. She said, 'The constitution says One nation under God, and that's a Christian God. These people have no right to be here.'" (Eck 2001, 309; cited from Hill Fletcher 2005, 56).

Whether ethnic or religious or other differences are the root of such prejudice is moot. The prejudice is all too frequent.

The pattern perdures even in the twenty-first century. Today, "illegal immigrants" enter the United States from Mexico in a constant stream. How many actually enter the country illegally is unclear (but see Hill and Wong 2005). They take the meanest jobs for the lowest wages and send money home, as did the nineteenth-century immigrants. They are often portrayed as unreliable laborers, thieves, and burdens on the social system because they have no health insurance and often drive uninsured, beat-up automobiles. And like the Irish before them, they are often portrayed as lazy drunks. Simultaneously, individuals and families who have emigrated from the Middle East, India, Pakistan, China, Japan, Southeast Asia, and the Philippines sponsor relatives and often support them once they are here, as did Irish and Italians, among others, in the nineteenth century. With a globalized culture and a globalized market, migrants are not as likely to be desperately poor or dependent as in the past. And these most recent immigrants practice religions that are even stranger today than the Catholicism of the Irish, Italian, or Polish immigrants was to the Protestant nativists whose parents, grandparents, and great-grandparents had earlier been immigrants.

The key exception to this pattern, both of immigration and of nativist prejudice, is the forced migration of African peoples, ripped from their families and unsupported by any mutual aid societies in the brutal slave trade. Those captured by the "peculiar institution" of chattel slavery in the United States and their descendants endured horrible conditions and a different form of prejudice, not only in the slave-holding South but also in the "free states" of the North, where freed slaves competed with new immigrants for work. Their "unnatural" situation was unlike that of most of the voluntary migrants. Forced migration and slavery shattered families, forced life-long servitude, enslaved children, and drove the slaves' cultures deep "underground," if they were maintained at all. Forced migration shaped African Americans' destinies in ways different from those who were voluntary migrants. Their lives were disrupted in ways that still haunt U.S. culture, including those who escaped slavery and those people of color who have immigrated over the last one hundred and fifty years. Like other immigrant groups, African Americans were despised and robbed, starved and persecuted. Unlike any other immigrant group, the slaves and their children were not as a whole nurtured by patrons or supported by extended families and friends as were voluntary immigrants by those descended from earlier immigrants.

Patterns of nativist prejudice conflict with a historic commitment to acceptance of diversity today as in the past. A report in 2001 showed 13 percent of workers in the United States were immigrants (Parker 2001). A recent study estimated that 8 percent of U.S. jobs are held by *illegal* immigrants (Justich and Ng 2005, 1). Most of the illegals, of course, work the dangerous or menial jobs that citizens spurn. Settled families that see their livelihoods threatened and political and other leaders who see the social fabric strained by immigrants call for an end to illegal immigration. Many of the jobs such immigrants hold, however, would go begging if immigrants did not hold them. Alternatively, to attract settled workers, the wages would have to be adjusted substantially upward. Whether immigrants remain an economic boon to the economy remains debated, but it is clear that one cannot assume that immigrants are a drag on the national economy.

In short, nativism in U.S. culture has been a characteristic response to immigration. Whatever ethnic or religious group is "new" provokes prejudice among the descendants of those who immigrated earlier (not people whose ancestors have lived in the land since early modernity). Nativist prejudices are an ever-present threat to the achievement of what Wuthnow calls the "reflective pluralism" he prescribes for the United States.

Nonetheless, the specific pattern of immigration—a nation in which all the inhabitants, not only some of them—are immigrants or descended from immigrants produces a distinctive, perhaps unique, pattern of religious diversity.

A *Pattern* of *Religious* Diversity

Unlike other cultural sites, the United States is now and has been *intrinsically* religiously diverse. Two major factors follow from this. The first, what Robert Wuthnow has called "reflective religious pluralism," may be considered not as much a condition as an achievement. The second is that religious diversity is not purely external to any religious community or person.

Religious diversity is the condition of the United States. The responses to this diversity have varied. One is nativism, discussed above. Wuthnow, however, noted that Americans have often been proud of the fact that we have managed to learn how to cope with religious diversity in our history. He found that this "history has affected our laws, encouraging us to avoid governmental intrusion in religious affairs that might lead to an establishment of one tradition in favor of others. And it has taught us a kind of civic decorum that discourages blatant expressions of racist, ethnocentric and nativist ideas" (Wuthnow 2005, 4). Yet this decorum may mask a grudging tolerance, a merely pragmatic coexistence that recognizes that members of all religious traditions have civil rights, including the right to worship.

Authentic religious pluralism remains elusive. As Wuthnow puts it, pluralism in general is "our response to diversity—how we think about it, how we respond to it in our attitudes and lifestyles, and whether we choose to embrace it, ignore it, or merely cope with it" (Wuthnow 2005, 286). For Wuthnow, authentic reflective pluralism is what pluralism ought to be. It is the embrace of diversity by people strong enough in their own character to understand, respect, cooperate with, and support others who belong to different faith traditions. "Religious pluralism involves more than the mere coexistence of multiple traditions. At the very minimum, it requires engagement across traditions. And such engagement necessarily challenges preconceived ideas about beliefs and values" (Wuthnow 2005, 104–5). Ignoring other traditions or simply coping with their challenges while not engaging those who bring those challenges is not authentic reflective pluralism. Persons of strong character can meet those challenges, sometimes by standing firm in their beliefs and practices, sometimes by changing to a religiously richer view. This sort of reflective pluralism is an achievement in a religiously diverse society, not merely another term for a society that happens to be religiously diverse.

Crucial to achieving authentic diversity is engaging in authentic conversation across and between religious traditions. Conversation is not debate. Rather, as Jonathan Sacks put it, it is a

> disciplined act of communicating (making my views intelligible to someone who does not share them) and of listening (entering into the

inner world of someone whose views are opposed to my own). Each is a genuine form of respect, of paying attention to the other, of conferring value on his or her opinions even if they are not mine. (Sacks 2003, 83)

Conversation is how we learn to live together peaceably in a pluralistic society. Only then can we engage in the needed "sustained act of understanding and seeking to be understood across the boundaries of difference" (Sacks 2003, 83). To engage in such conversations, we must recognize not only that we may have some things to teach but also some things to learn. We may even have to learn to change.

Such communication is possible because we are "hybrids," to use Jeannine Hill Fletcher's term. We are identified not only by a singular feature, such as our religion, but have other aspects to our identity. We have ethnic, economic, political, and other constituents in our identities. Though we differ in politics and religion, we may share enthusiasm for model railroading or knitting.

Overlapping concerns can spread wider the net of solidarity. Yet, while working alongside persons of other faiths, the distinctiveness of their religious perspective is not erased, and communication does not take place on some newly found sameness within the two religions. Rather, as members of multiple communities simultaneously, each possesses a multilingualism through which a shared language can be found. (Hill Fletcher 2005, 93)

Even as we recognize our religious differences, we can share in the dialogues of living together and of action (discussed in chap. 3 below) and come to learn and appreciate, even while we may disagree with, other perspectives. If we communicate well with others, we might even convert them to our views.

Wuthnow's call for reflective religious pluralism in the United States does not require or even recommend that particular religious communities water down their views or prohibit them from seeking to change others' views. Wuthnow, Sacks, and Hill Fletcher, in various ways, provide patterns for communication. Communication may include efforts at persuasion directed to overcome disagreements. But to persuade those of a different faith tradition, one must communicate effectively with them in ways that they can accept.

The second consequence of religious diversity is that however individuals may respond, ignoring others is not a live option for religious communities. A religiously isolated community simply cannot fit this site. There is no place isolated enough on which to build it. This is not to deny that monasteries or religiously homogenous communities can be built in dense forests or on high mountains or in barren deserts or even behind high walls in the heart of teeming cities. Trappists, Zen Buddhists, Carmelites, some Mormons, and others build such communities. Nor is it to deny that a relatively homogenous neighborhood can be built in the midst of a bustling metropolis. Orthodox Jews in Brooklyn and Muslims in Detroit have developed neighborhoods with distinctive cultures fitting their religious communities in the midst of busy diversity. Yet no such localized community is impermeable to the forces, for good or ill, characteristic of the broader American culture. And one of those forces is the reality of genuine religious diversity, an implicit challenge to the finality and sufficiency of one's own religious way of life. A living faith tradition can survive on this site only if it has a way of coping with the fact of being one of many traditions on the site, all of which have some good reason for being here.

Religious diversity on this site is not merely external to a particular tradition. It can be internal in at least two ways, geographic and ethnic. The Roman Catholic tradition, presumably the most extensive and seemingly rather "monolithic," provides a good example of both.

The Catholic Church comes in various "flavors" in the United States. The ways of "being church" vary by location. In the cities of the eastern United States, such as Boston, Philadelphia, and New York, the Roman Catholic Church has been a political and cultural powerhouse; in the South and the rural sections of the plains and mountain states, it has been politically and culturally marginal. In the middle of the twentieth century, newspapers in Chicago and Milwaukee, for example, grouped their real estate advertisements in the classified sections of newspapers geographically by Catholic parish, not by town or other neighborhood designator. This indicates a powerful cultural position for the Roman Catholic Church, one that it did not have in North Carolina, for example, where Catholics have historically been less than 1 percent of the population or in Utah where the dominant Mormon tradition demands that Catholics make sustained efforts to maintain and nourish distinctive Catholic communities.

The way "the same faith" is lived out in these and other varied contexts is quite different. To treat the matter somewhat simplistically, we can say that, in the areas with a dense Catholic population and a culturally visible institutional structure, the church as "institution" shapes the way people live in and live out the tradition; in those with a thin population where other churches, for example, Southern Baptist or Methodist, are the culturally dominant religious institutions, "the church as remnant community" characterizes the practical ecclesiology of the other faith communities. In the former, the Catholic Church can be powerful enough to function politically as if it were established (save for the lack of tax support). In the latter, the Catholic Church can be practically persecuted (save for the tax exemptions given to all "charitable institutions"). A map showing the proportion of students in Catholic school systems and the distribution of Catholic colleges and universities would give a rough depiction of the distribution of such different population densities and different ways of being church. The denser the distribution of such institutions, the more likely a church is experienced as institution. There are numerous other factors involved, of course, and there are no pure types of either situation. The point is simply that geographical location makes a real difference in social location of faith communities and in the way their members live in and live out their faith tradition.

Ethnically, the Catholic Church is becoming increasingly Hispanic. It has become a commonplace (whether entirely accurate is yet to be seen) that sometime in the next decade or so a majority of members of the Roman Catholic Church in the United States will be Hispanics, but the conversion of Hispanics to Evangelical, Holiness, and Pentecostal Protestant traditions is also significant. Moreover, there is cultural diversity within Hispanic Catholicism. In the Southwest United States, Mexican American culture is strong, while in the Southeast, Cuban American patterns are distinctive; and in the Northeast, Puerto Rican and Dominican Catholics tend to be more visible. Yet all these populations have the census designation "Hispanic," although their religious practices and devotions vary widely.

Groups of migrants may carry their own particular devotions with them. For example, Mexican and Mexican American migrants to the rural South keep devotion to Our Lady of Guadalupe. Santería is a live option for some Cuban and Cuban American Catholics, but less so for Mexican American Catholics. Devotional and institutional patterns in Roman Catholicism continually evolve. There is no one homogenous, nationwide ethnic pattern even among Hispanics, at least not yet; but the penetration of pan-Hispanic media such as Univision and Telemundo may change this (see Miller 2004, 70).

Varying geographical density is not limited to the various Hispanic communities. Filipino and Vietnamese Catholics are strongly represented in San Francisco and in other major metropolitan areas. Historically, Irish Catholics have held sway in Boston; Irish and Italians in New York and San Francisco; middle Europeans in the Midwest (Polish Chicago in the heart of the German triangle from St. Louis to Cincinnati to Minneapolis); Bohemians and Czechs in parts of Texas; and French-derived Catholics in the southern tidewater regions and northern New England. The French and Irish traditions are shaped in part by Jansenist tendencies brought from Europe; Hispanic Catholicism is relatively untouched by such a heritage.

While each of the diverse geographical sites retains some local characteristics and while ethnic groups maintain their traditions insofar as they can, these patterns are relativized by the overwhelming processes of ecclesial centralization under Roman jurisdiction and internal migration in the United States. Cuban American theologians, such as Roberto Goizueta write critically and constructively about Mexican American devotion to Our Lady of Guadalupe, which is not part of their traditional Cuban heritage. Various Roman offices work to make the practice of the faith, especially liturgical practice, consistent from place to place. The Roman Curia advises the pope to move bishops from Rome to St. Louis to Philadelphia, from New Jersey to Florida and back, from Philadelphia to Hawaii to Virginia (in three recent cases). Vowed religious, other than those committed to "stability of place," can be and are moved from coast to coast and border to border and beyond. Additionally, Catholics, like all Americans, migrate internally to pursue educational opportunities, to take better jobs, to accept military assignments, to live in a more suitable climate, and for a whole host of other reasons. Some traditional or ethnic local devotions fade and national devotions thrive. Robert Orsi (1998) shows this in his examination of the growth of the cult of the patron of "hopeless causes," St. Jude, that emerged as a national devotion in the middle third of the twentieth century among the children and grandchildren of immigrants. Problems such as the "sexual battery and episcopal complicity" scandal are national problems. People moving from one place to another may be delighted or disillusioned by the way a church operates in a new town or city and engage in parish shopping until a relatively satisfying way of being church is found. Anyone who has been active in the church and migrated internally—the common wisdom is that 20 percent of U.S. residents change residence in any year—can recognize the significant differences in ways of being church in these various locations, and yet also recognize that it is the same church.

Such geographic and ethnic diversity internal to this tradition is not being homogenized in a new papist melting pot in the United States. Rather, a very complexly flavored stew is being cooked up, with various ingredients contributing to the aroma of the whole, but the flavors of each ingredient not (yet?) being absorbed into the taste of the whole. After all, even if their archbishops are of Irish or German or Anglo stock, Milwaukee and Chicago still "must" have a Polish auxiliary bishop because of the concentration of Catholics of Polish heritage in these cities; and the ability to communicate in Spanish is increasingly a valued qualification for lay ministers, priests, and bishops throughout the United States.

If this diversity is internal to a monolithic institution, faith traditions with either a more congregational, locally administered polity or with a variety of ethnic groups forming the tradition—or with both—will have analogous characteristics that one would expect to be even more diverse. Internal diversity is a key factor in the religious culture of the United States. The mobility of particular families and the formation of national associations for the betterment of the traditions mean that an internal diversity that presents both challenges and opportunities for religious traditions is a characteristic of this site.

Hill Fletcher notes that this diversity means that each person is a "hybrid." Since we are "shaped by a multiplicity of stories the conditions for conversation

across difference are in place. Because our frameworks are created intertextu-
ally from out of many stories, while two people might not share the story of
their religious community, they may have in common some additional stories
. . . of culture or ethnicity, of profession or generational outlook" (Hill Fletcher
2005, 110). These other stories or traditions in which we live are part of who we
are and may be the places that we can meet those who are "other" than us religiously. The key point for present purposes is that we are composite. We are
not shaped merely by our religious tradition but by a whole host of communities to which we belong. Diversity is internal to our communities and to each
of us.

Religious diversity is also external in a very challenging way. Diversity is
found within every religious structure built on this site. Interethnic, interfaith,
and interracial marriages are becoming more common. Education at public
schools and universities means that children of parents from one faith tradition
rub elbows and may even live with other good people who do not share their
parents' traditions. Work environments are prohibited by law from religious
discrimination, unless belonging to a specific religion is a bona fide occupa-
tional requirement. Hence, one normally encounters people of other faith traditions in the workplace. The same neighborhood may have a Catholic church,
a Jewish synagogue, a Mormon temple, an Islamic cultural center, and a variety of Protestant houses of worship. Buddhist meditation centers and Hindu
temples are increasing in number as well. Any of these institutions may anchor
or co-anchor a neighborhood. Any may be a civically important place where
neighborhood concerns are addressed and plans for action formulated.

This internalization of external diversity is also seen in some exemplary
individuals. Some Jesuits practice yoga or Zen meditation. Pope John Paul II
prayed at Assisi in 1986 with other religious leaders. Women called to ordained
service migrate from the Roman Catholic to Episcopal or Lutheran Churches.
Married Anglican males who were ordained as priests in the Anglican communion have been accepted into the Roman Catholic Church and (re)ordained
as Roman priests despite the hierarchy's supposedly unwavering commitment
to a celibate, all-male clergy. What seem to many to have been hard and fast
walls between traditions are being broached in a wide variety of ways. Specific
identity markers are slipping in significance; new ones are emerging, and the
harsh light of internal diversity banishes illusions of isolated purity. One cannot live in and live out a faith tradition in isolation from the diversity of multiple faith traditions.

This pattern of internal and external religious diversity may not be unique,
but it is distinctive of the United States. The significance of this pattern is that
practicing *one of many* living faith traditions other than the one into which one
is born and bred is a cultural "live option" in the United States. Many countries
do not have such a diverse religious landscape; in them, choice of a faith com-

mitment may be possible only for an elite few (compare Cobb 2002, 20–22) or exceedingly difficult. Some states in India require a thirty-day notification of conversion. Other nations that follow Islamic *shariah* prohibit conversions away from Islam. The live option in most countries is to participate either in the faith tradition endemic to the region or to become secular. That is, the *only* live option for those who cannot or will not practice their inherited faith tradition in most places is secularism (or perhaps being a persecuted minority, that is, an oppressed group rallying around a distinctive religious identity against the regime). Secularization is not the only option to living in a specific faith tradition in the United States, but merely one of many possibilities for those immigrants who need to figure out how to live in and live out a religious tradition in this country, as well as for those of their descendants who are afflicted with spiritual wanderlust.

Religious leaders in Canterbury, Rome, Lynchburg, Jerusalem, Teheran, not to mention other religious centers on the Eurasian landmass and in nearby island nations, seem to engage in unending rhetorical warfare against secularization and modern secular humanism. These leaders seem to fear that antireligious secularism will seduce adherents of the various faith communities away from their religious homes. The attacks on secularism in the United States, where a quarter of the population or more participates regularly in worship, seem to have a different object and audience from those in France, where perhaps only a twentieth of the population engages regularly in worship.

The religious rhetoric protesting against secularism is often vehement. Vehement rhetoric reflects the perceived power of secularism as an antireligious "other." As terrorism is seen as a threat to the stability and power of the United States, secularism is seen as a threat to the politically or culturally established faith tradition. At times, as in renascent Islamic movements, secularism seems to be the "defining other" that sharpens the cultural identity of the battling faith tradition. "The secular," however, is no one thing that can be attacked straight on any more than terrorism is. Each enemy, whether terrorist or secularist, is particular to the place that cultures it. And, yes, we do think there are some similarities between rhetorical opposition to terrorism and to secularism; the rhetors and the target differ, but the rhetorical attacks are similarly structured.

In the United States, however, no single religious "other" undermines the allegiance of the faithful. Multiple faith traditions and a variety of secular philosophies vie with one another on the pluralistic playing field. Various forms of secular humanism, egoism, and religious indifferentism are only some of the many live options available, not the only alternative to one's natal tradition. However pernicious the various religious traditions and their theological elite find secularism, it occupies a very different cultural place in the United States from the rest of the world. Like the various living faith traditions, the patterns of secularity are many ways among many ways on the cultural landscape. Secularity is not the "single" other to be opposed. It is too diverse to be a defining other, despite the fact that some religious integralists and fundamentalists attempt to paint the secular as demonic, as unified, and as monolithic as patriots painted the so-called worldwide Communist conspiracy that was the defining other politically and militarily for the United States half a century ago.

In sum, religious diversity in the culture of the United States has a particular pattern that rules out religious isolationism as a live option, is both internal and external to the various living faith traditions, and puts secularization and secularity in quite a different cultural place in the New World from the place of secularity and secularization in the Old World.

Why is this pattern of diversity different in the United States from other cultural locations? One key issue is the specific political pattern of nonestablishment.

The Nonestablishment of Religion

One answer to a question common to trivia games was "antidisestablishmentarianism." The question, of course, was What is the longest word in the English language? The word means "the ideology of opposing the ending of formal political and financial support of a church by the government." Although disestablishment patterns vary from country to country, in general, the taxpayers no longer pay for erecting buildings for churches or religious schools or for maintaining worship spaces. Governments may pay teachers in religious schools for teaching secular subjects but not for catechetical instruction. Ministers are no longer paid their salaries by the state. Generally, governments also lose any rights they may have previously had to name or recommend people for leadership posts in the denomination that had been established.

Although there are earlier and later instances of disestablishment, the French ideology and polity of *laïcité* is the premier example of disestablishment. Europe was swept by waves of wars for a century after the Protestant Reformation. Although these are often called the "wars of religion" between Protestants and Catholics, the sufficiency of that perspective has been challenged recently (Cavanaugh 1995). These were not simply clashes between Catholics and Protestants. States whose rulers (and people) were Catholic sometimes were in alliance with nations whose rulers (and people) were Protestants. To simply call these battles "wars of religion" when alliances crossed the religious divide—and recrossed, and double-crossed, and triple-crossed again and again—is misleading, claim historical revisionists. That these clashes saturated European soil with blood is indisputable. That they did so in order to free political rulers from competition from religious bodies for sovereignty within a territory is less clear. Perhaps so, but the truly modern nation-state does not appear until the French Revolution of 1789, which overthrew the king and also—necessarily—the church (see Cavanaugh 2004, 260–61). The union of throne and altar meant that the king and the hierarchy of the Catholic Church united in ruling France. To overthrow one meant unseating the other as well. These wars may have been the first sign of the reshaping of Christendom into a new culture less dominated by international religious elites and more by local hereditary or democratic elites. They are not, however, the birthpangs of the modern nation-state as much as they are the first rumblings of a multicentury political process whose shape varies from place to place, whose shapes were not foreordained, and whose outcomes are still not fully determined.

Beyond France, Germany was not united as a nation until the late nineteenth century. Italy was united only in 1870. The Austro-Hungarian empire is hardly an example of the bureaucratic modern nation-state; modern countries were carved from it only after 1918. Most of the wars were fought on the lands that all these nations would eventually consolidate and hold at least until World War I. Although the standard account may blame too much bloodshed on clashes over religious ideology, religion was a key factor. The wars of religion did not result in the quick formation of the modern nation-state. It would take a century or two and a whole host of other factors for each modern nation-state to get organized in its modern European form and finally to "overthrow" the hegemony of religious authorities. The time lapse between the religious wars and the formation of actual modern nations suggests that any who claim that the wars of religion were really not about religion at all may be overstated at best. That religion was a key factor, certainly along with other motives, was recognized while they were being fought, for example, by Michel de Montaigne, who caricatured Protestant and Catholic polemics about God's supporting one side or the other in the wars of religion in his essay "We Should Meddle Soberly with Judging Divine Ordinances" (written 1572–74).

Throughout Europe in the nineteenth century, struggles continued between royalists and republicans. The settlement of the Napoleonic wars with the Treaty of Vienna in 1814 stabilized Europe until the revolutions of 1830 and 1848. In France, in the quarter century leading up to the law of separation of 1905, the government "gradually took over the running of most hospitals, banned catechism from state schools, legalized divorce, removed crucifixes from public offices and required civil weddings at the local town hall" (Heneghan 2005, 16) although it did not forbid religious solemnization of marriages. The Catholic Church did not accommodate itself with a unified Italy until the treaty with Mussolini in 1929.

The general pattern of disestablishment is clear. A perceived ecclesiastical (and therefore clerical) cultural hegemony was overthrown, sometimes along with a royal hegemony. The upper clergy, at least in Catholic countries, had been at least partially exempt from the law courts of the land—priests and religious were governed by canon law and Roman courts. The established church's institutions were supplanted by a functional, governmental bureaucracy in law, education, and in the care of the ill. That church was then forced to look to its own resources for its support (despite the fact that in many regions, property that church entities had owned and used for support were nationalized centuries or decades earlier and the church, in turn, came to receive governmental support). The particular ways for carrying out disestablishment and the cultural places of the churches made striking variations on this theme.

The pattern in the foundation of the United States is quite different. It is not disestablishment but nonestablishment. The difference is crucial. Although colonies persecuted different religious groups (being a Romish priest, for example, in Massachusetts in the 1640s was a capital offense) and churches were established politically in some states well into the Republican period (Connecticut being the last state to disestablish the Anglican Church in the state constitution of 1818), the national policy that emerged and became codified in the Constitution and the Bill of Rights was quite different. The first amendment to the Constitution codified the understanding of the Constitutional Convention that the nation was not to have an established religion. Robert Wuthnow summarized the standard story well. He wrote:

> The American system of government reflects the deep religious divisions that swept across Europe in the century following the Protestant Reformation. Those divisions, erupting in near-fratricidal war between Catholics and Protestants during the Thirty Years War, were in every respect as severe as any of the religious tensions in the world today. John Locke, David Hume, and others to whom America's founders looked for guidance were deeply influenced by those conflicts. American government was deliberately conceived as a system of checks and balances that would prevent any minority—religious or otherwise— from imposing its will on the people while at the same time guaranteeing all minorities freedom in matters of religion, speech, and assembly. The First Amendment embodies those principles. (Wuthnow 2005, 82)

Whereas the French goal was to banish an authoritarian religion from its public hegemony and to regulate a clerisy that had been in many ways above local law, the U.S. goal was not only to protect the people from potential religious tyranny but also to protect the various "religious denominations from the state. This fundamental difference creates trans-Atlantic misunderstanding to this day" (Heneghan 2005, 16). Thus, the U.S. Constitution is indeed the protector of smaller communal religious spaces. The culture grows out of common forms of life (*pace* Cavanaugh 2004, 266), even if the governmental administrations do not and cannot always protect all those religious spaces equally well.

Even if the wars of religion had little to do with religion per se, one outcome of those wars was disestablishment, removing an "alien" authority from having sovereign power in the emerging nations of Europe; the point of nonestablishment in the United States is not a removal of an established privileged authority but an innoculation against the tyranny of any one religious authority and the allowance of freedom to all religious bodies and individuals. "Nonestablishment" is not "dis-establishment."

The contemporary significance of this point is highlighted in an unstudied comment by Helmut Koester, a German born and trained scholar of early Christianity who taught New Testament and associated subjects for most of his career at Harvard Divinity School. In commenting on the fact that it was the *American*, not the German, scholarly establishment that understood the significance of Walter Bauer's claim that a doctrinal diversity ("heresy") preceded the establishment of a definitive orthodoxy by the early church and its leaders in postbiblical Christianity, Koester wrote:

> This was a finding more welcome to Americans than Europeans. In Europe, everybody belongs to some kind of orthodox establishment, either Protestant or Catholic, at least in theory. Few people want to disturb the delicate equilibrium of church-and-state concordats. In our "Christian" country [the U.S.], however, everyone is a heretic in the eyes of everybody else. (Koester 1991, 470)

The cultural pattern of diversity is simply different in the United States from in Europe. That difference means that European religious bodies protect themselves not through nonestablishment but by forms of establishment sanctioned by concordats, such as that between the Vatican and Nazi Germany in 1933 that is still in place, although significantly modified. The loss of ecclesial privilege is disestablishment; the refusal to privilege any ecclesial grouping from the beginning is nonestablishment.

One result of disestablishment has been said to be the privatization of religion. In France, of course, other factors were also important. With the collapse of state support and government control of health and education, churches became truly voluntary. Migration from countryside to city in France was a component in the Industrial Revolution of the nineteenth century. The Catholic Church did little to minister to the emerging proletariat, which found more support for its immediate needs in radical and communist labor organizations. By the time of the law of separation, city dwellers had become increasingly less involved in the life of the Catholic Church. The worker-priest movement in the middle of the twentieth century was a response to the "loss" of the laboring class (a class that the church had never "held" and thus could not really be said to "lose"). However, the movement was suppressed in 1954. Disestablishment, migration, and other social changes, and the secularization of bureaucratic and welfare functions are factors in the privatization of religion in France. In nations such as Germany and Ireland, where some forms of establishments still exist, religious bodies are clearly public actors, even if participation in the practice of those bodies by citizens is purely voluntary and, for many, a set of choices unconstrained by political power, and in that sense "private."

The result of nonestablishment in the United States, in contrast, has been the creation of legally voluntary, but nonetheless compelling, self-supporting charitable and civic associations with substantial political clout. Some religious leaders decry the privatization of religion in this country. This is confused if "privatization" in the U.S. is equated with "privatization" in Europe. Wuthnow's discussion of managing religious diversity can be adapted to make this point clear. The average *individual* may be able to pick his or her religion privately, that is, "quietly deciding what his or her personal stance will be . . . "; but the religious *institutions* are public institutions. They communicate their views about the good, the true, the just, and the beautiful through their ministers and through their very existence. Their witness is always, necessarily public (cf. Wuthnow 2005, 230). Their witness and influence was and is tremendous. The churches, rather than ignoring immigrants, supported them strongly as they settled in a new land—this is political action. Protestant church leaders led the way in the abolitionist movement of the first half of the nineteenth century and in the temperance movement in the latter part of the century. Churches were actively engaged in suffrage issues on both sides of the women's suffrage question. By the latter third of the nineteenth century, the Roman Catholic Church had offered a limited support for the labor movement and was developing an independent school system in many large Northeastern, Mid-Atlantic and North Central cities. These are public political practices.

In general, religious ministers were licensed to perform marriages. Congregations, dioceses, vowed religious communities, and other institutions sponsored health and welfare agencies as well as local "private" aid societies. Churches remain active in political debates about reproductive rights, same-sex marriages, and public support of religiously administered primary educational institutions. In sum, faith communities have been and remain significant public actors in the United States.

While not established, the churches in the United States are hardly private, save that they are legally precluded from formally endorsing candidates for elective office. Unlike in Europe, ecclesial leaders and institutions in the United States were never exempt from local civil and criminal law, but had to fit in with the national, state, and local legal systems—a fact that creates dilemmas for Catholic colleges and social service agencies that have to live in two very different legal systems: canon law and civil law. That there is something very important about private religious choice highlighted by the concerns over privatization is recognized in the next section of this chapter, but religious communities and institutions were not and are not politically private. They are mediating social and cultural institutions with significant social presence and political clout.

Some find, however, that the power of religious groups to shape public policy has been diminished. Over the past few decades cultural critics, especially on the religious right, have bemoaned the alleged disappearance of religion from the naked public square. These critics have claimed that religious people were forced to divest themselves of their distinctive religious views in order to engage in debate on political issues. Appeals to religious warrants were ruled out of court in these debates. This perspective misrepresents the situation.

While religious claims and religious rhetoric have ebbed and flowed over the last half century, religious concerns, arguments, and people have certainly not been absent from political debate. Faith communities have had significant impact in local politics in many locales. Religious elites have had significant political power, even if that power has not been clearly expressed in election-time rhetoric. Many churches—for better or worse—supported the national war efforts in World Wars I and II and in Korea. The Roman Catholic Bishops' 1919 Plan of Social Reconstruction had large elements enacted in the New Deal of the 1930s. In the 1950s and '60s, the civil rights movement was fostered by the black churches and their ministers. White Catholic, Protestant, and Jewish leaders as clergy or scholars of their own living faith tradition publicly supported the movement in demonstrations led by black Protestant ministers. When Martin Luther King, Jr., wrote his famous "Letter from Birmingham Jail" in 1963, it was addressed to clergy who had questioned his timeliness and wisdom in violating a court order. The tactics of the civil rights movement were debated in overtly religious and philosophical terms. Religious leaders from various traditions were leaders in the mobilization against the Vietnam War and the Supreme Court decision in Roe v. Wade handed down in 1973. President Jimmy Carter (1976–80) used explicitly religious rhetoric and was supported strongly by religious activists. When Ronald Reagan was elected in 1980, conservative Christians especially rejoiced because their man, for whom they had worked, had been elected. "The Challenge of Peace," issued by the National Conference of Catholic Bishops in 1983, fomented a national debate on the legitimacy of nuclear deterrence and the possibility of the moral use of nuclear weapons. The just-war language of that letter, based on the theological work of Augustine and Aquinas and presented in language that was not overtly sectarian but deeply religious, can be traced in the speech president George H. W. Bush gave on January 16, 1991, "Address to the Nation on the Invasion of Iraq," announcing the initiation of the first Gulf War. In that speech, the president appealed to all of the relevant just-war criteria from "The Challenge of Peace" almost verbatim to justify inaugurating that war (Bush 1991). Religious groups continued to influence public policy, especially on end-of-life issues, throughout this period.

The administration of George W. Bush has found the religious conservatives' influence waxing again. Indeed, it seems to some observers that one of the reasons for the political left to lose its own clout is that liberal politicians like John Kerry were simply incapable of communicating any connection of their political issues to their religious convictions or the religious convictions of the electorate. This ineptitude allowed the conservatives to hold the field of moral and religious issues to personal, individual morality. The intensity of the churches' historic support for social reforms and lively participation in debates on social issues declined while their support for "family values" considered in the narrowest way was the obvious religious agenda on the political stage.

That particular religious views have not always been successful in influencing public policy is certainly true. That those whose primary reference community is the cluster of institutions inside the Washington beltway have apparently little sympathy with particular religious views is also true. Yet these factors do not imply that religion is merely private or that secularism of some pernicious form has triumphed in the political sphere. Rather, the fact is that, in a pluralistic society, no institution or elite has hegemony over policy. Religious diversity and nonestablishment do not necessarily, or actually, lead to relegating religion to a purely private realm, but they do prohibit me from forcing my views on my political peers. To have my position accepted by my political peers, I have to persuade them in ways they can accept that my position is politically viable and appropriate. I cannot force my view on them against their consent.

Critics have claimed that religious leaders have been forced to translate their views into religiously neutral language in order to enter the public square. Much is said to be lost in such translation, especially the particular bite of religiously committed language. The rhetoric of prophecy loses much if adapted to secular requirements of the naked public square. However, this claim is confused. The problem is that the critics' claims involve an account of language that is simply inadequate. The root difference seems rather abstract, but the way that one understands the fundamental function of language—as a vehicle for signification or as a medium for communication—shapes how one thinks about committing religious talk in public.

The critics assume that language essentially functions to signify what we mean. When we talk of God, we mean God; when we talk of God's law, we refer to God's law. Thus, when we change our language to less religiously loaded language in the naked public square, such as that of natural law or human rights, we change the significance of what we say. On this assumption about language, the "translation" model means that churches cannot say what they truly mean "in public." Hence, if we are forced to "translate" our message to other idioms, the critics allege that we are being forced to water it down because we change its significance. Such translation allegedly runs a very real and severe risk of losing what we mean to signify.

If one assumes, however, that language fundamentally is a communication medium, then for communication (and signification) to be effective, the speaker (or writer) needs to consider the hearer (or reader) being addressed and her or his ability to understand what is being communicated. If a hearer has no concept of God's law or rejects such an idea, one may certainly communicate with that hearer. But language about God's commands is hardly effective for convincing an agnostic or atheist with whom one has to work politically that an act or policy is virtuous or vicious. That God requires or forbids an act or policy carries no persuasive force with someone who does not believe in God or who believes rather differently about who or what God might be! If the point is to preach the word, speakers can talk of God's law until they are blue in the face. If the point is to convince the hearer to support a specific policy or engage in a particular act, then the speaker will have to find some other way to convince the nonbelieving hearer. The use of less religiously inflected language is not the watering down of religious rhetoric, but a necessary strategy to communicate effectively and convince across ideological boundaries. In a pluralistic society, cross-traditional communication and persuasion require that a speaker or writer consider the audience one wants to convince. Given the patterns of immigration, diversity, and nonestablishment discussed above, such an approach is a necessary constituent of any communicative theology in the U.S. context.

The appropriate tactic is not to try to reword our claims in neutral language, but to seek to communicate with a particular audience at a particular time and place for a particular purpose. The difference may be subtle, but it is important. To illustrate this point, consider the popular sixty-four page, twelve-lesson publication meant to instruct non-Catholics seeking to marry Catholics, published by the Redemptorists, *How to Survive Being Married to a Catholic* (Henesy and Gallagher, 1997). It used humor to deconstruct caricatures of Catholic practices. Its twenty-four pages of illustrated cartoons clearly show how the Catholic Church is distinctive, but neither authoritarian nor irrational, in its views. It also used a persuasive approach to convey fundamental and distinctive Catholic teaching in more traditional catechetical sections. Contrast this with *The Catechism of the Catholic Church*, a tome meant for reference, neither humorous nor persuasive, but simply setting out a statement of the faith as determined by an international committee designed for those who instruct others. Both present "the faith," a fact attested by both having imprimaturs certifying that they are free from doctrinal error in their presentations. It is not that one is somehow watered down and the other the whole story, or that one is insider language and the other outsider language. Rather, each is constructed to communicate the tradition in different circumstances to different people for different purposes. Both signify with appropriate clarity for the purposes and contexts what the faith is, but signification is not the purpose of either. What a nonbaptized prospective bride or groom can be enabled to understand differs from what a Catholic high school religion teacher can be expected to understand. Even for college-age Catholics, *How to Survive Being Married* has been more effective than theological tomes in communicating the faith. The point is communication, and the ability of the audience to hear is a determining factor in how one communicates.

Our polity does not silence distinctive religious voices in the public square. Rather, some religious representatives have preached the word in ways that cannot be heard by their audiences. They have failed to persuade at least in part because they have failed to communicate their message clearly in a way that can be understood. A counterexample of a communicative and persuasive success is the Catholic bishops' pastoral letter of the 1984, *The Challenge of Peace*. It is not that religious leaders must divest themselves of religious language in the public square. Rather, they must use language that communicates to the target audience what they mean to convey *in a way the audience can understand*. Religious leaders like Martin Luther King, Jr., and the National Conference of Catholic Bishops provide examples of just this sort of effective communication in language appropriate to a diverse audience.

Nonestablishment does not privatize religion. Immigration is the key factor in establishing a culture of religious choice—a choice that is personal. On a personal level, one's choice of religion is private, that is, not legally constrained. Nonestablishment does not exclude religious language from the discourse of politics, but diversity may shape the way religious leaders need to talk if they are to be persuasive. Nonestablishment is intended to ensure that no particular religious institution achieves hegemony over a diverse population. Nonestablishment does not preclude religious leaders or constituents from participating in the political life of the nation (save that religious groups, like all charitable organizations, cannot make financial contributions to or endorse specific candidates for public office; the latter prohibition is easily and often avoided, while the former can be sidestepped by carefully setting up political action committees).

Religion is not private in the United States. Religious communities, institutions, and their representatives are constituent of and in the diverse commonweal, both locally and nationally. Nonestablishment is a distinctive way for religious institutions to be public, though not governmental, in this country.

Beyond the historic and ongoing factor of immigration, the cultural pattern of religious diversity, and the particular polity of nonestablishment, two other factors have emerged as crucial especially over the last half century or so if we are to understand the U.S. site on which we work to develop a Catholic Christian theology of religious diversity. *Commodification* has given rise to a shoppers' paradise in religion. Our free choice of faith traditions has been transformed. We have become consumers of religion in a veritable spiritual supermarket. Globalization in communication and commerce has made the world much smaller and more interdependent. Radiologists in India read X-rays taken in Boston in real time. U.S. goods (e.g., Coca-Cola) are produced, advertised, recognized, and sold around the globe; products and energy from half a world away are sold at the local mall or megastore. As immigration has repeatedly triggered nativist responses, so globalization triggers tribalist responses, even terrorist ones.

Commodification

The transformation of the family home from a site of production to a site of consumption is an oft-told tale (see Miller 2004, 46–54, and his sources). Some trace it to the end of the Middle Ages, when a commercial revolution occurred (Howell 1986); much of the domestic work of growing, preserving, and cooking food shifted. Consider bread. Wheat has to be sown, grown, harvested, threshed, winnowed, and milled before it can be used in making dough for baking bread. When these were household tasks in rural areas, a coordinated effort of a number of family members was needed. Now, even in rural areas, these tasks have been rationalized out of the household. Farmers, millers, and bakers each take on part of the work and accomplish it more efficiently. Householders no longer produce and mill grain, but use part of the income from their crafts or other businesses to buy bread.

Buying flour, preparing dough, and baking bread at home has become a less common practice. The same could be said for making cloth and sewing clothes. In general, as production became separated from particular households the market had to become a daily or weekly affair rather than an annual bazaar. Marketing became a regular household task as more specialized tasks were rationalized into industries that produced commodities for consumption.

About a century ago in the United States, the electrification of homes created a fundamental shift in householders' work. Labor-saving devices changed work patterns and shifted class boundaries. No longer did middle-class and upper-class women have to manage servants and oversee their cleaning or their production of food and clothing. The women assumed some of those tasks themselves; sometimes they were expected to use their new tools to do the work that two or three domestic servants had done. Baking became the work of the housewives of the growing middle class, no longer the work of cooks they hired to prepare food. Wood-fired ovens that demanded substantial labor to gather and prepare wood were replaced by gas (and eventually electric) stoves. Domestic work for lower-class women dwindled.

Housewives also used labor-saving tools to do jobs that their husbands or professional workers had done. Hoovering eliminated the necessity for men to carry out rugs too heavy for their wives so that the wives could then beat them out of doors. The refrigerator eliminated the necessity for strong men to deliver large blocks of ice for the icebox. Eventually housewives learned to drive automobiles and went shopping for commodities to be consumed at home. Rather than accepting delivery of a fifty-pound cloth sack of flour that she would use not only to bake into bread but also to cut and sew into her children's clothing, the housewife went to the store and bought sliced bread in a disposable (that is, useless) paper or cellophane package so that she and her family could consume the bread.

Whether this process is a good thing for women or men or children or anybody is not the issue here. A more reliable system for producing crucial foodstuffs seems an obvious good; the shifting cultural roles of women and men seems a blessing, if a mixed one. Decreasing independence meant increasing interdependence. The process also seemed to contribute to the destabilizing of the family, which seems a significant loss. The issue that concerns us is that bread is no longer an item that a household produces but a commodity that it consumes. And what is true of bread is true of ice cream, frozen fish, lettuce, shirts, children's underpants, and a host of other items: almost everything in our homes is now a commodity, wastefully packaged in useless material.

Modern commodities are brought into the household to be consumed or to improve consumption. This shift is a change even in who we are because we radically change what we typically do. We no longer add value to the commodities we buy (as in assembling flour, yeast, and water into dough for bread). We simply consume them more or less as is, with as little effort expended—and value added to them by our labor—as possible. Our labor-saving appliances such as electric stoves are designed to make consumption effortless. They accelerate the emergence of commodification: the separation of production from consumption. We are no longer connected to the people, the factories, and the land that produce the commodities we consume.

Abetted by the power of advertising, formerly homemade items, from food to music to clothes, became replaced by commodities such as entertainment and fashion that we may buy more when they please us than when we need them. The evolution of the space of the domestic home, from a site of production for consumption to a site of commodity purchase for consumption is one window onto a crucial factor in U.S. culture. Our culture is not merely one of consumption—all cultures seem to function to shape consumption—but one of the commodification of consumption.

"The commodity hides the conditions of its production" (Miller 2004, 37).

The brand new Chevrolet in the showroom hides the fact that its brakes and catalytic converter were made by Chinese laborers who were paid a tenth of what U.S. laborers had been paid to make the same item. We value the Chevy by its price, by the amount of cash we need to exchange for it, and the amount of income we have to generate to make that exchange possible. We enjoy the DVD or the rock concert or the professional football game or the loaf of bread or the coffee enough to pay good money to consume them, whether as entertainment or nourishment. We are no longer visible to ourselves or others as producers who have a connection, whether through barter, purchase, or production, with the goods we use and consume. We have unavoidably become shaped by a consumer culture that is unavoidably commodified.

Vincent Miller claimed that consumer culture is "a situation in which elements of culture are readily commodified. Cultural commodities, like literal products, are . . . abstracted from their conditions of production and presented as objects valuable in themselves, shorn of their interrelations with the other symbols, beliefs, and practices that determine their meaning and function in traditional contexts" (Miller 2004, 72). For most of us, how entertainment spectacles are produced, where our automobile is constructed, or how our bread is made is of no concern. Our material culture has become commodified.

This culture teaches us that making good choices to consume well is a prime value. For the past seventy years, millions of Americans have subscribed to *Consumer Reports*, published by the Consumers' Union. We subscribe to this "objective" magazine so we can make good choices among the many commodities we can buy. The evaluations in the magazine say little, if anything, about the conditions of the production of the commodities. The only relevant question to be answered for the consumer-reader is whether these commodities function well and are thus worth their cost. The annual automobile buying guide issue exemplifies perfectly this single concern: the fact that some automobiles may be produced in oppressive conditions is never mentioned; that some contribute excessively to polluting the atmosphere is rarely, if ever, noted. The only question is whether one car or another is a good commodity for purchase.

The prime value of good choice presumes a fundamental value of free choice. Unconstrained by anything except our own financial capacity to purchase commodities, we value being free to choose whatever we want. The rhetoric of choice dominates much public rhetoric about controversial issues. The success of pro-choice rhetoric in debates over reproductive technology, the presumption that a free market is a fundamental value, and the promotion of government support for private chartered grammar schools as a "choice" for parents all spill over into a presumption that religious freedom is freedom to choose. Religious freedom at root means that every person can choose privately among the religious commodities offered by religious leaders and institutions for sale in a spiritual marketplace.

In this culture where choice among commodities is a prime value, religion has become just another commodity (see Miller 2004, 73–106). Megachurches sell seekers entertainment as worship. Religious texts and symbols become disconnected from the traditions that give them their sense. Spirituality has become commodity, with intellectual property rights that prevent any unauthorized (read "non-paying") users from adapting or adopting the spirituality (see Effross 2003). One pays the spiritual guru just as one pays the trainer at the health club. Freedom of choice is crucial if one is to have the ability to obtain spiritual commodities (cf. Tilley 2004, 167–68).

In a commodified culture, it makes sense to see the key point of the nonestablishment of religion to be necessarily associated with the individual's freedom to choose one's own religion. And if we consider only the individual consumer, this seems true. The choice of a religious tradition or a spiritual path is a private choice in the sense that there is no serious legal constraint on that choice. However, if the argument made above about the significance of nonestablishment of religion in the U.S. polity is accurate, then there are other profound and fundamental values protected by nonestablishment: an innoculation against the tyranny of any religious elite and the protection of religious communities from the tyranny of the government. The primary contemporary challenge of U.S. culture to religious authenticity is not so much the privatization of religion, nor the nonestablishment of religion, nor the internal or external diversity of faith traditions, but the commodification of religion.

Wuthnow (2005) has characterized this pattern as that of the spiritual shopper. Christopher Lasch anticipated him by nearly three decades in his description of one emblematic figure:

> Jerry Rubin, having reached the dreadful age of thirty and having found himself face to face with his private fears and anxieties, moves from New York to San Francisco, where he shops voraciously—on an apparently inexhaustible income—in the spiritual supermarkets of the West Coast. "In five years," Rubin says, "from 1971 to 1975, I directly experienced est, gestalt therapy, bioenergetics, rolfing, massage, jogging, health foods, tai chi, Esalen, hypnotism, modern dance, meditation, Silva Mind Control, Arica, acupuncture, sex therapy, Reichian therapy, and More House"—a smorgasbord course in the new consciousness. (Lasch 1979, 45)

Rubin would today be confronted with a whole new range of spiritual commodities, including seekers' services, exorcism and deliverance ministries, herbal remedies, new forms of meditation and drug-induced euphorias, as well as those he experienced. Rubin, of course, is not typical, and there may be another way to construe spiritual shopping (see pp. 176 below). Yet it is clear that a vast spiritual marketplace attracts an uncountable number of shoppers.

The problem with the hegemony of the market is not merely the com-modification of religion but the replacement of a substantial self with a soli-tary Narcissus who shops around until she or he finds what satisfies, even if only for a brief time. The question finally is whether a commodified self can be narrated in a story coherent enough to be seen as worth living in and living out. Of course, some shoppers do settle into a way of life and live out the spir-itual path they initially buy into. Unless they do settle down, the problem of living coherently remains.

Moreover, the explosive growth of markets has had significant social effects. Jonathan Sacks put it this way:

The market . . . has subverted other institutions—families, communi-ties, the bonds that link members of a society to a common fate, and the moral discourse by which, until now, we were able to maintain a critical distance between "I want" and "I ought." By replacing a hier-archy of collective obligations with a supermarket of personalized lifestyle preferences, it has undermined our ability to talk of public goods—the things (from parks to public services to loyalties) we do not buy or own but share. (Sacks 2003, 35)

The market has undermined "'third-sector' or 'mediating' structures. . . . Oth-ers prefer the term 'civil society.' Yet others . . . speak of social capital." (Sacks 2003, 152). Those spheres of human community that give shape to our civic life have been increasingly diminished and treated as either part of the public, governmental domain or part of the private, free choice domain.

One appropriate way to respond to the challenges of commodification is, as Vincent Miller notes, to find tactics for "stewarding religious traditions in consumer culture" (2004, 177). His analysis, though seemingly pessimistic, accurately articulates the challenge. It deserves thoughtful contemplation:

Consumerist culture forms people in consumerist habits of use and interpretation, which believers, in turn, bring to their religious beliefs and practice. Thus, while theology can offer daring and radical coun-ternarratives by drawing on the rich wisdom of religious traditions, these responses are subject to the same fate as other cultural objects within consumer culture. For that reason, Christian counternarratives, metanarratives, or even master narratives are in danger of becoming ineffectual and, more than that, of functioning as comforting delusions that are nothing more than a way for religious believers to convince themselves that, appearances notwithstanding, their religious faith is impervious to the erosions of commodification. Indeed, such reassur-ing narratives are very marketable commodities in the cultural turmoil of advanced capitalism. Theology has to learn the lesson that the market has taught other subversives who have attempted to reach a mass audience: this system greets subversions and denunciation with mercantile enthusiasm. It welcomes the most radical denunciations of the shallowness of our civilization and its global excesses in the same way the sated gourmand welcomes the tartness of a sorbet between courses of a heavy meal. (2004, 179–80)

Even the slogans of the most radical critics can be mass-marketed as T-shirts— or WWJD bracelets. What is needed is conscious working to preserve mediating structures and other expressions of our shared social capital.

Yet a culture of commodification also presents an opportunity, even a mandate, for renewal of traditions. Miller notes that the practices that constitute a faith tradition are internally connected to the meaning of the beliefs, symbols, and attitudes that the tradition carries (2004, 179–228). Keeping religious traditions alive in the face of overwhelming and ubiquitous commodification means engaging in practices that keep those internal connections alive. Participating thoughtfully in sacramental and liturgical practices connects symbols to the tradition rather than letting them float free as disconnected cultural commodities. Engaging in craftlike practices that make evident the connections between products and the means of producing them can counter the ubiquitous cultural tendency to see all things as commodities abstracted from the conditions of their production and worth only what we will pay for them. Moral practices such as enacting a commitment to buy fair-trade products from the Two-thirds World whenever possible can also help undermine the seemingly inevitable disconnection of products from those who produce them. Creating sacred spaces and improving media communication are also practices that can counter the cultural pattern. All of these practices—not to mention traditional religious practices—help create spaces in which practitioners can keep their traditions vibrant.

Spiritual shoppers are often blamed by traditionally religious people for their preference for dabbling in religion, rather than for living in and living out a tradition. Yet vibrant traditions also do not produce legions of people who find them empty or meaningless. Spiritual shoppers have a spiritual hunger. Evidently many of them found that the traditions of their parents did not satisfy that hunger. It may not be that shopping is a pattern that is merely cultural. It may be that the faith communities themselves have gone stale. The dwindling numbers of mainstream Protestants, Roman Catholic vowed religious and priests, and observant Jews suggest not merely that the culture is undermining their ability to carry on, but that the forms of life incarnated in these traditions no longer communicate to their adherents the depths of the riches they have to offer. Commodification is clearly a cultural challenge; the question is how the faith communities will change themselves to communicate with and convert those who have drifted into the spiritual supermarket.

Globalization

It is sometimes difficult for college teachers to remember that contemporary freshmen have no recollection of any president before Bill Clinton or that the fall of communism is more ancient to them than the beginning of the Second World War for the boomer generation. Yet those of us who lived through 1989 as adults knew that the world changed that year even though we could not guess at the implications of the end of the Cold War era. Nearly two decades later, we still cannot understand all the ramifications of that momentous series of events. After that year, the United States was the only global superpower left. Globalization entered a new and definitive phase.

In one way, globalization is not a new phenomenon. The ancient Silk Road, the trade route between China and the Mediterranean, spread commodities, ideas, diseases, and religions throughout the "known" world. European expansion into, colonization in, and exploitation of the Americas, Asia, and Africa was a form of globalization. The twentieth century first witnessed wars on a global scale. International commerce and communication are not new; multinational corporations have brought weal and woe to the world for many decades, if not centuries. Yet the condition of a single nation's culture dominating the globe is quite new.

Although the diagnoses of and prescriptions for the woes of globalization differ widely (see the works cited by Mallon 2005, 156–59; also Huntington 1996a, Fukuyama 1992, Friedman 2000; for theological work, Mallon 2005, Schreiter 1997, Sacks 2003, Gerdes 2006), the relevant point is made best by one title: *Jihad vs. McWorld: How Globalism and Tribalism Are Reshaping the World* (Barber 1996; 1995 and 2003 editions have different subtitles). Globalization in commerce and communication is provoking resistance, even terrorizing resistance from those whose cultures are threatened by the global hyperculture. Some resist because of the effects of the global economic boom. Others resist because they are not part of the boom. Others resist the hegemony of U.S. "moral decadence."

An increasingly dominant American culture and English language, spread through international trade, science, and communication (especially through the Internet over the last decade or so), have provoked profound local resistance up to and including *jihad*. Distinctive religious communities and nations struggle to maintain their cultural identities in the face of the universal availability of denim jeans, white T-shirts, Coca-Cola, McDonald's hamburgers, Hollywood films, Web-based pornography, and other icons of American industry and culture. As the United States spends vast sums for energy in other countries, economic and political elites can obtain consumer goods that parade their elite status. Whether a Mercedes or a Lexus or a Hummer, owning a luxury car trumpets its owner's success in the global market.

Production has become globalized in ways unimaginable fifty years ago. Japanese- and German-brand automobiles are now produced in the United States of steel imported from around the world. This is just one example of the fact that complex commodities are increasingly "international in content." Capital and jobs flow easily across international boundaries as entrepreneurs seek to cut costs of production and increase both sales and profits. "Transfer pricing," a corporate practice of interlocked companies buying from and selling to one another as commodities move around the world such that the conglomerate's profit is taken on the transactions performed in a tax-haven state, becomes simpler and even harder for governmental regulators in any specific country to pick out as the volume of global trading increases and the creation of limited liability corporations proliferates. As the United States borrows vast sums from individual, corporate, and national investors to finance its increasingly bloated national debt, much of which is due to the endlessly confused "war on terror" (as if one could make war on a tactic, rather than on the specific people who use the tactic), the web of globalization is reinforced.

Global capitalism has emerged as a new phase in the late capitalist economy. Capitalism is a powerful engine for the creation of wealth. As Jonathan Sacks put it, capitalism has simply delivered higher living standards and greater freedom. In the countries participating in the global capitalist economy, there have been increases in political freedom and "spectacular rises in living standards. Improvements in agriculture have meant that while, prior to industrialization, it took the majority of a country's workforce to produce the food it needed, today in advanced economies the figure is around 2 per cent" (2003, 28). Sacks also noted that the spread of improved public health measures and medical care has reduced infant mortality and lengthened the lifespan of the average citizen. The range of goods available to ordinary consumers in modern successful economies was unthinkable a century ago.

Capitalism, however powerful as a wealth creator, is a poor wealth distributor. In fact, it concentrates wealth in the hands of a few. The differential distribution of the benefits of the increase in generated wealth is substantial enough to be morally appalling—a point made literarily by Charles Dickens and philosophically by Karl Marx in the nineteenth century. Globalization over the last fifty years or so, and especially over the last two decades, has increased our awareness of the huge differences between poor and rich. Many would argue that globalization has exacerbated the inequities. The rest of this paragraph adapts Jonathan Sacks's illustrations of the situation about the year 2000

(2003, 29). The average North American consumes thirty times what the average person in India consumes. Forty-four percent of the people of the world have no sanitation; 22 percent live in poverty; 22 percent do not have access to safe drinking water; 17 percent do not have adequate shelter; 15 percent have no access to medical care; 14 percent are malnourished; and 30,000 children a day die of preventable diseases. Much of this is due to the centralization of wealth. As Sacks noted:

> By the end of the millennium, the top fifth of the world's population had 86% of the worlds GDP while the bottom fifth had just 1 per cent. The assets of the world's three richest billionaires were more than the combined wealth of the 600 million inhabitants of the least developed countries. The enormous wealth of the few contrasts starkly with the misery of the many and jars our sense of equity and justice. (29)

In the United States over the past twenty years "97 per cent of the increase in income has gone to the top 20 per cent of families, while the bottom fifth have seen a 44% reduction in earnings" (ibid.). The wealth of the country as a whole has been increasing, but that wealth has accrued disproportionately to those already rich. The facts that a large percentage of the U.S. population lacks adequate health care and that approximately one out of five children in the United States lives in poverty are effects in large part of the increasing disparity between the rich and upper-middle class on one end of the scale and the working and welfare poor on the other. As the middle class is priced out of many cities by the affluent, a sharply divided two-class culture may be emerging.

It could be argued that globalization is not a characteristic of the U.S. site for doing theology, but an aspect of every other characteristic. Migration becomes easier as transportation becomes increasingly available and relatively cheaper. Migration becomes more difficult as nations put up physical and legal barriers against immigrants. Religious diversity is increased in the United States as an increasingly diverse immigrant pool brings increasingly diverse religious traditions with them and provokes a new wave of nativism. Legal nonestablishment is opposed by those theocrats of various stripes who would promote a cultural, if not legal, establishment of their own traditions. Global pathways hasten the commodification of all goods so that MacGregor athletic shoes are advertised in the United States with Scottish symbols but are manufactured in China. Whether globalization is a new phase in old trends or a new factor, globalization has had a profound effect on all the cultures of the world, including U.S. culture. It is a significant factor on our site.

Whether the global victory of modern (limited) free-market capitalism over the state-directed capitalism of the Soviet system is ultimately good or bad for humanity is moot; but that victory has been a prime constituent in the emergence of a new phase of globalization.

Conclusion

This chapter has surveyed some of the cultural factors that make the United States a distinctive site for constructing a Christian, and specifically a Catholic, theology of religious diversity. How do these factors shape the sort of theology we can construct on this site (and, obviously, on other sites that share some or all of these characteristics)?

First, immigration continues and problems of nativist responses remain. Religious prejudice may be most difficult to overcome in the face of immigration. Again, controversial views abound regarding immigration and the preservation of different traditions. Sociologist Wuthnow noted that "assimilation makes pluralism easier by creating commonalities that transcend ethnic and religious subcultures" (Wuthnow 2005, 73). Theologian Hill Fletcher recognized the same phenomena as "hybridization." However, the vanishing of distinctive traditions and values is also a loss. Oddly enough, our consumer culture may function to help preserve distinctive traditions of at least one group of immigrants. While the more typical pattern seems to be one of homogenizing distinctiveness and coopting diversity (who isn't "Irish" on March 17?), Miller noted with regard to one group an ironic countertrend that may also apply to other distinctive groups in a consumer culture that values particular niches in the marketplace:

> Thus, the assimilation of the Latino immigrants who have arrived in this country over the past several decades is likely to be very different from the earlier waves of immigrants, who became Americans by giving up their original cultural identities. A distinctive Latino identity will likely survive because the current marketing networks can cater to a lucrative cultural niche. There is now room in marketing structures and media bandwidth to recognize and give voice to different and dissenting voices, but their particularity or dissent is treated as a cultural product that is marketed like any other. (Miller 2004, 70)

How we should respond to this odd aspect of commodification in a "postmodern" culture is not clear. While it may be easy to proscribe prejudicial acts against those who are of different races and faith traditions, it is far more difficult to prescribe useful actions for and favorable attitudes to immigration and immigrants.

Second, religious diversity is an intrinsic constituent of this site that must be embraced. Such diversity is not an accidental factor or a regrettable aspect of this site. This means that our theology must actively encourage Christians to listen respectfully to those who live in and live out other faith traditions. That we have sometimes, at least, failed to do so is evinced by Wuthnow's reporting that the most important thing others want from Christian communities and individuals is "greater respect and understanding" (2005, 64). Participants in other faith traditions do not, for the most part, want to convert to Christianity. Nor are they dissatisfied with their own traditions, as some Christians seem to assume. As Wuthnow put it:

> What American Hindus, Buddhists, and Muslims most often say they want from American Christians is simply greater understanding. Some of them would like converts to their religion, but most are interested in gaining respect. They do not mean this only in a politically correct way, but in terms of greater familiarity and knowledge. . . . They do not expect Christians to give up being Christians or Christian leaders to fundamentally alter their teachings. But they realize that they are a presence with which Americans are going to have to come to terms. . . . They believe better understanding would be good for the rest of the population as well. (2005, 72)

The mere toleration rooted in indifference is not sufficient. The diversity of faith traditions is not something that we can ignore but must respond to positively.

Third, nonestablishment is a distinctive feature of our site that must be recognized and arguably supported. If the argument above is on track, then the main point of nonestablishment is opposition to the tyranny of a minority—or a majority. Nonestablishment does not canonize religious individuals' or communities' nonparticipation in the political debates of the nation as either a fact or a positive value. Religious traditions are not private even if legally speaking a person's choice to join or remain in a religious community is. The failure to distinguish the differences between what nonestablishment means for individuals and communities or institutions has led some to disparage nonestablishment as if it were disestablishment. The positive point must not be forgotten: nonestablishment functions to protect the civil rights of those who are not dominant in the culture (see Wuthnow 2005, 73). Whether Christian, Jewish, Hindu, Muslim, or Buddhist, a theocratic political regime run by another group (or, arguably, the elite of one's own) is not desirable. Whether religious institutions should continue to receive tax exemptions, whether explicitly religious grammar schools should receive governmental support, whether particular religious symbols should be displayed on government property, or how religious leaders ought to communicate the imperatives of their tradition in the public square are all issues that need to be explored but are far beyond the discussion here—not to mention specific issues that concern religious people. Especially if religious leaders see that other institutions such as corporations have achieved a tyrannical or hegemonic position because of their economic or political power, they should speak out—and indeed join hands with leaders from other religious traditions who might also oppose such economic, social, or cultural domination.

Fourth, the question of our response to commodification has been addressed above, as this issue is a factor that affects all people of all traditions. Again, following Miller, it is difficult to prescribe particular practices or actions, but proscriptions are possible: do not assume that a distinctive countercultural narrative is sufficient to block the slide into thoughtless pluralism, religious indifference, and religious commodification. After all, Christians know that "the line between the church and the world passes right through each Christian heart" (McClendon 1986,17). The complex stories of our religious lives include diversity, a diversity that may be insoluble by appeal to one narrative ingredient in that complex story or to an explanatory theory.

Finally, globalization affects our lives on this site in subtle and obvious ways and serves to qualify each of the site characteristics in multiple ways. The most obvious is that the necessity for immigrants to choose to remake or abandon their home religion has become even more complex in a world made a village by the Internet. But the crucial point for theology or culture studies is this: We not only live on this site; this site, for better or worse, lives in us. Whatever we do, intellectually, spiritually, or manually, the site in and on which we do it shapes the possibilities of our thinking, our praying, and our working.

3

A Building Code for a Theology of Religious Diversity

OUR BUILDING METAPHOR WILL SHOW SOME CRACKS IN THIS CHAPTER. For example, a home builder starts by laying a foundation. Human practices, however, need no foundation. One simply engages in the practices to learn whether and how they work. One does not need to proffer a transcendental analysis of the universal conditions for the possibility of getting on a bicycle in order to engage in cycling or for the possibility of engaging in high jumping so as to execute a high jump during a track meet. This applies as well to the practice of doing theology. One does not need to construct foundations in order to engage in seeking to understand the faith tradition in which one dwells.[1] Nor do worshipers require a firm philosophical foundation to justify their engaging in the practice of worshiping God. Like bicycle riding and high jumping, theology and worship are practices that one learns in doing; they do not need foundations. Foundational arguments cannot show the reasonableness of high jumping or praying—or of theologizing. Understanding the practices, what they yield, and how they shape practitioners are far more relevant to answering the questions of whether it is wise for someone to engage in them.

Practices are varied and malleable. The kind of bicycle one uses makes a difference to the speed and control one has in riding. The invention of the Fosbury Flop changed the practice of high jumping forever. And one might debate about the best ways to worship God or the methods for doing theology. When one is engaging in the practice of worshiping, however, foundational philosophical questions about the existence of God are as out of place as questions about the existence of bicycles or the Fosbury Flop while engaging in cycling or track meets.

One can always ask if it makes sense to spend one's time engaging in a practice, whether riding bicycles, high jumping, worshiping God, or doing theology. Yet proving the existence of God does not warrant worshiping God or doing theology; indeed, it might warrant returning the ticket to God (as Ivan Karamazov did) or calling God to judgment (as Job did) or in shaking one's fist at God. How does a philosophical foundation for a practice such as thanking God for favors received make worship more rational than a practice such as thanking one's lucky stars? And would proofs of the nonexistence of lucky stars or of God be worth much in showing that one should not spend one's time in such activity or in reflecting on such activity theologically?

Philosophical analysis of religious practices, including believing, is important work. Yet attempting to build a philosophical foundation for doing theology is a modern defensive strategy. Many modern philosophers attacked religious belief and practice as unfounded and irrational. Theologians responded to the skeptical intellectual culture of modernity by building foundations. The result was an intellectual stalemate, at best. Philosopher David Hume took his mind off insoluble problems about the foundations of knowledge by turning to backgammon. Religious folk might properly engage in religious practices to take their minds off the stalemate.

Of course, some practices, such as phrenology, may well be irrational or worthless. The value and reasonableness of a practice is shown by those who participate in it well. Participants come to have the goods the practice generates by engaging in the practice. The practice of the sciences—imagination, hypothesis, experimentation, and independent verification—have yielded new understanding. Astronomy has a good predictive track record. Astrology, however, yields rather random results. The former is a science; the latter an amusement. In general, particular claims are tested within the processes and methods that constitute the practice. Good practice ferrets out mistaken or bogus claims, such as "cold fusion." Scientific practices are "proven" by their effectiveness in yielding the goods they are expected to yield, not by their philosophical foundations.

Practices carry their own reward—and punishment. Paying attention to what particular practitioners do to and for both the community of practitioners and the human communities that extend beyond the communities of practitioners is further evidence of their worth. Looking at what practices do to people, for people, and enable people to do is a way to understand both the rational and the moral values of practices. That such evaluation may well be controversial, of course, seems rather obvious. As the last chapter noted, the extremely complex set of practices known as global capitalism provides a good example of a practice or set of practices that reasonable people may evaluate quite differently.

Practices are guided by rules (see Lindbeck 1984; Tilley 2000). An apprentice or novice in the practice has to learn not only the rules that shape the practice but also how and when to apply them. "Never move another's peg for marking the beginning of the competitor's run up to the high bar." "Sharpen your tools daily." "Genuflect on one knee when entering the pew unless the

Blessed Sacrament is exposed; then genuflect on both knees." A truly skilled practitioner—whether a cyclist, high jumper, woodworker, or Tridentine worshiper—can understand the rules so well that she or he can see how to change them to improve the practice.

A Catholic Christian theology of religious diversity requires principles for understanding the diversity of religions. The rules that articulate these principles guide Catholics—and, for the most part, we would argue, any Christian—who engage in interreligious practices, especially interreligious dialogue. These rules form a basic "building code" for constructing a theology of religious diversity. Like all building codes, they do not prescribe certain architectural features but prescribe what elements are needed and proscribe elements that are to be avoided.

These rules apply to Christians, not to members of other living faith traditions or of no faith tradition. Although derived from the tradition of Catholic Christianity, we think they apply more generally to guide the ways Christians interact with those of other living faith traditions.[2] Some Protestants would, of course, find additional rules needed and might have difficulty with some of ours.

It is very important to note that rules are not formulated as statements or truth claims. We are claiming that Christians ought to follow these rules, not that they should proclaim them as truth claims that others have to accept and apply to themselves. We may think we have such claims, but those need to be tested in dialogue. These principles are derived from our "best practices" and continue to shape our practice. They guide what *we* do and how *we* deal with others whom we encounter in interreligious dialogue and other practices. Principles are not a *theory* of or a *foundation* for interreligious practices, but provide rules to guide our engaging in those practices. As imperatives, they do *not make truth claims*, even if they suggest or imply specific claims. Rules *regulate* and *guide*; they do not *state* (even though they can *be* stated). These are the rules *we* have to apply to *our* practice of engaging with those of other faith traditions.

That there are analogous rules guiding other living faith traditions seems obvious, but those rules are not our concern here. That there are many further rules needed to guide engaging in interaction in general and conversation in particular seems obvious, but they also are not our concern here. We do not think it appropriate to apply these particular rules to others. These are the rules that shape *Christian* participation—at least Catholic Christians' participation. If they are unacceptable to others as guides to *our* way of engaging in a shared practice, then we have to withdraw from sharing in the practice or examine the rules and, perhaps, reform our own tradition.[3] If others' rules that guide their participation in the shared practices are unacceptable to us, then we have to withdraw from the practice or invite them to rethink their rules.

In what follows, we lay out four rules from the Catholic Christian tradition to guide a practical theology of religious diversity (and in our view, a theology that is unrelated to practice is little more than swamp gas). We find that these rules limn the grammar of many of the particular statements proclaimed by the magisterium of the Roman Catholic Church since the Second Vatican Council (1962–65). We give most of these rules as proscriptions rather than prescriptions. Prescriptions tell us what to do or believe. Proscriptions tell us what not to do or believe. Proscriptions do not prescribe the way to build a theology, but simply remind us not to make certain proscribed moves as we build a theology in and for our faith tradition. Proscriptions admittedly sound negative, but like municipal building codes they allow for creativity in construction; prescriptions are constraining. Proscriptions leave room within a tradition for constructing new theological understandings in a way that prescriptions seem at times to exclude. Perhaps this is why the classic councils precisely proscribed what Christians were not to say (*Si quis dixerit . . . anathema sit*) rather than prescribed what Christians were obligated to believe.

We have put each of these rules in the form of a commandment. We use this form as a tongue-in-cheek way to signal that there are other formulations of these rules possible. We do not take them as so hard and fast as to be final and complete, but as useful guides, subject to correction.

I. Thou shalt not deny God's universal salvific will.

This rule distinguishes our catholic and Catholic approach from the radical exclusivism characteristic of some evangelical theologies. Such exclusivist views imply that either God did not desire to save all people (impugning God's creative goodness) or that God is not able to make that desire a real possibility for all people (impugning God's power). We neither accept nor reject the proposition that people are able to refuse to accept God's will that they be saved, so we have to acknowledge that it may be possible that people have the freedom and ability to thwart God's will and do so. Hence, it may be possible that God's salvation is not universally effective. Even if it is possible for some to refuse God's grace, whether any actually do so is not a question relevant to our project.

In Paul's first letter to Timothy, we find a "proof text" for this injunction:

> I urge that supplications, prayers, intercessions, and thanksgivings be made for everyone, for kings and all who are in high positions, so that we may lead a quiet and peaceable life in all godliness and dignity. This is right and is acceptable in the sight of God our Savior, who desires everyone to be saved and to come to the knowledge of the truth. For there is one God; there is also one mediator between God and humankind, Christ Jesus, himself human, who gave himself as a ransom for all. (1 Tim 2:1–6, NRSV)

Of course, there are many other proof texts that proponents of almost any view on the range of God's offer of salvation can quote from the Bible. And some Catholics will wonder how this squares up with the tradition of *extra ecclesiam nulla salus,* but that issue is discussed when we address rule three, below.

The key to this injunction is the document of the Second Vatican Council *Nostra Aetate,* and the subsequent series of clarifications and expansions of that document. *Nostra Aetate* declared that "all peoples comprise a single community, and have a single origin, since God made the whole race of men dwell over the entire face of the earth . . ." (§ 1). It went on to state that "One also is their final goal: God. His providence, His manifestations of goodness, and His saving designs extend to all men (cf. Wis 8:1; Acts 14:17; Rom 2:6–7; 1 Tim 2:4)" (§ 1). The document further asserted that the church rejects nothing "true or holy" in other religious traditions (§ 2), and that Christ died for the salvation of all (§ 4).

This universalism is not unique to *Nostra Aetate* (see Lane 2006). In the Constitution on the Church, *Lumen Gentium,* the council declared that "all are called by God's grace to salvation" (§ 13). Members of other faith traditions are related to the people of God "in various ways" (§ 16). The Pastoral Constitution on the Church in the Modern World, *Gaudium et Spes,* noted that God's grace acts in people's hearts in unseen ways and that we "ought to believe that the Holy Spirit in a manner known only to God offers to every man [*sic*] the possibility of being associated with this paschal mystery" (§ 22), a theme taken up also in the decree on mission, *Ad Gentes,* which declared that Christians are to "share in cultural and social life by the various exchanges and enterprises of human living. Let them be familiar with their [others'] national and religious traditions, gladly and reverently laying bare the seeds of the Word which is hidden in them" (§ 11). A series of papal encyclicals and other documents from Vatican offices reinforced this point: God calls all people to union with God—God is the origin and the final end, the destiny, of humanity.

This is not a new position but a development of an ancient one. In his summary of the teaching of the church fathers before St. Augustine, Francis A. Sullivan, S.J., noted three points that they held in common. First, they had a "generally positive attitude on the possibility of salvation for both Jews and Gentiles who had lived before the coming of Christ" (1992, 27). While there was no clear consensus on just how God saved the holy ones of old, the ancient writers did not exclude them from salvation simply because they were not explicit members of the church. Second, they had a "uniformly negative attitude about the possibility of salvation for Christians who were separated from the great church by heresy or schism" (1992, 27). Those who refused to remain in the community enlivened by the love of God were effectively refusing God's love. So those who *put themselves* outside the church were putting themselves outside the community of salvation. Third, only when Christianity becomes established as the religion of the Roman Empire—and the actual, if perhaps all too often nominal, religion of most of its citizens—do writers claim that pagans and Jews are outside the circle of salvation. This is the point at which the motto becomes important. Sullivan concluded his analysis:

> If people were damned, it was not because God did not will their salvation; it was because they had refused the means of salvation he had provided for them. This does not mean that the judgment of guilt passed by Christian writers against heretics, schismatics, pagans and Jews was necessarily a correct judgment, or one that we can share. They may well have been wrong in their judgment about the guilt of the people who were outside the church. The important thing is that *if their judgment was mistaken, it was a mistake about the guilt of people, not about the justice or salvific will of God.* (1992, 27; *emphasis added*)

In sum, arguing that some were excluded from salvation was polemical rhetoric against those who left the church (before the establishment of Christianity as the official religion of the empire) or who would not join the church (after establishment)—and they were all "guilty" of refusing God's salvation by refusing to affiliate with the church.

We do not need to decide whether any humans have exercised their freedom to reject God's grace so thoroughly as to damn themselves. We can align our view with Karl Rahner's:

> Rahner has consistently described a vision of the universe in which all men and women ultimately will be saved by a loving God who is beyond our comprehension.
>
> "An orthodox theologian," Rahner says dryly, "is forbidden to teach that everybody will be saved. But we are allowed to *hope* that all will be saved. If I hope to be saved, it is necessary to hope that for all men [*sic*] as well. If you have reason to love one another, you can hope that all will be saved." (Kennedy 1979, 66–67)

The refusal to deny God's universal salvific will is rooted in our faith in God's love for all creation and our hope that God will bring each and every part of it to its ultimate fulfillment.

The contrary view that God's salvific will is not universal is rooted in a reading of St. Augustine, especially in his anti-Pelagian writings. As Sullivan put it, Augustine was understood to be claiming the following:

> that the universally contracted guilt of original sin was sufficient to justify God in condemning not only infants who died without baptism,

but also adults who died in ignorance of Christian faith. There is good reason to believe that it was his effort to reconcile the exclusion of these two categories of people from salvation with the justice of God that led St. Augustine to his theory about the consequences of original sin for the whole human race. (1992, 37)

Medieval theologians generally rejected this view regarding unbaptized babies (Sullivan 1992, 46) and only accepted that God would damn people for sin they actually committed.

Yet even Augustine, ever the rhetorician, is not certainly to be understood as making this point as one that Christians must believe. As a polemicist, Augustine is notoriously inconsistent across his broad range of writings. His understanding of the freedom of the will varied remarkably over the course of his long polemical career. In one of the few documents Augustine wrote as an instruction from him as a pastor and bishop rather than as a polemicist, the *Enchiridion*, a very odd rhetorical picture appeared (cf. Tilley 1991, 118–36).

Augustine's description of the way things have gone in the world in *Enchiridion* included the observation that not all people are redeemed. This leads to an obvious question: Why are some not redeemed? To deny that God could redeem them would deny God's omnipotence. To deny God's will to save all would deny God's benevolence. How did Augustine the bishop deal with this perplexity?

Augustine taught the resurrection of the flesh: all people are resurrected. He then responds to various questions about the resurrection of those who were miscarried, deformed, had their bodies dissolved, or deviated significantly from the norm in height or girth, etc. Having solved these problems he affirms that *we* will rise in our bodies without internal or external defect to ease and happiness. Augustine then turns to the resurrection of the bodies of the damned. Those who are not liberated by Christ will be raised to endless damnation.

There is a profound rhetorical difference here between the "us" who are to be saved and the "those" who are to be damned. If one is sensitive to the rhetoric of and audience for *Enchiridion*, the contrast is essential. Augustine is addressing a believer. His audience included only those who will be raised to felicity. Whosoever is not liberated by Christ is "them," outside his audience. Whatever Augustine may have written for other audiences, in this instruction, the audience's redemption is presumed. Hence, in *Enchiridion*, Augustine dismissed out of hand the importance of many of the speculative issues, especially those that have nothing to do with "us." They need not worry "us." Augustine never materially identified "them." Implicitly, all who read *Enchiridion* with the rhetorical force that he wrote it must read it as an instruction to "us."

After further dismissals of other uncertainties and speculation on the intensity of punishments, which vary according to the depths of sin to which each of the nonsaved had fallen, Augustine went on to teach how we are to be grateful for God's mercy, which we will see clearly only in our resurrected state.

The key point is that even Augustine did not—when he was writing as a teacher of the Christian faith—identify materially who is damned, *but only implied that they are not "us."* The extent of the "us" was left unclear; indeed, "us" may be so extensive as to include all just people at least since Abel. At one point he even described the church as beginning with Abel and consisting in all the just (Sullivan 1992, 30). And while Augustine is typically taken to be saying that God wills the salvation of all, but that "they" do not deserve it and God is justified in damning them, it may be better to understand him as saying that God wills the salvation of "all of us" and finally leave the extent of that "all of us" undetermined.

If one attends to Augustine's rhetorical subtleties, one notes that he is not *denying* God's universal salvific will but following a North African tradition of preaching to *motivate* "us" (and others) to avoid a dreadful fate. *Threatening* with fire and brimstone does not entail that one believes that God *will* actually throw some into eternal flames, just that God *can* do so if a person's life warranted it. All people may be part of "us" who are spared by a gracious God. There is no reason not to hope so, especially if we live well.

The universal salvific will of God may be universally effective, *pace* the typical reading offered of Augustine's theology. In line with the earliest tradition and with Vatican II, then, any account that actually denies the universal salvific will of God is "outside the camp." This does not rule out Augustine, but it does rule out some readings of his writings. What changes is that whereas some ancient and medieval theologians presumed the guilt of those who were outside the church, Vatican II along with some ancient theologians presumes that those outside the church are innocent and can be encompassed in the "us" whom God wills to be saved (see Sullivan 1992, 151). But that problem leads us to raise the question of *how* God saves and leads to our second rule.

II. Thou shalt not deny the sufficiency of God's salvation
    in and through Jesus Christ.

The Second Vatican Council put it this way: "Christ . . . is the one Mediator and the unique Way of salvation" (*Lumen Gentium* § 14). In his encyclical *Redemptor Hominis* (1979), Pope John Paul II noted that "every man . . . has been redeemed by Christ, and . . . with each man . . . Christ is in a way united, even when man is unaware of it" (§ 14). The International Theological Commission (1997) devoted a chapter of "Christianity and the World Religions" to the unique mediation of Jesus. It concluded that only "in Jesus can human beings be saved, and therefore Christianity has an evident claim to universality" (§ 49). It also stated that other "possibilities of salvific 'mediation' cannot be seen in isolation from the man Jesus, the only mediator" (§ 49). Numerous other texts might be cited, but they would simply reiterate the claim that Jesus Christ is the unique and sufficient mediator of divine salvation.

This affirmation is not always articulated clearly. "Christianity and the World Religions," for example, snips quotations about Christ as the mediator of salvation from earlier biblical and patristic authors but fails to follow its own rules for interpreting those texts. "The context—literary, sociological, etc.—is an important means of understanding, at times the only one, texts and situations; contexts are a possible place for truth, but they are not identified with truth itself" (§ 101). As they note, we cannot understand the meaning of an utterance, text, monument, artifact, life, or movement apart from the context(s) in which each lives and moves and has its being. However, in its section on "fundamental theological presuppositions" (§§ 32–49), the commission uses proof texts from the Bible and the fathers of the church as if these propositions extracted from their context simply showed Christ's universal normativity for salvation. They give little consideration to intratextual contexts, much less the situations in which and the purposes for which the texts were composed. For example, the document simply cites patristic authors Justin Martyr and Clement of Alexandria, who claimed that the Greeks stole ideas from Moses and the prophets (§ 44) without ever noting that those claims are defensive polemical rhetoric. These latter claims are not merely historically unverifiable, but likely to be simply false. By neglecting the opportunity to contextualize and analyze such claims, the ITC document is inconsistent with its own theory of interpretation.

The early Christian texts on salvation through Christ alone were worked out in crucibles of conflict. They are weapons in a rhetorical battle. The anti-Jewish polemics in the Gospels of John and Matthew are the products of young and marginal Jewish communities attempting to find their own identities as "Jews for the Messiah Jesus" within the wide range of possibilities present in Judaism before and after the fall of the Temple in 70 C.E. These texts, properly understood, do not license anti-Semitism or anti-Judaism. Similarly, the argument for the exclusive universality of salvation in and through Jesus characteristic of the patristic writers functions as polemics against apostates and opponents. Those who joined other sects, participated in mystery religions, or devoted themselves to the state religion were the targets of these blasts. It is an error to take them at face value as if they were carefully articulated statements of theological principle rather than as shots fired in hot rhetorical battles. It will not do to take them literally as articles of faith.

Our rule leaves open the question of how to understand the relationship between the salvation God wrought in and through Jesus Christ and the salvation that God wills for all of humanity. Beyond notions that salvation in Jesus Christ is in some way a fulfillment and completion of other patterns of salvation, theologians have proffered Spirit christologies and trinitarian accounts of God's salvific action (see Hill Fletcher 2005, 62, and below). What is precluded is suggesting that some other mediator is also a "Son and Word of the Father" (*Dominus Iesus*, § 10).

Vatican documents have criticized formulations of trinitarian accounts and Spirit christologies. Their critique generally can be seen as applying another classic maxim, *opera trinitatis ad extra indivisa sunt*. In a proscriptive form, we might formulate this as "Do not treat the work of one member of the Trinity in, on, and for the world as separable from the work of another." What is attributed to the work of the Father is also that of the Son and the Spirit. What is said to be the work of the Son is also that of the Father and the Spirit. The work of the Spirit cannot be separated from the work of the Son or Father. One cannot ascribe salvation outside explicit association with the Christian community to the Spirit *rather than* the Son. Nor can one *separate* the work of the Word of God from the actuality of the incarnate one. This proscription simply blocks the path of a theological view that would separate God's works for the world as if the persons of the Trinity could be said to be operating in some way independently of one another. This proscription does not block appropriate theological distinctions but reminds us that there are theological shoals in this area.

One shoal is easily avoidable. This is the shoal of theological imperialism. Even if rules I and II are to guide our theological constructions about religious diversity and our participating in interreligious practices including dialogue, we have to abide by them. However, as noted above, we do not have to assert them as universal or absolute truth claims.

First, it is not at all clear that Christian concepts of salvation are commensurable with notions of the final destiny of humanity found in other traditions. Although some philosophers and theologians use "salvation" as if it were a generic concept for "human destiny" issues, this is not a precise use. It is, rather, the extension of a Christian term beyond the bounds of the tradition in which it makes sense.

Properly speaking, coming to Nirvana or the Pure Land, being absorbed in the ocean of being, or fading from life in Hades are not concepts of salvation. Each of these concepts clearly obtains its significance from within the respective faith tradition that generates them. The generic use of "salvation" may be misleading or even intellectually imperialist. Such generic talk of salvation hides the fact that our talk of salvation in Christ may not have clear parallels in other traditions. The work of Di Noia and Heim, discussed in chapters 7 and 8 below, highlights the differences. The conceptual structures of the faith traditions that give these terms their sense may be incommensurable. It is not at all clear that they could properly understand or evaluate such assertions.

Second, these rules do not guide God's acts, but our claims. Some of our Buddhist friends might believe that the Buddha-essence within us needs to be brought out and that over the course of many lifetimes we might come to Nirvana or that Amidha Buddha will ultimately bring all into the Pure Land. Their rules guide them in their practices and relationships with those who share their tradition and those who do not; they do not guide the flow or power of the Buddha-essence or govern Amidha Buddha. These rules are not simple claims or "first order assertions" about the way things are but sophisticated theological guidelines for our practice, "second order rules." This is not to deny that we can and sometimes should make such claims about salvation in and through Jesus Christ. Just how those claims are to be formulated is a matter of significant theological debate.[4]

For Catholic theology, one cannot separate Christ from the church. The quotation that began this section is part of a more complex whole: "This sacred Synod turns its attention first to the Catholic faithful. Basing itself upon sacred Scripture and tradition, it teaches that the Church, now sojourning on earth as an exile, is necessary for salvation. For Christ, made present in His Body, which is the Church, is the one Mediator and the unique Way of salvation" (*Lumen Gentium* § 14). Nor is it possible to separate the church from the universal salvific will of God. Pope John Paul II wrote that "it is necessary to keep these two truths together, namely, the real possibility of salvation in Christ for all humanity and the necessity of the Church for this salvation" (*Redemptoris Missio* § 9). Hence, we propose a third rule.

III. Thou shalt not deny the necessity of the church for salvation.

This rule recapitulates what Sullivan (1992) found was articulated in *extra ecclesiam nulla salus*. Sullivan's analysis suggests that the way in which the church is necessary is not a settled issue (1992, 156).[5] As the Congregation for the Doctrine of the Faith wrote in *Dominus Iesus*, quoting Pope John Paul II, "'the action of Christ and the Spirit outside the Church's visible boundaries' must not be excluded" (§ 19). How this action and how the church's involvement in it is to be understood remains open. The key may be found in the Second Vatican Council's Pastoral Constitution on the Church in the Modern World:

> While helping the world and receiving many benefits from it, the Church has a single intention: that God's kingdom may come, and that the salvation of the whole human race may come to pass. For every benefit that the People of God during its earthly pilgrimage can offer to the human family stems from the fact that the Church is *the universal sacrament of salvation*, simultaneously manifesting and exercising the mystery of God's love for humanity (*Gaudium et Spes* § 45; referring to *Lumen Gentium* § 15; *emphasis added*).

By introducing the idea of the church as a sacrament, the council effectively opens up the issue of how the church as sacrament of God is necessary. Regarding the ways in which God's saving grace comes to people, the "Council limited itself to the statement that God bestows it 'in ways known to Himself'" (*Dominus Iesus* § 21; citing Vatican II, *Ad Gentes* 7).

Yet because the church is the universal sacrament of salvation does not mean that other faith traditions are not in some sense willed by God to make available in some way the grace and truth of salvation. A key argument of Jacques Dupuis, discussed in chapter 5 below, is that the various faith traditions can be construed as willed and used by God for the salvation of humanity. Tilley (2006) has argued that this interpretation of the efficacy of other traditions is compatible with official Catholic teaching as presented in *Dominus Iesus*. One need not—and must not—assert that other religious traditions are sacramental as is the church. One can also affirm, however, that in some way these traditions can be willed by God as vehicles of some sort to bring those who have no access to the church (or perhaps those who are so appalled by some of the actions of members of the church) and thus cannot participate in the sacramental life of the church directly.

An implication of this rule is that we cannot deny that the church has and ought to have a mission *ad gentes*. One of the concerns that arises in discussions of the logic of interreligious dialogue is that it evacuates the work of evangelization of its appropriate urgency. There seems to be an inconsistency between the practices of interreligious dialogue and evangelization. However, the Pontifical Council for Interreligious Dialogue construed this issue differently: "Proclamation and dialogue are thus both viewed, each in its own place, as component elements and authentic forms of the one evangelizing mission of the Church. They are both oriented towards the communication of salvific truth" (*Dialogue and Proclamation* § 3). These items need to be unpacked in the context of understanding the necessity of the church.

First, dialogue takes four forms. The dialogue of life is the very practice of living together and supporting one another in a local context of religious diversity. The dialogue of action is the practice of collaboration across faith traditions to work for justice and development for all people. The dialogue of theological exchange is the practice of scholars seeking to understand more clearly their own heritage and to appreciate others' heritages as well—and, clearly, we can learn much about our own tradition by listening to and appreciating the testimony and criticism of others. The dialogue of religious experience emerges in the practice of sharing spiritual values and practices across traditions, as when Tibetan Buddhist and Western monastics share their traditions and practices (cf. *Dialogue and Proclamation* § 42). The significance of recognizing that dialogue takes multiple forms will appear below as we assess the various theological proposals regarding religious diversity.

Second, in the processes of evangelization, the most effective proclamation is witness. As Paul Knitter put it, "Witnessing is based on the desire and need to share what one has found to be true and precious" with others (Knitter 2005a, xi). Our practices, including the practice of believing, are our primary form of witness. The saying attributed to St. Francis of Assisi, "Preach the Gospel always; if necessary, use words," is relevant here. The way we use words and the purposes for which we use them vary. Christians want to evangelize the unchurched, spread the Good News in lands that have never heard it, re-evangelize lapsed Christians, and may even delight in the conversion of others to Christianity. Yet even if there may be times that explicit proselytizing is counterproductive, other forms of proclamation may well not be ruled out. What is ruled out is coercion or tactics that undermine others' integrity.

Recognizing and affirming the necessity of the church do not demand verbal proselytizing, but clearly demand witness. Members committed to the church witness in all they do to the beauty, truth, goodness, and justice that they find in the Christian tradition, and that they find the tradition advocating in and for the world. Alas, Christians' moral failures also function as witness to Christianity, but a profoundly negative witness. If our witness is not positive, our church loses credibility. This is not a claim about the way things should be, but about the way things are. That each form of dialogue calls for evangelization in the appropriate forms of witness seems obvious. Such witness makes the message credible in the context of dialogue.

Walter Ong, S.J., has suggested that the use of the Greek term *katholikos* as one of the marks of the church is significant (1996, 31–33). Using Greek when formulating the marks in Latin, when the Latin form *universalis* was available to complement the other three marks ("one, holy, apostolic"), suggests that "catholic" and "universal" are not quite the same thing. Ong suggests that the universality of the church consists not in the extent of the church but in its distribution as "the leaven in the lump." The church does not cover the world or own the world, nor is it simply worldwide. Rather, it is to be found everywhere that the breath of the Spirit raises the lump of the world into the bread of life. In this sense, the church may be a sacrament not by its universality understood as a characteristic of its extensiveness, but by its catholicity, by its obligation not to be the world, but to raise the world into new life in the Spirit. This is another way of suggesting that the center of evangelization may not be proselytizing but witness.

The necessity of the church is a sacramental necessity. God acts in and through the church as God acts in and through the bread and wine of the Eucharist. This necessity can be understood in a number of ways. Just as the sacrament of Baptism classically was construed as having three modes depending on the circumstances (baptism of water as the ordinary way, of blood for those catechumens who were martyred before being baptized, and of desire for those who were not Christians but oriented to the Good that is God in their lives), so perhaps we can think of the sacramental presence of the church as multimodal depending on the circumstances.

Realizing this sacramentality in practice may well require different practices to represent and effect the grace of God in the world, to be the leaven in the lump. To reduce this sacramentality to one mode, for example, proselytizing, would certainly not be required by the present rule and, arguably, would be an inept way of living by it—especially in light of our fourth and final rule.

The necessity of the church is connected with the sufficiency of Christ for salvation and the universal salvific will of God. The first three rules are clearly internal to the Christian tradition. The fourth rule is also internal to the tradition, but also seems one we ought share with those who are not Christians.

IV. Thou shalt affirm the dignity of each and all human persons.

One significant theme of the Second Vatican Council was the dignity of the human person. Descriptions of human dignity, its rootedness in God, and its implications for our life together are sprinkled through many of its documents. *Gaudium et Spes* proclaimed:

> [T]here is a growing awareness of the exalted dignity proper to the human person, since he stands above all things, and his rights and duties are universal and inviolable. Therefore, there must be made available to all men everything necessary for leading a life truly human, such as food, clothing, and shelter; the right to choose a state of life freely and to found a family, the right to education, to employment, to a good reputation, to respect, to appropriate information, to activity in accord with the upright norm of one's own conscience, to protection of privacy and to rightful freedom in matters religious, too. (§ 26)

This affirmation of this dignity is rooted in the Christian conviction that all people are created in the image of God and called to communion with God (*Gaudium et Spes* § 12, 19). *Nostra Aetate* found that there is no basis

> in theory or in practice for any discrimination between individual and individual or between people and people arising either from human dignity or from the rights which flow from it. Therefore, the Church reproves, as foreign to the mind of Christ, any discrimination against people or any harassment of them on the basis of their race, color, condition of life or religion. (§ 5)

Perhaps the strongest, and most astonishing (at the time), affirmation of human dignity as expressed in diverse religious traditions can be found in *Dignitatis Humanae*, the Declaration on Religious Freedom:

This Vatican Synod declares that the human person has a right to religious freedom. This freedom means that all men are to be immune from coercion on the part of individuals or of social groups and of any human power, in such wise that in matters religious no one is to be forced to act in a manner contrary to his own beliefs. Nor is anyone to be restrained from acting in accordance with his own beliefs, whether privately or publicly, whether alone or in association with others, within due limits.

This Synod further declares that the right to religious freedom has its foundation in the very dignity of the human person, as this dignity is known through the revealed Word of God and by reason itself. (§ 2)

The commitment to recognizing human dignity, not merely on the basis of philosophical theory but also on the basis of the Catholic Church's understanding of divine revelation, is at the heart of Catholic teaching on social, political, and economic matters.

How to understand this rule and put it into practice remains underdeveloped. As we noted in the previous chapter (pp. 45), Wuthnow reported that participants in other faith traditions found Christians rather ignorant about other traditions (2005, 72). The point is that Christians have not yet done a good job of recognizing the dignity of religious others. If they had, members of those faith traditions would not be calling for the increased respect and understanding that is needed to show that Christians accept their human dignity.

In the previous chapter we noted Rabbi Jonathan Sacks's call for genuine respect among those of differing faith traditions through the practice of listening and speaking that forms authentic conversation. The root of this call is a profound understanding of creation. Sacks wrote:

God, the creator of humanity, having made a covenant with all humanity, then turns to one people [the Jews] and commands it to be different, *teaching humanity to make space for difference. God may at times be found in human other, the one not like us.* Biblical monotheism is not the idea that there is one God and therefore one gateway to His presence. To the contrary, it is the idea that *the unity of God is to be found in the diversity of creation.* (2003, 53; *emphasis in original*)

The greatness of the God of Abraham, Isaac, Jacob, and Jesus is that the divine unity is great enough to encompass and even love diversity. "*God is the God of all humanity, but between Babel and the end of days no single faith is the faith of all humanity*" (Sacks 2003, 55; *emphasis in original*). Like Vatican II, Sacks called for respect for and positive appreciation of the human search for God in all its forms. "The challenge to the religious imagination is to see God's image in one who is not in our image. That is the converse of tribalism. But it is also something other than universalism. It takes difference seriously" (Sacks 2003, 60). The challenge to those of us who believe in the intrinsic dignity of humankind created by God is to recognize "the dignity of difference."

Like Vatican II, Rabbi Sacks recognized that our faith traditions are not private. They are involved in the social, economic, and political dimensions of our existence. Hence, as the council did, he noted that our faith "involves justice, not merely in the narrow sense of the rule of law and the transparency of procedures, but also in the substantive sense of conferring on all members of society an honoured place" (2003, 121). The rule that we are to affirm human dignity means that as we cherish our own lives, "then we will understand the value of others. We may regard ours as a diamond and another faith as a ruby, but we know that both are precious stones" (209). What Wuthnow values as the achievement of authentic pluralism and Sacks finds to be real tolerance (not the demeaning attitude of mere toleration) is found not in the absence of faith, but in its full richness. "Difference does not diminish; it enlarges the sphere of human possibilities" (ibid.).

Difference also must shape our understanding of the God who created each and all of us. The fact is that we belong to different faith traditions. However we may think God is working within and through those traditions, if we fail to recognize the intrinsic dignity of all as created in God's image and destined for communion with God, then we fail to observe this rule.

This difference prohibits religious imperialism. For to claim that our tradition is a diamond and the other traditions not precious stones is to deny the dignity of those whose lives have been shaped into what they are by their participation in those traditions. While we have significant difficulties with S. Mark Heim's position (see chapter 8), we recognize that Heim reminds us that the unity of humanity is a unity of diversity. Those who would reduce our diversity to a minimalist vapid sameness in effect deny the dignity of each particular person. We are social by nature; part of who we are is materially shaped by the traditions and narratives that we live in and live out. The reductionism of "sameness in essence" neither respects the dignity of each and all nor avoids the most obnoxious form of intellectual imperialism, masked as "acceptance" of "what's the same as us." In doing so we disrespect the other as us and accept the others only as our mirror images, not as having the dignity of God's creatures, of being created in the image and likeness of God. They may be our opponents, but they should not be our enemies; indeed, they may well become our friends.

As Christians committed to human dignity, we must act in such a way that we respect the dignity of difference. This is not a flaccid relativism. Part of respecting another is confronting them in conversation when they have done what we find wrong. Withdrawing into fideism, sectarianism, or solipsism is ultimately a terrible failure to recognize the dignity of others who are different from us. It is to cut them off from our part of the human community because their faith communities are not ours. That, in effect, is to deny them a place in God's community, the community of all of humanity. We may disagree profoundly with others in our community and work to change their minds and hearts on particular issues. We cannot abandon them. Abandonment of others affirms them as worthless to us; it is the ultimate denial of dignity.

Toward Evaluating Theologies of Religious Diversity

In these first three chapters we have engaged in a series of tasks. We first laid out our claim of what a sited or local theology is. We then highlighted the most significant characteristics of the site on which we do theology. In this chapter we have analyzed what we find to be the most salient rules in the Catholic Christian tradition for building a theology of religious diversity on our U.S. site. In the next seven chapters we analyze and evaluate contemporary theologies of religious diversity as candidates for a Catholic theology of religious diversity.

As a preview, we have come to see that each of these theologies tries, as a theological construct, to follow the rules discussed in this chapter. Each of them, however, seems to place a priority on one or two of these rules. Each fits some rules better than others. We ask how faithful each approach is to the rules we have outlined as our building code. If we have misconstrued the tradition in forming these rules or have omitted some rule of importance, then our evaluations will be flawed. Of course, we think we have been on target in formulating this code.

A second issue is the appropriateness of the proposals for this site. As we argued in the previous chapter, the religious diversity of the United States makes this a distinctive site. It has, in our judgment, some real strengths. Foremost is the fact that the United States is a nation of immigrants without a dominant ethnic group that marginalizes other ethnic groups simply because of their status as a minority group. Consequent upon this is a tradition that teaches us to tolerate religious diversity and makes room for the development of real religious respect and pluralism, in part because of nonestablishment. It also has, in our judgment, some real challenges, especially the challenges of the commodification of religion, which can lead to an increasing individualization of spirituality and the privatization of religious traditions and of globalization, which can lead to profound inequalities and the reaction of "tribalism" as a protective strategy—and not only by renascent nationalist and religious movements but also by shaping an appropriate patriotism here into an American tribalism. We evaluate each of the constructs for its ability to recognize and support the strengths of this site and to respond to and overcome the challenges we face today. Chapter 11 discusses the way the accounts fit the site in which we work.

4

Classic Inclusivism

Does God Go Incognito?

with John F. Birch

An orthodox theologian is forbidden to teach that everybody will be saved.
But we are allowed to hope *that all will be saved.*
If I hope to be saved, it is necessary to hope that for all . . . as well.
If you have reason to love another, you can hope that all will be saved.
—Karl Rahner, S.J.

THE HOPE FOR UNIVERSAL SALVATION IS DIFFICULT TO ARTICULATE IN AN orthodox manner. Inclusivism attempts to do just that. It seeks to balance commitment to God's salvific presence in non-Christian religions and to Christ's distinctive, definitive place as God's effective self-revelation to the world. Inclusivist positions arose as alternatives to an exclusivism that denied the possibility of salvation to anyone who was not explicitly Christian and to indifferentism, which regards no particular faith tradition as better than another. Inclusivism has become the "default position" of many mainstream Christian churches, including Roman Catholicism.[1]

The model of classic inclusivism, represented in this book by the work of Karl Rahner, is marked by three central characteristics. This model construes Christianity as completing or fulfilling other religions. It recognizes that other faith traditions can contain divine truth. It finds that non-Christian religions may serve as ways or instruments of salvation for their adherents.

Rahner develops two key themes in his model of inclusivism: the possibility of salvation for non-Christians and the presence of Jesus Christ in other religions. This chapter analyzes Rahner's position, examines critiques of and responses to Rahner's work, and evaluates his view in light of the criteria developed in chapter 3.

Rahner's Classic Inclusivist Model

Karl Rahner (1904–84) was born in Freiburg, Germany, and entered the Society of Jesus at the age of eighteen. From the age of twenty-five to twenty-nine he studied theology at a Jesuit school in Valkenburg, Holland. After being ordained a priest in 1932, he returned to Freiburg to study philosophy, taking courses with Martin Heidegger (Livingston 2000, 206). He completed doctoral and postdoctoral studies in theology in Innsbruck in 1936. He taught before and after World War II at various universities, including Innsbruck, Munich, and Münster. He lectured around the world. During World War II he engaged in pastoral work and, clandestinely, taught in Vienna. He also did pastoral work in Austria after the war. He was a *peritus* (expert) at the Second Vatican Council (1962–65) and wrote over sixteen hundred books, articles, and essays. He died in Innsbruck.

As a Jesuit, Rahner was influenced by the mystical orientation of the *Spiritual Exercises* of St. Ignatius of Loyola (1495–1556), founder of the Society of Jesus (Di Noia 1997), as well as the work of St. Thomas Aquinas and German philosophy, especially from German philosopher Immanuel Kant (1724–1804) through Martin Heidegger (1889–1976). The root of Rahner's theology is that all human beings do have freedom and knowledge, but all also experience limits to both. We finite and restricted beings are aware of those limits. Any finite limit implies an "other side" of the limit (as a wall always walls something off from something else). The "ultimate" "other side" of any finite experience of limitedness is the infinite. We are thus oriented, however dimly, however impenetrable the wall seems, to Being as limitless, unrestricted Absolute Mystery, that is, to God. Rahner called this orientation "a pre-apprehension (*Vorgriff*) of 'being' as such, . . . an unauthentic but ever-present knowledge of the infinity of reality" (Rahner 1978, 33).[2] This orientation is ultimately a gift of God, who creates and sustains every finite being. For God, there is no wall, but simply creation into which God as creator flows as gracious presence.

What we call "grace" is God's creating and sustaining everything. It is God's presence to every creature. The presence of the infinite creator does not overwhelm or annul what creatures are. It does not obliterate nature. Rather, grace fulfills or completes nature, especially human nature. Contrary to those who would find that sin is so pervasive and destructive that nothing is good in nature without a supernatural intervention, Rahner finds that creation—however distorted by the power of sin and evil—is good, but imperfect and fractured. Rahner encapsulated this view in his term the "supernatural existential," which stresses the continuity of God-created human nature with God-graced human nature.[3]

This fundamental orientation implies that divine grace and divine revelation are universal. No human being has not—even if unaware—met God. Every human being is graced by God. No human being fails to encounter the Absolute

Mystery, though anyone can suppress or fail to thematize the unthematized experience of encountering the divine. For them, either the wall seems impenetrable or they find there is no wall and no "other side." For Rahner, the history of revelation and the actuality of grace cannot be separated from the history and actuality of the world (Di Noia 1997, 130). This position implies that religions, then, have the potential of serving as habitations of the divine presence (Knitter 2002, 70–71).

Rahner maintained that in the past, a religion other than one's own "was in practice the religion of a completely different cultural environment. It belonged to a history with which the individual only communicated very much on the periphery of his own history" (Rahner 1966, 116). He contrasted this state of religious diversity with the contemporary situation, which he characterized as a world in which "everybody is the next-door neighbor and spiritual neighbor of everyone else" (1966, 117). Rahner recognized that the diversity of faith traditions is not a new development, but that what we have called "globalization" in chapter 2 is a radically new context for diversity. The fact of religious diversity has given rise to numerous theoretical approaches that attempt to account for and explain it. The new context helps explain why diversity seems something new in theology; in the past, physical distance buffered us from others unless we encountered them in trade, migration, or war.

Rahner also found that Catholic theology had not given sufficient thought to religious diversity. Hence, he did not offer his views on religious diversity as "the common thought of Catholic theology" (1966, 117) because Catholic thought on the topic was not mature. Yet Rahner accepted the notion of God's universal salvific will for all people, while also maintaining that salvation comes only through faith in God through Jesus Christ (1966, 123, 124).

The problem is that it seems inconsistent to assert both the universality of God's saving will and the particularity of salvation in Jesus. Rahner showed how they fit together by exploring four core theses. He offered these not as an empirical historian of religion, but rather as a dogmatic theologian speaking within Christianity and offering only a potential "self-understanding of Christianity," not a settled position (1966, 118). His approach is rooted in his fundamental vision sketched above of the universal graciousness of God present to all people.

The first thesis, which Rahner regarded to be the most basic, is that "Christianity understands itself as the absolute religion, intended for all men [sic], which cannot recognize any other religion besides itself of equal right" (1966, 118). In other words, Christianity is not one tradition among many. Nor is it a valid, but incomplete, religion. A "valid and lawful religion" is one that is rooted in God's self-communicative action, not in peoples' attempts to get to God or to interpret human religious experience. Rahner maintained that God's communication is addressed to all people because of the universal import of the incarnation, death, and resurrection of Jesus Christ.

This relates to the question of how Jesus Christ can be present for or in other religions. If God's self-revelation is not only intended for all people but also involves the same relationship for all people *because of* its grounding in Christ, then how does Christ become present in the other religions of the world? Rahner answers that Jesus Christ can be present in other faith traditions in and through the Spirit of Christ, which is the Holy Spirit.

Rahner's three key moves to explain this vision must be understood in the context of his trinitarian theology: For Rahner, *opera trinitatis ad extra indivisa sunt*, that is, the acts of members of the Trinity on what is not God are indivisible. Rahner does not *separate* the works of the Trinity in what follows but *distinguishes conceptually* among them to make sense of an inclusivist model of salvation. However it may be *ad intra*, there are not three agents acting on the world, but God's agency in and for the world manifests itself in three distinctive gracious ways.

First, the incarnation and the death of Jesus (the cross) are "final causes"[4] of God's universal salvific will and self-communication to the world (Rahner 1978, 317–18). The Holy Spirit is and has been at work in the world, but not in an abstract, transcendental way. Rather, the Spirit works in historical, concrete mediations. God is present and communicating in and through historical events, specifically the incarnation, death, and resurrection of Jesus. God's action in and through Jesus is both tangible and irreversible.

Second, the Holy Spirit is the "efficient cause" of the incarnation, death, and resurrection of Jesus Christ. God as Spirit brought about the event known as Jesus Christ—his birth, life, death, and resurrection—and yet the latter is distinguished as the final cause of the former who "always and everywhere brings justifying faith, this faith is always and everywhere and from the outset a faith which comes to be in the Spirit of Jesus Christ" (Rahner 1983, 291). Therefore, the Holy Spirit can be said to be the Spirit of Jesus in that the Holy Spirit is the efficient cause of the incarnation of the Word, while Jesus Christ the incarnate, redeeming Word is the final cause—the point or purpose of the action—of the Holy Spirit.

Third, Jesus Christ is present in other religions not by incarnation but by way of the "memory" of those religions. In this context, Rahner defined memory as "the a priori possibility for historical experience precisely as historical, as distinguished from the a priori conditions of possibility for the a posteriori knowledge of things in the natural sciences" (1978, 319). What this means is that we cannot have a history without a memory. Yet memory is rooted in every person's hope; the point of remembering the past is to understand how we got to the goods and evils in the present and to look for the enhancement of the good and the overcoming of evil in the future. Such hope opens a person to perceiving divine salvific action in particular historical experience. No one lives without a fundamental hope, even though particular situations may seem hopeless. Memory is rooted in hope. It is a searching or groping that ultimately anticipates—sometimes inarticulately or even in a negative way—God's salvific work. However, God works in and through Jesus Christ. Since this salvific hope is universal, and God's universal salvific will is accomplished in Jesus Christ, the universal hope is fulfilled by the particularity of salvation in and through Jesus Christ.

Rahner thus identified Jesus Christ as the "Absolute Savior," that "event in history in which a free decision about the salvific outcome of history is made and becomes tangible" (1978, 320–21). Building on the traditional Christian affirmation of two natures in one person in Jesus Christ, Rahner finds that in Jesus Christ the human and divine wills are free, yet in perfect accord: Jesus Christ as divine and as human freely wills universal salvation. Thus, the hope-rooted memory of any historical faith tradition finds its ultimate fulfillment in the person and work of Jesus Christ. In Rahner's words, "the absolute savior is the God-Man who reaches fulfillment through death and resurrection" (1978, 318).

Of course, one might raise questions about this thesis. Admittedly, this theology sounds numbingly speculative, an abstract theory. Rahner, however, thought that accounting for the fact of religious diversity requires a theory. That theory will inevitably be speculative because it is dealing with a fundamentally speculative problem—how a universal hope and a universal encounter with the gracious God is consistent with the particularity of Jesus Christ. This is a theoretical problem. A theoretical problem requires a theoretical answer.

Other questions still remain. What about the non-Christian religions that make no acknowledgment of Jesus Christ as God's self-revealing agent? If Jesus Christ is said to be present for and in other religions by way of the work of the Spirit, and by way of a particular religion's memory, then what about the claims of non-Christian religions that omit Christ or run contrary to the claims of Christianity? Rahner claimed that Christianity fulfills its role as the "true and lawful religion" whenever it existentially interacts with other religions, questions them, and judges them by Christianity's own self-understanding. For Christians, it is an open question whether any other tradition is a vehicle of divine grace. The answer requires inquiring about actual religious traditions and what they do to and for their adherents, not by purely theoretical reasoning. Speculation shows grace is possible in other traditions; investigation seeks to find whether that possibility has been actualized in a particular faith tradition.

Since Christianity began at a particular point in time it cannot be said to have always provided the way of salvation for humanity. There was a time when there was no Christianity. Likewise, there is some point in time practically when individuals become fully and irreversibly Christian, a time when it becomes a historical reality to them. For Rahner, then, an important question is whether this point in time is the same for all people or whether it possesses a unique history that is based in cultures and historical eras. The question that concerned him was, Does Christianity's call on the individual human soul have a history? Without giving a definitive answer to this question he offered the possibility that "the beginning of Christianity for actual periods in history, for cultures and religions, could be postponed to those moments in time when Christianity became a real historical factor in an individual history and culture—a real historical moment in a particular culture" (1966, 119). Although grace is universal, the realization of God's grace in history is particular. God's grace is there, but it may not yet be recognized. In practice, this is not a theoretical issue. Concrete judgments in concrete circumstances based on a critical and empathetic understanding of the Christian tradition and the other traditions under question are required.

That Christianity bears a history among other religions is related to the question of the reach or extent of divine grace. Rahner held that grace is always and everywhere available as a real and present possibility for people to experience the salvific relationship that God desires for them (1983, 291). This understanding of grace relates directly to his second thesis.

Rahner's second thesis with respect to non-Christian religions is that elements of grace exist in non-Christian religions. Thus, any of these religions might be recognized as being valid and lawful. Of course, even valid religions may contain error and depravity. With respect to pre-Christian religions he maintained that a lawful religion is "an institutional religion whose 'use' by man at a certain period can be regarded on the whole as a positive means of gaining the right relationship to God and thus for the attaining of salvation, a means which is therefore positively included in God's plan for salvation" (1966, 125). Notice the difference between this definition of lawful religion and the definition he offered for lawful religion in the context of Christianity, above. For people living prior to Christianity, lawful religion offered the possibility of entering into a right relationship with God according to God's salvific will and plan. This means that there existed in pre-Christian religions a real possibility of divine grace.

This is not to say that there are no unlawful religions, for Rahner maintained that lawful/unlawful boundaries existed in religions prior to Christianity. As he put it:

> It would perhaps be possible to say in theory that where a certain religion is not only accompanied in its concrete appearance by something false and humanly corrupted but also makes this an explicitly and consciously adopted element—an explicitly declared condition of its *nature*—this religion is wrong in its deepest and most specific being and hence can no longer be regarded as a lawful religion. (1966, 127)

He did not argue for a universalism; he argued for the *possibility* that gratuitous, salvific elements of grace are present in religions that preceded Christianity in time and space. He acknowledged that the existence of lawful elements in a religion does not necessitate that all of that religion's elements are lawful, nor did he infer that all religions are lawful. For Rahner, the universal salvific will of God means that individual persons have the opportunity to enter into a right (salvific) relationship with God at all times and in all places of human history. "Otherwise there could be no question of a serious and also actually effective salvific design of God for all men, in all ages and places" (1966, 128). This relationship was not a totally interior experience, as if it occurred apart from the religious traditions in which people live their lives. It is mediated by the traditions that people live in and live out, Christian or not.

Considering other contemporary faith traditions (as opposed to pre-Christian traditions), Rahner regarded them also as possibly containing elements of divine grace. Again, relying on theological considerations, he maintained that the universal salvific will of God must entail the possibility of salvation of all people of all times and places, including those who live long after the coming of Jesus Christ. He could not reconcile God's salvific will with the Christian belief that salvation is found only in Christ after the incarnation. Every person "is really and truly exposed to the influence of divine, supernatural grace which offers an interior union with God and by means of which God communicates himself whether the individual takes up an attitude of acceptance or of refusal towards this grace" (1966, 123).

Rahner viewed God's grace to be effective as necessarily existing in material form or embodied. Therefore, it is possible that the various faith traditions of the world provide some of the most effective embodiments that divine grace assumes (Knitter 2003, 70–71). Nature and grace can be distinguished in the abstract, but not separated in actuality.

Accepting and refusing God's salvation are not two equal options for human choice. For Rahner, "Christ and his salvation are not one of two possibilities offering themselves to man's free choice; they are the deed of God which bursts open and redeems the false choice of man by overtaking it" (1966, 124). God's abundant love does not annul our choices, but redeems them. To choose against God is difficult, if not impossible. It requires that one be and choose to remain fundamentally depraved.

Human nature as constituted by God in creation is human nature transformed by grace. That is, human nature was historically and concretely created by God, yet with an intended, specific purpose and goal: God. The participation of the supernatural order of grace with the natural order of creation brings us back to the fundamental root of Rahner's thought, the "supernatural existential." The reasoning might be circular, but it is a virtuous, not vicious, circle.

The third thesis supporting Rahner's inclusivist view states that Christianity encounters members of non-Christian religions as potential "anonymous Christians." If one starts with the term "anonymous Christian," one will misconstrue Rahner's work; this term can be understood correctly only in light of the previous two theses. Since people encounter the universal grace of God present in the world, it is not really possible to regard the non-Christian as one who has in no way been affected by divine grace. Everyone we meet has been affected in some way by divine grace. This means that every non-Christian is potentially one who has accepted this grace as the "entelechy of his existence by accepting the immeasurableness of his dying existence as opening out into infinity" (1966, 131). To use our earlier metaphor, there is finally no wall between us and the infinite, but a bridge to our ultimate goal. In accepting the grace of God, the non-Christian accepts God—Father, Son, and Spirit—perhaps without naming God. That is to say, an individual may be touched by God's grace, accepting it in the only way she knows, and therefore become someone who is in a saving relationship with God. At the same time, salvation reaching one in this manner is Christ's salvation, which means that the person in this state is in some measure connected or related to Jesus Christ. Therefore, she is not merely an anonymous theist, but rather an anonymous Christian.

Although this follows nicely from Rahner's fundamental theology sketched above, one evaluative question is obvious: What does this imply with regard to the Christian missionary effort? Some might say, and have said, that the notion of the anonymous Christian makes Christian missionary efforts superfluous. Since God's grace is there in other faith traditions, why should we bother to witness and proclaim? Rahner did not agree with this inference from his work. He maintained that explicit preaching of the Christian message makes possible the conversion of others that is "demanded 1) by the incarnational and social structure of grace and of Christianity, and 2) because the individual who grasps Christianity in a clearer, purer and more reflective way has, other things being equal, a still greater chance of salvation than someone who is merely an anonymous Christian" (1966, 132). Christian mission was as important for Rahner as it has traditionally been for the church because it enables the individual touched by divine grace to be more conscious of her relationship to the Absolute Savior, who she comes to know in the person of Jesus Christ. The difference in theory between an exclusivism that finds those outside the pale doomed and an inclusivism that finds those outside the camp touched by grace but possibly insufficiently aware of God's graciousness and how to respond to it in their lives warrants no significant difference in appropriate missiological practice.

This brings us to Rahner's fourth thesis, that the church expresses the divine grace hidden in other religions. Other faith traditions can be regarded as containing partial or incomplete truth. Members of other faith traditions must be encountered as those who may well be affected by, and accepting of, divine grace "anonymously," and thus possessed by and in the light of divine truth. Rahner maintained that there is a unity between "objective" or "this worldly" knowledge and "transcendental" knowledge (1966, 132). Hence, that "which is capable of being expressed in 'this worldly' categories mediates the transcendental and *e-converso*, although this mutually conditioning relationship is itself to be thought of not as a fixed entity" (1976, 287). We do not have immediate access to the transcendent. Our knowledge of God is truly knowledge but always mediated and expressed in particular historical contexts. Some of these contexts that truly express transcendent knowledge may be other faith traditions. Hence, our ordinary experience is at root the experience of God naturally acquired by people in life, which would seem to include non-Christian religious knowledge (see Kilby 1997, 8). Since anonymous Christians have access to such knowledge, yet can be perfected by encounter with the preaching of the church, then the church should regard herself as "the historically tangible vanguard and the historically and socially constituted explicit expression of what the Christian hopes is present as a hidden reality even outside the visible Church" (Rahner 1966, 133).

The church no longer exists in the context of a relatively homogeneous culture, but rather in a variegated global culture characterized by religious diversity. Various religions and cultures confront one another. Furthermore, there is every reason to believe that the religious diversity evident in our world today will not dissipate in the future. This reality prompted Rahner to warn the church about the possibility of extinction unless Christians broke free of the mindset that sets them against everyone else who is not explicitly a member. In other words, the church needs to be "not the communion of those who possess God's grace as opposed to those who lack it, but is the communion of those who can explicitly confess what they and the others hope to be" (Rahner 1966, 134). He perceived this attitude or mindset to be modeled by St. Paul in his address to the non-Christians on Mars Hill when he told them that the Unknown God to which they dedicated a monument was in fact the God that he was going to make more fully known to them, the true God for whom they were yearning all along.

Rather than standing in opposition to the world and to other faith traditions, Rahner believed that the church should be present in the world as a community explicitly aware of graced nature. There it stands as concrete, historical evidence of the divine desire for the salvation of all people as well as the missionary voice that this salvation is found in Jesus Christ. Because it is the explicit expression of divine grace hidden in other religions, and because transcendental knowledge can be mediated through natural knowledge, other religions can possibly serve as potential pathways to salvation for their adherents. As these religions point to, or are oriented toward, divine salvation, which is most perfectly revealed in Christianity, they may become paths by which their adherents find salvation, which ultimately comes through the person and work of

Jesus Christ. In short, Rahner finds that other religions can potentially serve as ways of salvation because of their (implicit) orientation to Christianity.

We can summarize Rahner's classic inclusivism in four statements:

- Christianity understands itself as the "absolute religion, intended for all men, which cannot recognize any other religion besides itself of equal right" (Rahner 1966, 118).
- Elements of grace exist in non-Christian religions so that any of these religions can be recognized as being valid and lawful without denying that it contains error and depravity.
- Christianity encounters members of non-Christian religions as potential "anonymous Christians."
- The church is the expression of divine grace hidden in other religions.

Thus, for Rahner, Christianity perfects or completes other religions. Christianity recognizes that other religions can contain divine truth. Christianity acknowledges the possibility that non-Christian religions serve as pathways to salvation for their own adherents. This is classic inclusivism; Rahner draws a circle from the heart of Christianity that is as wide as the divine.

Critiques, Criticisms, and Problems

Rahner was a pioneering theologian with respect to giving serious thought to the relationship between Christianity and other religions. That is not to say that his approach is without problems or criticisms. Indeed, he acknowledged inadequacies in his view. Others found further problems. Some problems center on his understanding of the relationship between philosophy and theology, or the relationship between nature and grace, while others have to do with specific notions (e.g., anonymous Christianity) that he used in articulating his view. A look at every conceivable criticism is beyond the scope of this chapter, but we can examine some of the more prominent criticisms and problems with his approach that have been given considerable attention by Rahner as well as by his critics.

The French Jesuit Henri de Lubac (1896–1991) maintained that Rahner's use of the term "anonymous Christian" was valid because it recognized the penetration of the light of the Christian gospel into dark places, or the hidden work of the Spirit of Christ in the lives of people of varying cultures. Yet he also found the term misleading because it could hide the newness and singularity of what Jesus did and taught. Using the term "anonymous Christianity," according to de Lubac, "would be as much as to say that the revelation we owe to Christ was no more than the surfacing of something that has always existed" (de Lubac 1969,

87–88). He feared that the term could be taken to imply that the work and message of Jesus Christ merely surfaced something latent in the lives of people and the cultures in which they live.

Rahner recognized the ambiguity in the term "anonymous Christianity." He pointed out that there are two meanings applied to the term "Christianity." One is equivalent to Christendom or the church. The other is a characteristic, "the 'being Christian' of an individual Christian" (Rahner 1976, 281). For Rahner, "Christian" in "anonymous Christianity" characterized a person who had the characteristic of being and living Christianly. He was open to other terminology that might be less misleading, but in the absence of better terminology, he continued to use the term.

Hans Urs von Balthasar (1905–88), a Swiss theologian and former Jesuit, was critical of the term "anonymous Christian" because of Rahner's christology. Von Balthasar believed Rahner's christology was evolutionist, implied a reduction of the importance of sin and redemption, and devalued the theology of the cross. While von Balthasar found the doctrine of an anonymous Christianity "so urgently required in the present situation," the cross faded out because "man [*sic*] does not owe his redemption actually to Christ, but to the eternal saving will of God" (von Balthasar 1966, 65). Von Balthasar found Rahner's perspective to be an "anthropological narrowing of theology" (Livingston 2000, 209)—a critique common among positivist theologians evaluating correlationists' theologies.

Von Balthasar's concerns might cause one to rethink whether or not Rahner was merely using the term "anonymous Christian" in reference to any and every person, but that was not his intent. Rahner put it this way:

> Merely in passing it may be remarked that we might actually apply the term "anonymous Christian" to every individual who, in virtue of God's universal will to save, and thereby in virtue of the "supernatural existential," is inescapably confronted with the offering of God's self-bestowal and is totally unable to escape from this situation. In other words, according to this terminology absolutely every man is also an "anonymous Christian" but we prefer the terminology according to which that man is called an "anonymous Christian" who on the one hand has *de facto* accepted of his freedom this gracious offering on God's part through faith, hope, and love, while on the other he is not yet a Christian on the social level . . . or in the sense of having consciously objectified his Christianity to himself in his own mind. (Rahner 1976, 282–83)

Therefore, the term did not apply to every actual person, although every non-Christian person is potentially an anonymous Christian.

Being an anonymous Christian requires faith. Faith is always necessary for salvation; it is a free gift of God. For one to understand and come to know how to live Christianly in history, that faith orientation to Christ must be a reality of that person's life. That the person could not formally "name" the source of the gift of faith does not mean the person was without faith.

Hans Küng (b. 1928), a Swiss Roman Catholic theologian, regarded the notion of anonymous Christianity as a theological sleight of hand. His view is displayed in his question, "But is not the whole of good-willed humanity thus swept with an elegant gesture across the paper-thin bridge of a theological fabrication into the back door of the 'holy Roman Church,' leaving no one of good will 'outside'?" (Küng 1976, 97). Küng evidently doubted that a march across the "paper-thin bridge of a theological fabrication" is a real movement. Küng's doubt has to do with whether there is anything at all like what Rahner describes, since Küng's pluralistic view treats adherents of other religions as outside the church, unwilling to enter into the church, and therefore actually "unanonymous" and "unChristian," but certainly not damned because they are outside the church.

Rahner was aware of such concerns. He addressed the question "How could it be possible for there to be an 'anonymous Christian'" in *Theological Investigations* 14 (1976). He argued that divine grace is constantly present in the life of individuals. Rather than merely designing a way to speak or conceive of the possibility that adherents of other religions may gain access to salvation in Christ, Rahner's argument begins with the reality of divine grace and God's universal salvific will. Divine grace is actually present (existentially) in the lives of individual people. He takes this further, however, by saying that not only is divine grace constantly present in individual lives, but individuals are aware of this even though they may be only implicitly aware, not objectively aware. This implicit awareness occurs at a deeper level and shows itself in one's orientation "towards the immediacy of God as his final end" (1976, 288).

Rahner regarded this implicit awareness to be revelation. As he put it, "when man of his freedom accepts himself together with his *a priori* awareness which is already revelation, then that is present which can in the true and proper sense be called faith" (1976, 290). Faith is the state of receiving revelation. Divine revelation is just what authentic human faith, wherever it is found, accepts. Even an inchoate awareness of God can be implicit faith.

Karen Kilby has shown that Rahner's theology reversed the traditional understanding of the relationship between uncreated grace, the grace by which "God actually 'bestows himself' upon us and 'dwells in us'" and created grace, which is that "kind of grace, by which God alters and transforms us" (1997, 22). Theologians had typically understood uncreated grace to follow on created grace; Rahner reverses this order. God's self-bestowal is the ground for God's transformation of us. Rahner's notion of the anonymous Christian is not an ad hoc fabrication, but an implication of his reversal of the relationship between created grace and uncreated grace. In his view divine grace is a reality at work in the lives of individuals in that the "spirit of God dwells in us, and as a result, 'as a consequence and a manifestation' of this divine self-communication, we are transformed concretely and in particular ways" (Kilby 1997, 22). Küng's criticism, while highlighting the danger of "homogenization" in the concept of anonymous Christianity, does not undermine Rahner's work.

Not only was Rahner's notion of the anonymous Christian a result of his reversal of the traditional understanding of the relationship between created and uncreated grace, he intended the notion to be strictly internal to the Christian faith. In other words, adherents of other religions should not have been offended by the terminology because Rahner meant it to be used exclusively by Catholic theology in an attempt to articulate a Christian understanding with regard to how God is working and continues to work in the individual lives of non-Christians, as well as the non-Christian religious traditions in which they live. He never intended that the non-Christian be asked to regard herself in this way, as he acknowledged that "the subject being treated of here is first and foremost a controversy internal to Catholic theology" (Rahner 1976, 280). Küng's objection can be seen more fundamentally as an objection to this theological approach. In a sense, he saw Rahner as finessing the issue of the salvation of non-Christians, but seems to have neglected the derivation of Rahner's view from his basic anthropology.

American Dominican theologian J. A. Di Noia pointed out that Rahner tended toward a universalism with regard to his view of the relationship between grace and nature (Di Noia 1997, 130). Rahner, indeed, does not separate nature and grace, but does distinguish them. The problem Di Noia saw was that he did not offer clear delineations between them. In fact, Rahner was not sure that a useful theoretical delimitation of nature from grace was possible. In the actual world, nature just is graced (see McCool 1975, 186). Rahner's point was not to weld nature and grace into one realm with two aspects, but to correct the traditional Catholic neoscholastic view that nature and grace "appear as two layers so carefully placed that they penetrate each other as little as possible" (McCool 1975, 173). For him, nature is touched by and affected by grace so that nature itself becomes graced: "Our actual nature is *never* 'pure' nature. It is a nature installed in a supernatural order which man can never leave, even as a sinner and unbeliever. It is a nature which is continually being determined (which does not mean justified) by the supernatural grace of salvation offered it" (McCool 1975, 183–84).

This understanding of nature and grace allowed Rahner to account for the working of the Spirit of God in the lives of all people, not just those who are explicitly members of the church. Because grace is operative in human life, "every morally good act of man is, in the actual order of salvation, also in fact a supernaturally salutary act" (McCool 1975, 182). So a morally good decision can become a saving act, not because it is a naturally good act, but because it is an action impelled by a *graced* nature. For Rahner, grace *is* universal, but it is not indistinguishable from the natural realm. It is just that the set of ungraced entities is empty. Perhaps God could have made a world that was natural, but ungraced, but that possibility does not license the sort of radical separation of grace and nature posited by his mid-twentieth-century neoscholastic opponents. Like the other criticisms, Di Noia's concern has a point. Yet they all warn more against drawing inappropriate implications from Rahner's work rather than against accepting the work itself.

A Catholic Theology?

God's universal salvific will is one of two axioms that formulate the starting point of Rahner's view (see Keathley 2000). Rahner explicitly states "that, if we wish to be Christians, we must profess belief in the universal and serious salvific purpose of God towards all men which is true even within the post-paradisean phase of salvation dominated by original sin" (Rahner 1966, 122). It was his belief that "Our whole spiritual life is lived in the realm of the salvific will of God" (McCool 1975, 182). Therefore, with regard to the universality of God's salvific will, Rahner's classic inclusivist view aligns itself well with the tradition of the church.

That Rahner maintained his belief in the necessity of faith for salvation is probably most clearly evidenced in his doctrine of the anonymous Christian. Because grace is universal, Christians must regard each and every person they encounter as already on the path to salvation even without having heard the gospel message. Rahner's view of the necessity of Jesus Christ for salvation, along with God's universal salvific will, is what led Keathley to claim that there are the *two* axioms that constitute the starting point for Rahner's view (Keathley 2000). Therefore, the importance of faith in Jesus Christ for salvation, an established doctrine on which the church has repeatedly relied over the years, is also a doctrine upon which Rahner relied for articulating his view of anonymous Christians. Classic inclusivism fits well with both our first and second principles.

Rahner's fourth thesis had to do directly with the church in that he claimed that the church is the expression of divine grace hidden in other religions. By claiming that it is "the historically tangible vanguard and the historically and socially constituted explicit expression of what the Christian hopes is present as a hidden reality even outside the visible Church" (Sullivan 1992, 133), he seemed to be claiming a necessity for the church, even if it is a hidden necessity. Rather than a communion of possessors of divine grace as opposed to those who lack it, Rahner held that the church is the "communion of those who can explicitly confess what they and the others hope to be" (Sullivan 1992, 134). The inclusivist view, as seen through Rahner, fits with the necessity of the church, even though Rahner did not seem to give the same emphasis to the church that he did to God's salvific will and Christ's role as savior of the world. Rahner emphasized the necessity of the church for the salvation of people by virtue of the church's sacramental role as the continuing presence of Christ in the world.

Finally we come to the fourth rule, which affirms "the dignity of each and all human persons." Küng criticized Rahner because adherents of other religions do not regard themselves as anonymous Christians, and for Rahner to do so was intellectually imperialist. Implied in this criticism seems to be the charge that Rahner did not regard the dignity and differences of others sufficiently. Though he intended this notion as strictly internal to the church, as a way to aid its understanding of God's salvific work in the lives of all people, Rahner did not give detailed consideration to the perspectives and understanding of others in his reply to this criticism.

Rahner believed in maintaining the dignity of others. Rahner's response to the Japanese philosopher Keji Nishitani, who at the time was head of the Kyoto Zen Buddhist School, indicated that he accepted others' treating him as he had treated them on this topic. When Nishitani asked Rahner for his reaction to being regarded as an "anonymous Buddhist," Rahner replied:

> Certainly you may and should do so [i.e., call me an anonymous Buddhist] from your point of view; I feel myself honoured by such an interpretation, even if I am obliged to regard you as being in error or if I assume that, correctly understood, to be a genuine Zen Buddhist is identical with being a genuine Christian, in the sense directly and properly intended by such statements. Of course in terms of objective social awareness it is indeed clear that the Buddhist is not a Christian and the Christian is not a Buddhist. Nishitani replied: Then on this point we are entirely at one. (D'Costa 1986, 90–91)

Though Rahner did seem to allow for and desire mutual respect and dignity, the inclusivist view that he developed did not explictly account for the perspective of adherents of other religious traditions. As Rahner desired to articulate a distinctly Christian theology in his effort to enable Christians to understand that God works and how God works in the lives of others, an explicit account of other perspectives did not seem crucial. Yet its absence is at least a defect, and one of the reasons more contemporary models of inclusivism have been developed.

Rahner's claim that the Christian does not encounter the adherent of another religion as merely a non-Christian or unbeliever, but as someone who may have had an experience of God's grace and truth, makes his concern to respect others clear. He promoted a dignity for the other as one who may be touched by divine grace, while at the same time pointing out that the other's experience of divine grace can be perfected by becoming a member of the church. While Rahner maintained a certain respect for those who are members of non-Christian religions, his theology implies that God may work in participants in other religions, and perhaps even through these traditions, but these traditions are not part of God's plan of salvation for humanity. If the incarnation and the death of Jesus (the cross) are final causes of God's universal salvific will and self-communication to the world (Rahner 1978, 317–18), then the other traditions are effective only because their goal is really in Jesus.

Contemporary models of inclusivism have reworked the status of other traditions in God's plan. For example, Jacques Dupuis maintained that "if religion has its source in a divine self-manifestation to human beings, as we have shown, the principle of plurality will be made to rest primarily on the superabundant richness and diversity of God's self-manifestations to humankind. The divine plan for humanity, as we have explained, is one, but multifaceted" (Dupuis 2001, 387). For Dupuis, unlike Rahner, the world's faith traditions are willed by God for the salvation of their adherents (see Tilley 2006).

Classic inclusivism has become the "default view" for mainstream Christianity with regard to religious diversity. That it aligns with the first three rules is evident. This is not to say that classic inclusivism follows them all perfectly. No position could do so without some strain. The rules themselves are difficult to align with one another. Rahnerian inclusivism may not fit the fourth rule as well as it fits the first three, not so much because of any explicit denial of dignity and respect to those of other faith traditions, but rather because it is not directly concerned with the issue and suggests that the other traditions may not be part of God's plan for humanity. As classic inclusivism was developed with little interreligious interaction, this is not surprising. Insofar as traditions shape people into who they are, classic inclusivism's respect for the dignity of diversity may not be mere tolerance, but its respect is theologically grudging. As long as inclusivists require others to become members of the church, or at least oriented to the church in some way, inclusivism may be inadequate to fulfill the rule of affirming the dignity of each and all in their particularity.

Rahner's theology is a bridge from an intolerant view of other faith traditions and an extrinsicist view of the relationship of nature and grace to a positive appreciation of non-Christians by Christians and an integrated theological understanding of grace and nature. Both moves were needed and were timely. That classic inclusivism has become standard teaching in many traditions pays tribute to the usefulness of the model. Yet its commitment to the finality of Christianity, in some sense fulfilling or completing the other traditions, may not play well in the present environment of globalization and international migration. It is not surprising that another model of inclusivism has arisen, to which we turn in our next chapter.

5

Contemporary Inclusivism

Does God Give and Gather the Traditions?

with Matthew G. Minix

The diverse paths are conducive to salvation because they have been traced by God himself in his search for people and peoples; and even though not all have the same meaning or represent the same depth of divine involvement with people, yet all converge in the one plan designed by God eternally.
—Jacques Dupuis, S.J.

W E HAVE DIVIDED THE INCLUSIVIST CATEGORY INTO TWO DISTINCT models (classical and contemporary) in order to help clarify the way that shifts in the cultural landscape have affected the inclusivist model. Over the last two decades, increasing global awareness has brought a genuine dissatisfaction with the classical model of inclusivism, especially among those actively engaged in interreligious dialogue. A few Catholic theologians have responded to this challenge by developing a more contemporary model of inclusivism. These contemporary inclusivist theologians try to build a theology with an inclusivist shape in an environment that is quite different from that of their classic inclusivist predecessors, especially Karl Rahner. We retain the term "inclusivism" to emphasize the continuity between these approaches, even as the analysis of the models clarifies their differences.

Contemporary Inclusivism: New Approaches?

Contemporary forms of inclusivism share many of the same concerns as those forms of classic inclusivism that preceded them. All forms of inclusivism agree that God's saving activity cannot be confined to Christians alone. They oppose exclusivist positions that limit the possibility of salvation to explicit believers in Jesus Christ (or, in one particular Catholic form, baptized members of the Roman Catholic Church). Both classic and contemporary inclusivists affirm that God's gracious gift of salvation "includes" those who do not explicitly profess faith in Christ (D'Costa 1986, 112).

In opposition to a pluralist position, classic inclusivism viewed Jesus Christ as playing an "absolute" role in the salvation of all human beings. In contrast to the classic inclusivist position, contemporary inclusivists see Jesus Christ playing a "normative" role in the salvation of all human beings. While all inclusivists find that it is possible for people who are not explicitly Christian to be saved and that Jesus Christ has a genuine role in human salvation, contemporary inclusivists explain that role differently from the classic inclusivists.

It is important to understand this distinction in terminology between the two models. In contemporary ecumenical dialogue, Karl Rahner's explanation of Jesus Christ as "the absolute savior ... who reaches fulfillment through death and resurrection" (Rahner 1978, 318) can appear to imply a type of exclusivism that Rahner himself may not have intended.[1] Contemporary inclusivists maintain that to speak of Christ as the absolute savior is not only a barrier to religious dialogue, but is, in fact, simply wrong. They argue that the term "absolute" is uniquely "an attribute of the Ultimately Real; only the Absolute is absolutely." Contemporary inclusivists argue that terms like "normative" and "constitutive" indicate the true Christian understanding of Jesus Christ, "that the world and humankind find salvation in and through him" (Dupuis 1997, 292) better than the absolutist language of classic inclusivism.

Contemporary inclusivists differ on various issues, such as the role that other religions (and, possibly, other saviors) can play in salvation history. To show these differences, we consider two contemporary inclusivist models: the inclusive pluralism of Jacques Dupuis and the trinitarian exclusivism of Gavin D'Costa.[2]

Jacques Dupuis: Christocentric, Theocentric Pluralism

Belgian Jesuit theologian Jacques Dupuis (1923–2004) worked throughout his life to engender religious understanding between Christianity and other faith traditions. He spent more than thirty years living and teaching theology in India (Phan 2003a, 72). He advised the Indian Catholic Bishops' Conference during and after the Second Vatican Council. In 1984 he was assigned to teach in Rome at the Gregorian University. When the Congregation for the Doctrine of the Faith investigated his book (1997), he was removed from teaching. He continued to lecture and present papers until shortly before his death (Kaiser 2003, 222–25).

Dupuis sought to reconcile official Catholic teaching on other faith traditions with the genuine respect required for practical dialogue with members of those traditions. He transformed existing forms of inclusivism into what he termed a "Christocentric, theocentric pluralism," a contemporary Christian model of inclusivism. This approach continued to focus on Christ's own normative saving activity while also recognizing that God, the true source of salvation, works intentionally through all the major religious traditions of the world. The CDF ultimately vindicated Dupuis of suspicion and any "cloud" over his work dissipated.[3] His form of contemporary inclusivism has been very influential in current (Catholic) theological conversations, although his Indian confreres found him too conservative (Kaiser 2003, 224).

An essential component of Dupuis' form of contemporary inclusivism is that, in order for respectful dialogue to occur, Christians must recognize that other religious traditions could be part of "God's own plan for humankind" (Dupuis 1997, 11). Christians must accept that the existence of other religious traditions could be in some way an expression of God's will and that God could use these traditions to mediate salvation to their adherents. To fail to acknowledge that such a role is possible for other faith traditions would be to see them as ultimately opposed to God's plan for all of humanity. Christians could not then consistently truly respect and engage in dialogue with participants in other traditions.

Dupuis sought to explore the history of Christian theological interaction with non-Christians by building on the Old Testament idea of covenants with the nations. He noted that God made universal covenants with Adam and Noah, and then later made specific covenants with Abraham and Moses. Dupuis understood Christ as operating in all of these covenants through the forms of "Word (*logos*), Wisdom (*sophia*), and Spirit (*pneuma*)." Thus, diverse covenants were divinely established to play a real role in the saving mediation of Christ (1997, 42–44).

God never revoked the covenant that God made with the Jewish people. They are saved "through the covenant made by God with Israel *and* brought to perfection in Jesus Christ" (Dupuis 1997, 233). If God did not revoke the covenants with Abraham and Moses, why would one think that God revoked the covenants made with all of humankind through Adam and Noah? If God has not revoked the covenants with Adam, Noah, Abraham, and Moses, it is possible that God may also have made and kept other covenants with people in and through their own faith traditions. Other religious traditions can be seen to converge around Christ, who offers the concrete embodiment of that divine word, wisdom, and spirit present in their traditions and who is "the cornerstone that supports the whole process, its interpretative key" (Dupuis 2001, 161). God's diverse (pluralistic) plan for salvation is thus God's (theocentric) one plan because it is centered in Christ.

Dupuis claimed that the coming of Christ gives a particular fulfillment to these covenants. Christ's coming does not abolish or supersede their value for members of other covenantal traditions. His theology focused on "one God–one Christ–convergent paths." Dupuis supported this approach by citing authoritative texts from the Christian tradition that describe Christ as having been active in other traditions in various ways prior to the incarnation. These passages support a favorable understanding of other traditions from within the earliest Christian heritage. In invoking the *logos spermatikos* of Justin Martyr, for example, Dupuis showed that early Christian tradition saw a positive value in some of the beliefs of non-Christians (Dupuis 2001, 149). Using the thought of Irenaeus of Lyons, Dupuis could see Christ as present in non-Judeo-Christian *logophanies*, or manifestations of the Divine Word, while maintaining the incarnation as the "Father's climactic manifestation through the visibility of the Logos" (Dupuis 1997, 66). Christianity's heritage is more diverse regarding other religious traditions than exclusivists or classic inclusivists have shown.

Dupuis also found traditional notions of "substitutions for the Gospel," such as notions of evangelism beyond death (that those who had died not knowing of Christianity would be given a chance to choose for Christ in the afterlife) and implicit faith in Christ (which might characterize many or all people of good will who followed their consciences as well as they could), as exercises of the church's inclusivist impulse (Dupuis 1997, 112–20). He explored the theological considerations operating around Vatican II, from Jean Daniélou's fulfillment theory to Rahner's account of the anonymous Christian, as indicators that the Catholic Church was moving to a greater acceptance of other traditions (1997, 134–43). Dupuis also cited documents of the Second Vatican Council to warrant his claim that authentic truths and values exist within other religious traditions (1997, 162–70). Finally, Dupuis used the writings of Pope John Paul II to support a claim that the Holy Spirit could truly be said to be "mysteriously present in the heart of every human person" (1997, 175).

In all his theological writings, Dupuis' concentration on Christ remained particular and distinct. Yet Dupuis found orthopraxy more important than orthodoxy. As he put it, "'The discovery of the person of Jesus is more important than teaching doctrines about him, and must in any case come first in a context where experience is paramount in religious endeavor'" (Kaiser 2003, 227). However, christocentric inclusivism as a theory often tends to appear as no more than exclusivism with a happy face. Other traditions are seen at best as satellites or derivatives of the one true way. Dupuis preferred to construe the uniqueness and universality of Christ in a way that is "neither 'relative' nor 'absolute'" but rather "'constitutive,' insofar as Jesus Christ holds saving significance for the whole of humankind" (Dupuis 1997, 283). Dupuis advocated a trinitarian christology that recognized in Jesus both the *logos sarkos* (the enfleshed Word) and the active presence of the Spirit.

Dupuis was unwilling to limit either of these divine activities to the human Jesus alone. His understanding of the multiple covenants God made with humanity implies this. Dupuis wrote of other saving figures as manifestations of the *logos asarkos*, the nonenfleshed activity of the divine Logos. He argued that the *logos asarkos* uses other religions as vehicles of salvation, through the presence of the Spirit in the hearts of those believers. These traditions offer a salvation that will converge with the salvation offered through Jesus Christ. Dupuis also claimed that explaining Christ as a normative rather than as an absolute savior provided a place for the major religious figures of other faith traditions that were not in decisive opposition to the Christian tradition (1997, 295). Nonetheless, Dupuis maintained that this relationship between Christ and other such figures is ultimately "asymmetrical," and so affirmed a unique fullness of salvation through the incarnation of the Logos in the person of Jesus Christ, in which God's saving activity "reaches its greatest intensity in history" (2001, 186). Late in his life, Dupuis called this delicate balance an "inclusive pluralism" (2003, 1).

Dupuis argued for "a mutual complementarity, by which an exchange and a sharing of saving values take place between Christianity and other traditions and from which a mutual enrichment and transformation may ensue between the traditions themselves" (1997, 326). He maintained that other religious traditions should be seen not merely as the products of human attempts to reach God but as resulting from God's genuine attempt to reach human beings in their own particular histories and cultures. Dupuis asserted that for Christian belief "God—and God alone—saves," so that the title of "savior" is only applied to Jesus Christ "in a derivative manner which does not prevent God being the root-cause and the source of salvation" (1997, 306). The result is that saviors of other religious traditions can be understood to play a role in the salvation of their adherents, just as individual Christians are able to act as mediators of grace within the Christian tradition.

Not all forms of contemporary inclusivism are as open on the question of other religious traditions as the "christocentric, theocentric pluralism" of Jacques Dupuis. The "trinitarian exclusivism" of Gavin D'Costa, for example, is particularly hesitant when it comes to seeing other religions as vehicles of salvation. At the same time, there is an almost greater desire for mutual, interreligious transformation within D'Costa's theology than in Dupuis' theology. This seeming contradiction shall be explored at some length in the following two sections.

Gavin D'Costa: Trinitarian Exclusivism

Born in Kenya, theologian Gavin D'Costa moved to England in 1968. He was educated at Birmingham and received his doctorate from the University of Cambridge. He has taught at the University of Bristol since 1993. He has advised the Anglican and Roman Catholic bishops of the United Kingdom, and the Pontifical Council for Other Faiths in Vatican City, and was visiting professor at Rome's Gregorian University in 1998.[4]

The central premise of D'Costa's form of contemporary inclusivism is his belief that "Christian theology must be articulated within the horizon of its own histories and story (which has always been an interaction with other histories and stories) and the contemporary histories and stories of the societies in which it finds itself" (D'Costa 1990, 17–18). This perspective requires that D'Costa's form of contemporary inclusivism seek both to be true to the fundamental distinctiveness of the Christian revelation and to be willing to dialogue with other traditions. For example, D'Costa claimed that while Christianity must not insist that "its own particular revelation is the only important one," it must nevertheless assert that "if the particularity of Christ discloses God then it must hold to the normativity (not exclusivity) of its own particular revelation, thereby maintaining its universal claims" (D'Costa 1990, 16). To put it simply, if Christian revelation is taken seriously, then those who adhere to the Christian tradition must take the truth claims of the revelation seriously.

D'Costa is concerned to be faithful to the Christian tradition. In contrast to Rahner, who began with the "supernatural existential," described in the previous chapter, D'Costa began with a theology of the Trinity. He found that a "trinitarian perspective" is actually a better stance for Christians to take when entering interreligious dialogue than "the various strategies . . . which either ignore, abandon, or under-utilize this most central Christian doctrine of God" (D'Costa 1990, 16). D'Costa's understanding of the Trinity was shaped by decades of theological work that went beyond Rahner's approach to the Trinity (e.g., Moltmann 1993, LaCugna 1991, and the literature they cite).

Both D'Costa and Dupuis place a special emphasis on the Trinity in the structure of their theologies, apply that trinitarian structure to their understanding of christology, and give that christology an important place in their work. In the case of Dupuis, of course, this structure is found in an explanation of Christ as the God-sent, Spirit-filled, *logos sarkos* that converges with the God-sent, Spirit-filled *logos asarkos* of other religious traditions. D'Costa's trinitarian structure contains five explanatory theses that are intended to aid in "an authentically Christian response to the world religions because it takes the peculiarities of history entirely seriously" (D'Costa 1990, 17). A truly trinitarian theology of religions actually requires that the church must be open "to genuine change, challenge, and questioning." The model of interpenetration within the Trinity itself must therefore become the model for the way religious traditions relate to one another (D'Costa 2000, 133).

D'Costa's first thesis is that "A trinitarian Christology guards against classical exclusivism and pluralism by dialectically relating the universal and the particular." He argued that a proper understanding of the Trinity (and its relationship to christology) overcomes "christomonism"—by which he seems to mean not only a kind of fundamentalist theology that demands an explicit appeal to Jesus for salvation but also a Rahnerian understanding of Jesus as the only savior, a position that can become exclusivist, too. Only when it is clearly recognized that Jesus is not the Father can it become possible to understand that the Father "is not known exclusively through him" (D'Costa 1990, 18). This approach is akin to Dupuis' earlier points that in Christian theology "God—and God alone—saves" and that "only the Absolute is absolutely" (Dupuis 1997, 292, 306).

D'Costa's second thesis is that "Pneumotology [*sic*] allows the particularity of Christ to be related to the universal activity of God in the history of humankind." In emphasizing pneumatology, the theological study of the Holy Spirit, D'Costa is simply restating a position that we have already seen repeatedly in the section on Dupuis. The Spirit may be active in other religious traditions and we should be aware of that existence. D'Costa repeatedly affirms that, while it may be "sometimes painful," the church has much to learn from the elements of revelation given in other religious traditions and "will, itself, undergo fulfillment through dialogue" (D'Costa 1986 ,131).

D'Costa's third thesis is that "A Christocentric trinitarianism discloses loving relationship as the proper mode of being. Hence love of neighbor (which includes Hindus, Buddhists, and others, especially in a pluralistic society and a globalized world) is an imperative for all Christians" (D'Costa 1990, 19). This thesis essentially proposes an "ontology of peace" between Christianity and the other religions of the world, rather than the "ontology of violence" that often seems to characterize their relationship. D'Costa is arguing that the relationships between the members of the Trinity models the pattern of peaceful love that Christians should have with those of other religious traditions. This thesis articulates D'Costa's fundamental point that Christians should find the means to engage other religious traditions through the Christian understanding of the Trinity, rather than through some supposedly neutral, "pluralist" tradition.

D'Costa's fourth thesis is that "The normativity of Christ involves the normativity of crucified self-giving love." D'Costa intended this thesis as a clarification of what it means for a Christian to "love the neighbor." He claimed that it is through both personal suffering and a willingness to see "the real needs of our neighbors, especially in their marginalization, suffering, poverty, and vulnerability" that a Christian follows the pattern of Christ. D'Costa asserted that a Christian effort toward liberation ought to be "properly grounded in a Christocentrism (Christ's pattern) and theocentrism (for God's kingdom) and pneumatology (promoted through the power of the Spirit)." He appears here to anticipate Dupuis' move toward a "Christocentric, theocentric pluralism" (D'Costa 1990, 20–21) and Paul Knitter's turn to *soteria* (see pp. 98–102 below).

D'Costa's fifth thesis is that "The church stands under the judgment of the Holy Spirit, and if the Holy Spirit is active in the world religions, then the world religions are vital to Christian faithfulness" (D'Costa 1990, 22). That the church carries the fullness of revelation in Jesus Christ does not mean that the church has nothing to learn from other religious traditions. The church has a responsibility to seek out the truth contained within other religious traditions so that the church may fully become what God intends it to be. To fail to engage in dialogue with other traditions in which the Spirit is active would be to fail to revere and obey God properly. Hence, interreligious dialogue is a necessary part of faithfulness to divine revelation.

The different theological and philosophical traditions that inform Dupuis and D'Costa provide a key to understanding their differences. Jacques Dupuis approaches theology historically and inductively, a way particularly emphasized after the Second Vatican Council. Gavin D'Costa is influenced by conversation surrounding the formative power of tradition initiated by philosopher Alasdair MacIntyre. As Dupuis has moved an inclusivist position toward pluralism, so D'Costa has moved closer to particularism (discussed in chapter 7 below). Nevertheless, despite this difference in perspective, there is fundamental agreement between their two contemporary inclusivist positions on a trinitarian focus and an acknowledgment of the work of the Spirit in non-Christian faith traditions.

Are Contemporary Inclusivisms Suitable Catholic Positions?

In one sense, the answer to the question that heads this section should be obvious. If classic inclusivism is the "default position" for mainstream Christianity, contemporary forms of inclusivism should fit, too. The distinguishing feature of inclusivism in general is the priority that it gives to God's universal salvific will. For contemporary inclusivists, whatever the second or third rules mean, they must mean it in such a way as to "not deny God's universal salvific will." This priority sheds light on a key difference between classical and contemporary models of inclusivism: the cultural (including ecclesial) context within which each model developed.

Classical inclusivism emphasized God's universal salvific will in a context in which various forms of *exclusivism* appeared somewhat tenable. At the very least, it was not uncommon fifty years ago to find American Catholics who would argue vehemently that only Catholics could be saved. They seemed to have little or no acquaintance with the church's teaching of God's universal salvific will (Sullivan 1992, 4). In contrast, contemporary forms of inclusivism exist in an ecclesial environment in which God's universal salvific will is practically taken for granted. The cultural environment, especially in the United States, is so pluralistic that exclusivist positions have little cultural credibility, require extensive explanation by theologians and church leaders to get a hearing, and must necessarily be modified in everyday practice (Wuthnow 2005, 186). These differences in context cannot be overemphasized.

The best argument against classic inclusivism is that it is literally too parochial in outlook. Classic inclusivist theologians had little practical experience of non-Christian religions and interreligious dialogue, but much experience in intra-Christian, ecumenical dialogues. They responded to challenges to the credibility of the faith from non-believing Westerners, rather than from those of other faith traditions. Contemporary inclusivist theologians such as D'Costa and Dupuis lived in contexts that made the experience of de facto pluralism and the need for interreligious dialogue highly desirable. Their philosophical opponents were not so much nonbelievers as believers who believed differently. These differences lead to the different emphases and strengths of classic and contemporary inclusivisms.

The differences appear most clearly in considering the latter three principles discussed in chapter 2 above. With regard to the second rule, "Thou shalt not deny the sufficiency of God's salvation in and through Jesus Christ," the use of the term "absolute savior" may be attributable to the "internal Christian" concerns of Rahner and classic inclusivists. The problem with this term is that it not only minimizes the saving value of other traditions but also that it attributes a greater ("absolute") character to the saving activity of Christ than is proper for the Christian tradition. "Absolute" language not only fits better with exclusivism and intolerance than is appropriate but also cannot be heard without reference to G. W. F. Hegel's (1770–1831) philosophy of the "Absolute Spirit," which still shapes much European philosophy and theology—and the attacks on Hegel's work. Interreligious dialogue has helped shift the concept. Calling Christ a "normative" and/or "constitutive" savior avoids the problems of absolutist language (although these terms may bring problems of their own). Thus, we have a clear, concrete example of a form of growth in the tradition that has resulted from the practice of interreligious dialogue—supporting D'Costa's fifth thesis that the church can and must learn what God wants for it from interaction with other living faith traditions.

It is also possible that the third rule, "Thou shalt not deny the necessity of the church for salvation," may eventually become better understood as interreligious conversation increases. The CDF had been concerned that Dupuis could be interpreted as diminishing the role of the church. Dupuis became convinced that, for contemporary inclusivist theology to be done properly, it needed "to look at religious pluralism not merely as a matter of course and a fact of history (pluralism de facto) but as having a raison d'être in its own right (pluralism de jure or in 'principle')" (Dupuis 1997, 11). He was aware that his emphasis on other traditions could make the Catholic Church appear to be redundant. That was not his intent. While the church cannot have a role equal to that of Christ for salvation, it cannot be reduced to merely having a saving role only in the lives of its own members (unless one expands the concept of membership to include anonymous Christians, a move that also paradoxically reduces the significance of the church). Dupuis emphasized the necessity of the church in the documents of the Second Vatican Council in terms of "sacrament of salvation," and spoke of an "orientation" of non-Christians to the church. For Dupuis, the church is a sacrament in that it is a particular sign of God's grace. On his account, non-Christians are primarily oriented to the church eschatologically. Participants in other traditions are oriented to the church more in the finality of convergence than in the efficacy of its presence. Dupuis' understanding of how the church as sacrament of salvation mediates salvation for non-Christians does not deny, but seems to minimize, the present role of the church.

Classic and contemporary inclusivisms agree that respect is due each and every human person. They differ regarding how that respect is understood. In large part because of their intra-Christian focus, classic inclusivists did not pay serious attention to the dignity of the other as other in their diversity. Contemporary inclusivists' interreligious focus forced them to recognize the depth of diversity in ways that the classic inclusivists did not. Contemporary inclusivists also disagree among themselves on the correct emphasis and interpretation to give the fourth principle. This divergence shows the difference of forms within contemporary inclusivism.

Dupuis' theology, developed in the minority situation of Christianity on the Indian subcontinent, adheres to our fourth principle. Dupuis construes others as saved by God not as anonymous Christians but as participants in their own faith traditions. This focus means that Dupuis simply had no need to focus on the necessity of the church. Indeed, although the notifications from the Vatican were not written in precisely this way, they can be interpreted as reminding Dupuis not to give observing the fourth rule priority over observing the others. The notification suggests that Dupuis' work fits quite well with the rule to respect the dignity of each and every person as they are actually constituted in their own faith traditions, but may do so at the expense of not recognizing the necessity of the church as clearly as it should.

Dupuis and D'Costa diverge over the capability for other religious traditions to be vehicles of salvation. The crucial issue is how Dupuis' and D'Costa's models construe the dignity of humanity. Dupuis claims that God can use other religious traditions as vehicles of salvation. Dupuis does this in order to show proper respect for other religious traditions. As noted above, it is unclear if the church plays an effective role in the salvation of non-Christians, but only operates as a "final cause" in the sense of a form of eschatologically oriented convergence. If other religious traditions operate as vehicles of salvation distinct from the church, then it seems that the church may not actually be "necessary" for salvation in a strong sense. Dupuis presumed that the church was fulfilling God's purpose. He claimed that the "Church must show forth for all people the presence in the world of the Reign which God has inaugurated in Jesus Christ; it must serve the growth of the Reign and proclaim it" (Dupuis 1997, 356), but how the church in its witness, work, and proclamation is an effective sacrament of that reign remains undeveloped.

D'Costa's position proceeded primarily from his understanding of the documents of the Catholic Church and the theology of Pope John Paul II (D'Costa 2000, 113). He argued that neither the documents of the Second Vatican Council nor postconciliar encyclicals advance the position that other religions can be understood as vehicles of salvation. D'Costa did not argue that they are not vehicles of salvation (although this seems to be his view), but merely that church teaching has decidedly not addressed the question. His response, therefore, is to assume that other religions are not vehicles of salvation, as the church has not indicated that they should be viewed in that way; D'Costa leaves open the possibility that this may yet occur, though he doubted that it would (2000, 109).

The subtlety of D'Costa's position could easily be missed. Although he does not assume that other religions are vehicles of salvation, he does so from *within* the Christian tradition. This is a crucial aspect of his theological approach because it is intimately related to his central premise that "if the particularity of Christ discloses God then it must hold to the normativity (not exclusivity) of its own particular revelation, thereby maintaining its universal claims" (D'Costa 1990, 16). D'Costa did not claim that other religions do *not* possess revelation. In effect, he maintains silence on the matter. Since he affirms the presence of the Spirit in at least some of the traditions, he implied that they do possess some form of revelation. Yet a Christian does not have a clear basis from which to make a claim about whether or not other religions can be vehicles of salvation distinct from the church. In this D'Costa takes a page from the particularists' book, to be discussed in chapter 7 below.

In disavowing any knowledge of whether or not other religious traditions are vehicles of salvation, D'Costa observes the principles developed in chapter 2 in a way different from Dupuis. The practicing Christian knows that in the church there is at least one genuine vehicle of salvation. While there might be other vehicles of salvation, an argument can be made that the practicing Christian cannot truly know of any other vehicle of salvation and truly continue to be a practicing Christian. Through this careful balancing, D'Costa is clearer about the necessity of the church for all human beings than was Dupuis. D'Costa's church has no sharp boundaries in that its members are to show what it is to live in the love of God and thus, if they do so well, God can use them as instruments to inspire others "outside the church" to whom they relate. More clearly than Dupuis, D'Costa centers on the concerns articulated in *Dialogue and Proclamation,* as discussed above (p. 58).

Yet there is a serious tension in D'Costa's position. If other religions can be considered distinct mediators of revelation, how can they not also be considered distinct mediators of salvation? Does not the first conclusion imply the second? D'Costa does not think so. At the same time, because D'Costa affirmed the likelihood of revelation within other faith traditions and a type of dialogue in which all participants can be transformed in their beliefs, he must logically be open to the possibility of change in the Catholic Church's tradition on this point.

Just as the Christian tradition prohibits anyone from certainty about the salvation or damnation of anyone, so one cannot definitively say whether a person is or is not a member of the people of God. If the church were to explicitly recognize other religions as vehicles of salvation, then D'Costa would have to affirm that the divine truth contained in other religious traditions helped to contribute to this understanding, in much the way that they helped the terminology of Christ as a normative savior to develop. It is not clear, therefore, that D'Costa's position on salvific efficacy is consistent with his view of revelation in other traditions. If the issue of salvific efficacy were settled definitively, then what would Christians have to learn from other traditions about who God wants them to be and what God wants the church to be? The tension between revelation and salvation in D'Costa's view needs to be resolved.

One way of solving the tension would be to say that the Spirit present in the other traditions is the Spirit who constitutes the church. Hence, the tension between revelation and salvation could be resolved—it is the Spirit of God who always surprises us and teaches us and whose movement we can never predict and who also saves whom God wills saved. The price of this resolution, however, is to return to a classic form of inclusivism, which construes members of other traditions as anonymous Christians at best.

Conclusion

Contemporary inclusivism is founded on the belief that God's salvific will extends to all human beings. Like classic inclusivism, it seeks a middle path between the extremes of exclusivism and pluralism that will allow it to remain faithful to the Christian tradition. It seeks to explain the role that Jesus Christ plays in salvation as normative: we cannot claim that there are other saviors but can acknowledge the possibility that there might be, for we cannot know just how God as Spirit and *logos asarkos* works, but only that God as *logos sarkos* in Jesus is the heart of that working. It acknowledges the place of the church in salvation history. Finally, contemporary inclusivism seeks to respect the dignity of the human person and the other religious traditions to which people belong.

Contemporary inclusivism does not perfectly fit each of the rules, although it comes remarkably close. The form proposed by Dupuis seems to weaken the role of the church in the plan of salvation, although it skillfully preserves the role of Christ. The form proposed by D'Costa recognizes the possibility of revelation within other traditions, but it does not recognize what would seem to be a corresponding affirmation of them as vehicles of salvation and thus as respecting as well the dignity of all persons in their historical difference constituted, in part, by their participation in their religious traditions. At the same time, much like the theory of the anonymous Christian proposed by Karl Rahner, Dupuis' inclusivist pluralism and D'Costa's Trinitarian exclusivism seem to offer internal, Christian explanations of salvation within other religious traditions.

If inclusivism is the default position of mainstream Christianity in general and Catholicism in particular, the positions identified as "pluralist" seem to fall outside the pale because they deny the second and third principles that constitute the Catholic building code. The next chapter examines one exemplary pluralist position and asks whether that evaluation is accurate.

6

From Pluralism to Mutuality

Does God Cherish All the Faith Traditions?

with Daniel E. Martin

*Pluralists do not want simply to affirm the diversity and
the value of many religions;
the pluralist agenda is also the attempt to bring these many
and different religions into conversation.*

— *Paul Knitter*

A Desire to Communicate

PLURALISTS DIFFERENTIATE THEIR APPROACH FROM BOTH CLASSIC AND contemporary inclusivism by refusing to make claims of religious superiority for any religious tradition (Knitter 2005a, ix). They call for a "move away from insistence on the superiority or finality of Christ and Christianity toward a recognition of the independent validity of other ways" (Knitter 1987a, viii). The pluralist project is often described by its adherents as "crossing a theological Rubicon" (Knitter 1987a, viii) or of offering a new paradigm for understanding religious diversity.

The departure from claims of religious superiority is a profound shift. Pluralists find this shift necessary if productive interreligious dialogue is to move beyond tolerance toward interreligious mutuality (Knitter 2005a, ix–x). For Christians, pluralist positions require revising our view of the relationships between faith traditions, focusing how we think about the salvific aspects of the life of Jesus, and exploring new ways to think about the divinity of Jesus.

93

Given that classic inclusivism remains the default position in mainstream Christianity, pluralists have a burden of proof to bear against the accepted wisdom of inclusivism. Pluralist positions have found much disfavor in more traditional theological and ecclesial circles, which find that these positions simply fail to fit with the second and third principles regarding religious diversity. Yet it is not so clear that pluralist views are "outside the camp," as we shall see, especially as Paul Knitter has developed a position that moves beyond the classic pluralist approaches.

The Motivation of Peacemaking

The pluralist response to religious diversity is largely driven by concerns over what Indiana University professor of International Relations William Thompson has dubbed the Cool Hand Luke syndrome of failing to communicate (1983, 369). As noted in chapter 3, globalization has made communication necessary and isolationism impossible. Pluralists focus on dialogue and engagement. They refuse to construct Catholic religious identity by drawing sharp boundaries and valuing internal cohesion. They recognize that we inhabit a context that has spawned two opposite responses to the presence of religious diversity in the world, one focusing on differences, the other on commonalities. They begin with the latter.

Some contemporary Christian theologians focus on differences between faith traditions. Roger Haight, S.J., noted that they have "a hard time finding any common substrate represented by the word 'religion.'" He contended that this group tends toward isolationism because of a belief that religious differences offer a chasm that is too great to bridge. A second response by some theologians to religious diversity seeks commonalities among faith traditions. They look for what various traditions teach regarding what it means to be human at the most fundamental level and what moral responsibilities we bear. Haight invokes a Catholic sensibility when he describes the pluralist response to religious diversity as looking "for potential commonalities that reflect the ontological unity of the race" (1999, 396–97). It is precisely this choice between focusing on commonalities rather than differences that make some uneasy about the pluralist position.

Why focus on commonalities rather than difference in regard to the question of religious diversity? The simple answer is that this is what the contemporary situation demands.

Consider, for instance, Samuel Huntington's essay "The Clash of Civilizations?" (1996b). He offered an argument to show why some might view the firm assertion of religious identity markers as dangerous. The essay pointed out that during the Cold War international conflict centered on promoting political ideologies. In the post–Cold War world, conflicts are now being generated around questions of preserving a people's identity. Huntington claimed that religion serves as an even stronger determinant of cultural identity than ethnicity. The conflicts in the former Yugoslavia support this claim. In Yugoslavia, Western Europe and the United States were quick to support Slovenia and Croatia, whose populations are predominantly Roman Catholic. Russia attempted to make sure that Serbia, whose population is Eastern Orthodox, received a fair shake. Iran, Saudi Arabia, and Lebanon supported the predominantly Islamic Bosnian population with weapons. In this case, Western Europe and the United States assisted Slavic Croatians and Slovenians who followed a form of Western Christianity. Slavic Russia aided the Slavic Serbs, who followed a similar form of Christianity to that found in Russia, but not Slavic Croatians and Bosnians. Persian and Arab Muslims decried the treatment of Slavic Bosnians who follow Islam. Huntington concluded that religion was indeed a greater identity marker than ethnicity in the contemporary world (1996b, 14–15) because it was religious, not ethnic, markers that loomed large in determining which particular (foreign) government would aid which particular group in the former Yugoslavia.

Jonathan Sacks, chief rabbi of the United Kingdom, crafted his 2004 Grawemeyer Award–winning text (Sacks 2003) to show how religious traditions could help us *avoid* the clash of civilizations even in a world wounded by the events of September 11, 2001, and the U.S. invasion of Iraq. Sacks noted that religion can produce conflict, but religious traditions also offer paths to peace. Sacks's positive proposal is one in which various faith communities engage in conversation and seek a consensus on issues of peace, human dignity, and ecologically responsible behavior. Rather than simply aid those like one's own group, the quest to promote the conditions that promote the common good can be religiously warranted—a call similar to the Catholic concern with the dialogue of everyday life and the dialogue leading to action for justice (see *Dialogue and Proclamation* § 42). This quest for solidarity, justice, and ecological awareness is also at the heart of the projects of Paul Knitter and Roger Haight.

Seeking the common good of peace is not an easy task. Sacks warned that seeking peace may create a "profound crisis of identity" because of the inherent need for compromise between parties with their own interests at stake as they attempt to attain peace. Such identity crises do not leave the proponents of peace unbloodied. Martin Luther King, Jr., Anwar Sadat, and Yitzhak Rabin bear witness to the violence that peacemaking and reconciliation can evoke.

As one might expect, practitioners of peacemaking are rarely rewarded. Too often, making peace can seem like a betrayal of identity (Sacks 2003, 15, 7–10). Peacemakers such as Sadat and Rabin were killed for giving up land precious to their people in an effort to reconcile with enemies. One might surmise that giving up claims to Christian superiority in the name of peace might arouse similar reactions. As we explore pluralist approaches, it is crucial to ask if opposition to pluralist views is rooted in an excessive concern over losing identity markers. For such concern with the good of identity may waylay the good of working for peace. Single-minded focus on the former runs the danger of leaving no time to work on the task of making peace between religious traditions and their adherents.

The classic pluralist philosophical position has been modified substantially by Catholic theologian Paul Knitter. While committed to a version of the pluralist project, Knitter turned the project intellectually on its head. Knitter continues to give primacy, as do other pluralists, to our first and fourth principles, which affirm God's universal salvific will and the dignity of each and every person. Pluralists tend to deny Christ's unique role or the church's necessary role in human salvation, making pluralist positions unsuitable for Catholic theology in particular and mainstream Christian theology in general.

The most visible proponent of pluralism has been philosopher John Hick. Yet over the last quarter century, theologians influenced by him have developed rather different approaches to religious diversity. Paul Knitter's way of talking about religious pluralism once resembled Hick's much more so than it does today. Knitter has recently moved beyond the classic pluralist approach to discern a "mutuality" model for relationships between faith traditions (2002, 109–69) that places the practices of mutuality and solidarity before any theory of religious pluralism. To take practice as primary and theory as derivative—a typically postmodern or postliberal "nonfoundationalist" move—opens up the mutualist position to fitting the second and third principles better than classic pluralism. To understand contemporary mutualist (instead of pluralist) theology we must begin where the mutualists did, with pluralism.

John Hick's Pluralism

Pluralist theories do not originate in the Catholic tradition. Their intellectual impetus comes, in large part, from the work of philosopher, theologian, and former Presbyterian pastor John Hick. Hick articulated an early pluralist response to the religious diversity he encountered in Birmingham, England (1980). Hick's encounter led him to believe that Christianity could no longer maintain claims to an exclusive hold on salvation or inclusivist notions of fulfilling or completing the world's other religious traditions. Over the last half century, he has worked to develop a philosophy of religion that recognizes the value of the great faith traditions without privileging one of them as simply "true" or the "only path" to human fulfillment. Hick's Copernican revolution is the paradigm of pluralism.

Considered philosophically, the great faith traditions are roughly on a par with one another. This does not mean that they are in some way "the same" at root. Nor does it mean that a person should regard one tradition just as good as another. Rather, Hick—along with a number of other philosophers of the late twentieth century (e.g., Penelhum 1983)—found that no one tradition can show that it has an insider's track to ultimate truth or better means for developing good and holy people than any other. Hick also saw that adherents in all the great traditions could have experiences of the divine. Given this parity among the traditions in warranting truth claims, producing sanctity, and having religious experiences, Hick concluded that no tradition could reasonably sustain a claim of epistemic, moral, or spiritual superiority.

Hick used distinctions from eighteenth-century philosopher Immanuel Kant to explain this parity. The key distinction is between the *noumenal* and the *phenomenal*. We cannot know things as they are in themselves (*noumena*), but only as they appear to us (*phenomena*). God-as-God is beyond our ability to know. God can appear only in the particular historic faith traditions (the phenomena). Inevitably, these phenomena are at least incomplete, if not distorted, representations of God (the noumenal). Hence, any particular doctrine of God in any and every faith tradition is at best incomplete, if not partly false. Hick then posits an infinite God that is behind each and every partial or distorted finite model of what God is like. All of the traditions, in various ways, seek to reflect and reach the infinite (noumenal), but cannot do so because they are inescapably part of the phenomenal realm.

Hick has been roundly criticized by those who strongly support particular religious traditions on philosophical grounds (see pp. 111–14 below). Theological critics have also found his approach demeaning. Its strength, however, is calling Christianity to adapt to the reality of the profound depth of religious diversity. Hick finds that Christian theology needs to make a paradigm shift from a christocentrism that gave credence to classic inclusivism to a theocentrism that supported pluralist positions to account for this diversity (1980, 52–54).

Theocentrism (rather than christocentrism) makes it possible to envision all phenomenal religious traditions as pointing toward the same noumenal divine mystery or absolute reality. Each provides a particular perspective on what is divinely ultimate. The parity of the particular traditions entails that all have the right to be heard. For Catholic theologian Paul Knitter, this equal right to be heard is key to Hick's position because it simultaneously attempts to respect the differences found among the religious traditions but also argues that religions must have something in common to make dialogue possible (Knitter 2002, 110–11).

Hick did not mean for the shift to theocentrism to happen only to Christianity. All religious traditions would have to recognize that exclusivist and classic inclusivist theories were philosophically untenable. Either they begged the question by using their own standards to understand and judge other traditions or they simply construed other traditions as completed or fulfilled in their own. In either case, they did not give other traditions a fair hearing.

Hick has used distinctions other than that between the noumenal and the phenomenal. He has distinguished poetic from technical language. Working in a Christian context, he has attempted to make dialogue between faith communities easier by claiming that the language used to describe Jesus has been misunderstood. Believers' affirmations of Jesus' saving power are not technical theological language but poetic expressions of love and commitment. Christian attempts at doctrinal precision have forced Christians' commitment to Jesus, expressed in metaphorical and poetic language, into a quasi-scientific language systematized and universalized in philosophically inflected dogmatic theology. However appealing to Christian systematic thinkers, such translating of poetic evocations into universal and exclusivist claims could not be justified in the face of the claims of other traditions (Knitter 2002, 120).

Theologians have responded to this sort of challenge in various ways. The development of contemporary forms of inclusivism attempts to respond to the central significance of pluralist theories without going "all the way" to Hick's form of pluralism. Dupuis' combining christocentrism with theocentrism and D'Costa's trinitarian exclusivism were both developed because their authors recognized the importance of the key points pluralists and particularists have developed, even as they could not fully accept a pluralist or particularist model.

Many might concur with John Hick that translating poetic language into technical language creates problems for interreligious dialogue, However, Hick's main work was concerned primarily with "beliefs" or "claims." It is theory-centric. While recognizing these concerns and the situation of epistemic and moral parity that Hick described philosophically, Knitter has moved away from Hick's philosophically based position on religious diversity, which influenced his early work (1985). Knitter's stance has become much more informed by the prophetic and mystical elements of religions than by a philosophically based position rooted in Immanuel Kant's epistemological theory; it has become more praxis-centric. Whereas theory was key for Hick, and the early Knitter, the later Knitter is concerned with working for justice.

Paul Knitter's Understanding of Soteria

Knitter now prefers to call the pluralist approach to religious diversity an approach of mutuality because finding such common areas of concern fosters solidarity between divergent religious groups (2002, 109). Knitter describes his 2002 work, *Introducing Theologies of Religions,* as an update of his 1985 book, *No Other Name?* (2003, 126). In 1985, Knitter also described himself as adhering to the theocentric model, which he viewed as offering the most promise for interreligious dialogue. In *No Other Name?*, Knitter described the theocentric model using Hickian terms such as "paradigm shift" and "Copernican revolution" (1985, xiv, 165–66). By 2002, Knitter's position had come to focus on praxis much more than theory. As noted, Knitter offers mystical prayer practices and prophetic pursuits of justice as more viable avenues for arriving at religious mutuality than pluralistic theories (2002, 123, 125–48). By seeking common problems as a starting point, Knitter has both maintained Roman Catholic notions that common ties run throughout humanity and remained true to the contemporary imperative to take particularity and locality seriously.

Knitter has proposed that critiques of injustice by prophets and silent responses to the divine mystery by mystics found across cultures and religions can help form a concrete community to support mutualist responses to religious diversity. This understanding takes religious traditions as fundamentally rooted in mystical and prophetic practices rather than in theological systems. Mystics and prophets can be found in most, if not all, faith traditions. The practices of this dispersed group do not require that they have a "foundation" for dialogue. Even a thin, abstract philosophical position is unnecessary (2002, 123, 125–26). Knitter's mutualism is practice centered, not theory centered.

Knitter's move toward a religious mutualism based on working for justice began as a result of his own collaborative pursuit of greater justice in the 1980s. Knitter recounted meeting two refugees from El Salvador in 1983 who had been persecuted for fighting for human rights in their home country. This encounter changed Knitter's entire posture for dealing with the question of religious diversity. Within a year he and his wife were participating in an ecumenical group attempting to assist political refugees in war-torn Central America. Knitter followed this ecumenical experience by participating in a Hindu-Christian dialogue in India that viewed the promotion of justice as an indispensable component of meaningful dialogue (Knitter 1995, 1–22). These real-life collaborative pursuits of justice impacted Knitter's own scholarly writing. His essay "Toward a Liberation Theology of Religions" (1987b, 186–88) documented his evolution from a theologian who grounded his theory in philosophical principle to a theologian who reflected on the practices of Christian groups working for justice.

Knitter's use of liberation as a starting point for interreligious dialogue and cooperation is significant for several reasons. First, unlike Hick, Knitter is a Roman Catholic. He was influenced by the recent tradition of liberation theology, which refuses to separate liberation in this world from salvation in the next. Second, Knitter's shift from a theocentric pluralism toward a justice-based mutualism should force his critics to rethink their standard critique of pluralism. It may no longer apply to his work. Pluralists may violate our second and third principles; Hick certainly has no use for them. Yet this does not necessarily apply to Knitter's mutualism. Although classic pluralist theory cannot fit the principles

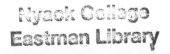

we have articulated, Knitter's moves bring him more in line with classic Catholic principles, while retaining many of the gains that pluralism sought. Finally, Knitter has taken the lead in attempting to show that the mystical and prophetic strands in non-Christian religions provide practical starting points for interreligious cooperation and dialogue. This last point is particularly important if Knitter is to preserve respect for the dignity of others (Knitter 2005b, 39).

Knitter has argued that concerns with salvation or soteriology are a point of convergence between religions. In Knitter's usage, "salvation" is a very broad concept, entailing liberation from suffering and oppression in personal, social, political, and religious spheres of life. Knitter names this orientation toward human well-being *Soteria*, or "the ineffable mystery of salvation." He defined *Soteria* as being fundamentally concerned with "bringing about liberation with and for the poor and nonpersons."

Concern for human welfare is common to many faith traditions. This concern with and action to realize human welfare provide ground, properly "'shaky' ground," for interreligious cooperation. This ground is shaky because it is no foundation but is the ad hoc practice of mutual cooperation. Such interreligious cooperation becomes more solid with dialogue. That is, the point is not to engage in a dialogue to find common ground to get started. The "starting point can be clarified or corrected after one starts" working for common goals (Knitter 1987b, 187–88). The point is not to build intellectual edifices, but to feed the hungry and understand how to overcome the social evil of hunger. In such cooperative action to ameliorate particular evils, shared understandings can emerge. Interreligious dialogue is not a necessary foundation for cooperation, but the result of sharing the work and talking about it.

Knitter's contribution is to reverse the presumed order of theory and practice. Like some postmodern theologians, Knitter has moved away from the concern to find foundations for what we do and believe, and moved to a position that recognizes the primacy of practice over theory.

Knitter's use of the word "ineffable" in describing salvation recognizes that no particular faith can express the entire mystery of salvation: Who knows how to describe with any reliability the furniture of heaven, the temperature of hell, the bliss of Nirvana, or the identity of Atman with Brahman or, finally, even whether these concepts refer to one or many forms of salvation? (A much different response to this question is found in chapter 8.) By focusing on the promotion of justice, Knitter's approach avoids the traps of taking one's own ideological or religious commitments as a foundation for cooperation. Rather, the very work helps participants to understand what *Soteria* is both for themselves and for others.

Knitter's focus on *Soteria* does not impose any specific views of God on potential participants in cooperative efforts between different religious groups. Knitter also recognizes that not all faith traditions understand salvation the same way, but that this is to be expected if salvation is an ineffable mystery. He simply proposes that "shared praxis" offers a starting point for discussion that contains a smaller threat of ideological hegemony (1987b, 187).

Knitter discussed the divine in Jesus in terms of a Spirit christology (2002, 142–45) rather than a Logos christology. He noted that attempting to preserve the uniqueness of Jesus without diminishing the importance of religious figures found in other traditions forces one to walk a tightrope. He argued that conceiving of Jesus as spirit filled is helpful because Jesus is an essential but not exhaustive representation of the divine mystery available to all religious traditions. Jesus was focused on instituting the reign of God in his preaching and life. He did not focus on his own status or establishing a religious tradition separate from Judaism. Jesus' emphasis on establishing the kingdom of God mirrors the role of the Hebrew prophets who were moved by the Spirit.

Knitter's position has continued to evolve. Knitter has added an explicit concern for ecological well-being to his understanding of *Soteria*. Knitter, like any good pluralist, has tended to focus more on what unifies than on what divides the world's religious traditions. In this quest for commonalities, Knitter came to the (rather obvious, but often ignored) conclusion that the earth itself provides the common context for all human religious experiences. The divine is experienced in different ways at different times and places. Expressions so different as to be incommensurable speak of those experience. But the earth, in all its limited diversity, is the common site for all religious reflection. Hence, ecological concerns are an area for forming a common purpose among differing religious communities (Knitter 1995, 112–13).

One only need survey the locations in which religious communities function and one can easily find common problems that face multiple religious communities. Knitter identifies poverty, victimization, violence, and patriarchy as common sources of suffering confronting most religious communities (Knitter 2002, 136–37). Increasingly, degradation of the environment—natural, political, and social—is a concern of all. Religious cooperation in particular places to understand and alleviate these problems can lead to dialogue. Common understanding of what is wrong about poverty or patriarchy cannot be guaranteed, but even small ameliorations of patterns of oppression can be celebrated as signs of hope.

Knitter's focus on common problems reflects the "can-do pragmatism" of his nation. The U.S. context certainly features both religious diversity and serious obstacles to justice. Pursuit of justice is a practical staring point, not a theoretical foundation, for interreligious cooperation (1987b, 188). However, as the cooperation of many from different faith traditions in the civil rights movement showed, focus on a goal on which diverse folk can agree can promote deeper understanding through witness and action. In this sense, Knitter's evolution toward praxis has produced a serious "sited" theology of religions.

The mutualist starting point for liberating praxis has not only afforded Knitter a different place for analyzing religious diversity than John Hick, but it has also provided him room for critiquing Hick's position. Even in 1984, Knitter had critiqued a recent work of Hick as slipping into an unsatisfying toleration (1984, 267–68).[1] Knitter's turning to praxis, his moving away from philosophical foundations, and his using mysticism, liberation, and ecology as fundamental points for connections and for common effort between religions give credence to his construing this approach as "mutuality" rather than "pluralism." Philosophically, Knitter is no longer moored to Hick's Kantian foundationalism. Theologically, this move offers his position the opportunity to avoid denying Christ's uniqueness or traditional ideological views of God or the church (2002, 146–48).

Haight's Christological Contributions

Roger Haight's work in christology in large part complements Knitter's approach. Where Knitter focused on Jesus' work promoting salvation, Haight focused on the person of Jesus through whom God saves. It is not that Knitter's soteriology requires or matches Haight's soteriologically oriented christology. Nonetheless, both have a concern for respecting religious diversity as well as for developing the Catholic tradition in new directions. In that, they can be seen as complementary.[2]

Haight's christology attempted to situate reflection on Jesus in a postmodern context. Haight argued that scientific information about the vast and ancient nature of the cosmos must be accounted for when doing christology (1999, 396). Our global culture and global interdependence helps us become aware of the ways religious diversity affects christology. Haight sought tools from within the Christian tradition to help understand diversity.

The Christian scriptures display a plurality of christologies (see Dunn 1980, 2003). This internal diversity has implications in and of itself for Christian responses to religious diversity. All christologies have a soteriological component (Haight 2005, 152–54). In his work, Haight does not move from christology to soteriology, from the person of Christ to the work of Christ, but from the work of Christ to Christ's person. In this move to the priority of practice, Haight's work parallels Knitter's in its fundamental soteriological orientation.

Haight sought to construct a christology especially applicable in the situation of religious diversity. While Haight uses the term "symbol" for describing Jesus' relationship with God, this does not mean that Jesus is "merely a symbol" for Haight. Haight claims that symbols are the powerful medium by which transcendent reality is historically mediated (2005, 152). Haight used the term "symbol" much as did Avery Dulles. For Dulles, symbols participate in and manifest the reality they mediate (Dulles 1983, 132–41; Tilley 1999b).[3] Haight's account of symbol is similar to Dulles's.

Haight importantly notes that in Jesus, God is truly encountered because anything less than this would mean salvation was not mediated by Jesus. Haight extrapolates from Jesus' divine nature important factors to consider when evaluating other religions. Haight notes that in Jesus, Christians encounter an active God who desires the salvation of all (2005, 155–56). Haight also determines that because God's revelation and action must be mediated via historical symbols Christians should expect religious diversity if they believe God wills the salvation of all people. If God has a universal salvific will, then it must be mediated to people concretely. A truly effective and active God would have to have as many diverse mediations as there are particular contexts in which God could act (2005, 156–57).

This notion of multiple mediations is particularly important for interreligious dialogue. If we view the diversity of faith traditions as consistent with rather than a frustration of God's will, as did Haight and Dupuis, talking to our non-Christian neighbors ought to proceed more smoothly. A Christian expectation of diversity among faiths also opens the door to appreciating the possibility that God's salvific will is active in other faith traditions because no one historically conditioned manifestation of God can mediate everything there is to say about the ineffable mystery of salvation (Haight 2005, 157).

Haight's Spirit christology grounds the understanding of how God might be active in other religious traditions. He developed his Spirit christology in contrast to, rather than in conflict with, a Logos christology (Haight 1999, 445). Such a Spirit christology understands Jesus' divinity as "empowerment by the Spirit" (Knitter 2002, 154–55). Haight favored emphasizing this model because in his view it clarifies the co-existence of Jesus' human and divine natures more easily than a Logos christology can (Haight 1999, 439; Buckley 2000, 555). God acted in and through Jesus. Our era understands "person" and "nature" quite differently from the fourth- and fifth-century fathers of the church who developed the normative christology of "one person with two natures." A Spirit christology may communicate the difficult doctrine of Jesus Christ being truly human and truly divine better than some incarnational logos christologies that can be heard as drifting into tritheism or subordinating the divine to the human in Jesus Christ (see Haight 1999, 451). Haight sought both to protect the presence of the divine in Jesus and to create space for the work of salvation in other religions.

The Catholic tradition has held that the Holy Spirit is present to all humanity. The presence of the Spirit who is active and eminent in Christ allows Haight to contend that mutualists hold out the possibility that other salvific mediations of the spirit might be "on par" with Jesus (1999, 399). This parity, however, is quite nuanced. Jesus is normative for Christianity. "But this normativity functions within the context of historicity. . . . Historical relativity forces the Christian to define more exactly the content of what is mediated by Jesus" (1999, 410). Jesus as norm for Christians does not preclude other figures, texts, or practices being normative for participants in other faith traditions. A Christian can come to judgment that another tradition was incompatible with God's revelation in and offer of salvation through Jesus. Given that such a judgment may be possible, it may not be necessary. Rather, Christians can see that "Jesus opens the imagination to God's presence to the world and guides Christian perception to recognize that what is revealed in him can be enriched by other religious truths" (1999, 410). Like contemporary inclusivists, Haight finds that Christianity needs to learn from other traditions, even those that are "contrary to," but not necessarily "contradictory to" Christianity (see p. 127 below).

With regard to other traditions, other salvific paths may be normative for their adherents. As a Christian theologian, Haight wrote that Christians can find that other traditions "can truly mediate God's presence even though they do not perfectly represent it. Every actual religion is historically limited, ambiguous, and possibly erroneous in any given practice or belief. Yet even as such it can be an instrument of God's saving grace" (1999, 416). Whatever salvation there is in the world, God is its primary agent; in that Haight is in agreement with Dupuis. That the incarnation is the only way God could and does work in the world seems confused. It limits an unlimited God. Nor is denial of divine grace in other traditions in accord with the heart of the Christian tradition.

How God works in other traditions remains a speculative matter. Positively, Haight claimed God does. Negatively, he found that Jesus reveals God's universal salvific will but is not necessarily the efficient cause of the salvation of all (1999, 353). In effect, Haight seems to agree for the most part with Rahner's view except that he does not actually assert that the Christ event is the final cause of salvation (see pp. 67, 79, 90, 212).[4]

Haight offered three criteria for judging the orthodoxy of a given christology: intelligibility in the contemporary world, faithfulness to the Christian tradition, and empowerment of human life (2005, 158). Haight took historical consciousness, globalization, and even cosmic awareness into account while constructing his christology. Thus, he meets his own first rule. Haight has argued that Christians should look for a unity of being in humanity and approves of Knitter's emphasis on interreligious collaboration that seeks liberation from suffering (1999, 398). Thus, he easily meets his third requirement for orthodoxy. It is his second requirement of faithfulness to the tradition that has generated the most controversy.

Haight reasoned that his christology is faithful to the christological elements of the New Testament, Nicaea, and Chalcedon. He first argued that a christology must accept the divinity of Jesus to be considered orthodox and that the New Testament primarily portrays the action of the divine using the language of Spirit. Haight also noted that because salvation is mediated through Jesus, construing Jesus as a human so radically different from other humans makes no sense because the destiny of Jesus must correspond to humanity's destiny. Haight finally argued that without the salvific action of God in other religions the saving acts of Jesus become less intelligible (Haight 2005, 158–60).[5] Whether this formulation communicates well what the tradition has said remains debated.

Can Catholics Accept Mutualism?

When formulating our four principles, we intentionally formulated them not to define what we must say, but to show what we ought to avoid. This approach is especially important in evaluating mutualism. That salvation and true experience of the divine are available to all seems to squelch any doubt that the first rule is violated by mutualist theologians. The heart of mutualism is God's universal salvific will. Hick, Knitter, and Haight would all agree on this.

Our second rule is "Thou shalt not deny the sufficiency of God's salvation in and through Jesus Christ." The basic pluralist move from christocentrism to theocentrism appears to contradict this principle. Jacques Dupuis criticized this shift from christocentrism to theocentrism as forcing a false choice on Christians. Dupuis argued that, while pluralists do not intend to diminish the faith of practicing Christians, their christological claims carry with them implications that would indeed alter and likely diminish Christian adherence. Dupuis further claimed that christocentrism and theocentrism are actually compatible because being christocentric merely reaffirms God's action of making Christ the center of God's salvific plan. Dupuis asserted that being christocentric should reinforce theocentrism (Dupuis 1997, 186–91).

John Hick's philosophical account of religious pluralism is not compatible with this principle. However, the status of Roger Haight and Paul Knitter's Spirit christologies remains an open question. This position does hold that Jesus is a unique and necessary mediation of God's salvific will, but it also holds open the possibility that other mediations are or can be on a par with Jesus Christ (Haight 1999, 399; Knitter 2002, 154), at least for adherents of other faith traditions. The christological postures of Knitter and Haight do seem to deny "the sufficiency of salvation in and through Jesus Christ." Such a denial, if it has been made, seems to have proceeded from the goal of giving full recognition to the globalized and religiously diverse world in which Knitter and Haight work.

However, the issue is not settled. In an era when understanding salvation as wrought by the blood sacrifice of Jesus is less than credible, the issue of what salvation means must be reconsidered. Liberation theology revamped soteriology to include social and this-worldly components as well as individual and next-worldly components. Knitter's understanding is worth considering:

[F]ollowers of Jesus would be better off if they understood (and felt) Jesus more as a *sacrament* of God's love than a *satisfaction* for God's justice. In the technical language we've already encountered, the way Jesus "saves"—that is, the way he enters people's lives and connects them with God—can be understood better as a *representative cause* rather than as a *constitutive cause*. More simply: Jesus "saves" people not by fixing something but by showing something. He doesn't have to fix or rebuild the bridge between God and humanity by responding to God's demand for satisfaction for humanity's sinfulness. Rather, his task is to reveal or show humanity that God's love is already there, ready to embrace and empower, no matter how often humans have lost their way in selfishness and narrow-mindedness. In other words, Jesus shows that the "bridge," or the relationship between God and humans, already exists; they just don't know where to find it or are not able to trust that it can be found. (Knitter 2002, 152–53)

In this passage are the seeds of a possibly orthodox flower.

One can understand Knitter's concept of a "representative cause" as merely showing the way. Indeed, if one assumes that representation signifies as a text does, then what Jesus does is simply to reveal what is already there, as Knitter puts it. In that case, the mutualist position is in serious tension with, or even in serious violation of, our second principle.

However, if Jesus is truly a *sacrament* of God, then Jesus does not merely *represent* but *empowers* those who walk in his way. For a representative cause can also be understood as a form of *agency*. As argued in chapter 2, the contemporary view of language as fundamentally communicating rather than signifying sees language as "trans-actional." To communicate successfully is not merely to represent well but to bring about a change in the hearer. The "showing" of a bridge is not a mere pointing out but is an exercise in enabling people to find it and to learn how to walk on it. When Jesus shows us the way, he also gives us the way. As any extremely powerful exemplar does, Jesus showed people how to live in and live out the reign of God and in that showing enabled them to do just that if they would but respond to his action. If this is a form of "exemplarism" in christology, it is not the sort of exemplarism that is merely exemplary, but is powerfully, empoweringly exemplary. As such, it may not fall under the strictures raised against exemplarism, that the redemption in Christ is merely an ethical model of what love means.

Neither Knitter nor Haight denies that Jesus is unique. That Jesus is God's symbol or sacrament is affirmed by both. In the context of contemporary understandings of language such as speech act theory (see Tilley 1991), symbols and sacraments are never *mere* representations, but, when effective, literally *effective* communications that change the receiver. Given this understanding of language, the salvation wrought in and through Jesus is clearly sufficient.

Whether a Spirit christology is orthodox is another question. Haight himself mentions that many do not accept Spirit christology as orthodox (Haight 1999, 445). One must conclude that Haight's Spirit christology is at least theoretically different from the Logos christology that is the mainstream of the tradition. However, once again the move toward Spirit christology seems to be made out of motivations to uphold God's universal salvific will and respect the dignity of the non-Christian other rather than an attempt to "demote" Jesus. If a Spirit christology is seen as an alternative model to a Logos christology, rather than a substitution for it, then it is possible that this sidestream of the tradition is a viable course. In short, it is possible that the mutualist tradition—though with some tensions and some questions still needing exploration—fits the second principle.

Our third rule is "Thou shalt not deny the necessity of the church for salvation." Once again various tenets expressed by Knitter and Haight seem to conflict with this rule. Knitter has claimed that Jesus' focus was "kingdom centered" rather than "church centered" (2002, 145). Haight has argued that insights within other religions can be universally applicable to Christians (Haight 2005, 157). Neither of these claims directly denies the necessity of the church for salvation. That they deny the sufficiency of the church for salvation is not startling and puts them in the company of most contemporary inclusivists.

However, if Jesus is understood as the sacrament of God and the church as the sacrament of salvation, then it is the duty of the church to show as an effective sacrament, as Jesus did, the salvation wrought by God. Again, this showing is not simply proclamation of truths, but transforming witness. If the church's communication is to be effective, that is, to be the means that God uses to change others, then the church is necessary to continue that divine communication. The image of the church as the body of Christ is important here. In this world, we can do nothing without our bodies. If God in Christ shows how God saves, then the church is necessary to keep hope alive and to remember in powerful practices, not just empty words, the way to life eternal.

The 1991 Vatican Council for Interreligious Dialogue document *Dialogue and Proclamation* reaffirmed four forms of interreligious dialogue: dialogue concerning life, liberative action, theological exchange, and religious experience (*Dialogue and Proclamation*, § 42) Knitter's and Haight's projects promote all four of these types of dialogue. This document also makes clear, however, that a scriptural mandate exists for the church to proclaim and serve the kingdom of God (*Dialogue and Proclamation*, § 59). This proclamation of the kingdom of God is far more christocentric than Knitter's *Soteria*. However, Knitter has pointed out that Christians working for *Soteria* need not jettison their specific beliefs and practices (Knitter 1987b, 187).

Robert Schreiter has questioned Knitter's distrust of formal authority. Knitter found that authority structures stifle dialogue. Schreiter countered that Knitter banished authority structures, but then gave more influence to non-Christian conversation partners than Christian partners in his mutuality model. Knitter seems to assume that formal authority is oppressive, but he offers no critique of the new authoritative demands being made by Christianity's conversation partners. Schreiter's criticisms suggest that Knitter's position may have more trouble with rule three than suggested above, if one takes his reaction to authority as a general point rather than as a reaction to specific authoritative acts of the Catholic magisterium (Schreiter 1992). Thus, we can conclude that neither Knitter nor Haight has formally violated the third principle, but that their positions need some clarification if they are to fit its injunction.

That pluralism and its mutualist offshoot both pass with flying colors the rule regarding human dignity seems obvious. Pluralism's general recognition of a "rough parity" among religions and the ability of non-Christian believers to encounter the transcendent seems to avoid any form of religious prejudice. In fact, the fourth rule is at the heart of the pluralist search for commonalities among religious traditions. This does not mean that naive pluralism is not prone toward errors and even perhaps toward rendering differences among faith traditions superfluous (Fredericks 1999, 116). This erasure of difference would indeed be an imposition of a universal that exterminated the value of the particular. It would also undermine the human dignity of many religious practitioners who hold their particularity dear. Thus, pluralism in general can tend toward imperialism, but the mutualist model has safeguards to avoid such charges.

Knitter's pursuit of human welfare and liberation is motivated from a deep commitment to the universality of human dignity. It also allows for him to focus interreligious activity on a common problem rather than on an "absolute reality" that erases difference. In this way, Knitter's mutualism and Haight's "pluralism" fall well within the accepted territory staked out by our fourth rule.

Knitter's and Haight's christological and ecclesiological claims seem to be in some tension in that they don't represent as well as some think they ought the principles of a Roman Catholic theology of religions. This raises the question of whether a mutualist approach can fit the four rules. James L. Fredericks has argued that Paul Knitter's liberative pluralism is so nuanced that it is beginning to occupy a different space than other versions of the pluralist response (Fredericks 1999, 119, 132, 135), a position with which we obviously agree. We think Knitter's position can dispense with foundationalist, pluralist theory and focus on the practices of solving problems obvious to adherents of many living faith traditions. John Paul II and Benedict XVI have stated that the impulse toward peace and human welfare is present within all faith traditions and open to all peoples. This means that one could engage in Knitter's collaboration on common problems even if one possessed a more traditional christology and eccle-siology. Thus, Knitter's move toward common problems as a source of common ground among divergent faith traditions has provided the church with a great gift. Moreover, even if the words are not traditional, it remains possible that a mutualist model communicates the heart of the tradition well. Certainly Haight and Knitter would claim so; the issue is moot, however, as it is not clear just how their points are heard by those who are the audience for their work—save for those who have another approach to language, which cannot be taken for granted.

As Robert Wuthnow noted, interreligious cooperation must be focused on a specific problem and local if it is to be both productive and sustained (Wuthnow 2005, 303). Knitter's practical approach to religious cooperation meets Wuthnow's criteria. The mutualist model for understanding religious diversity also challenges Catholics to be judged by the fruit the church bears (Knitter 2002, 135–36). In this way the model can serve as a corrective to any prideful tribalism that might contribute to global angst and bear bad fruit. It also can serve as a promising bridge to the world. Working for liberation and justice might be one way in which the church can bear effective witness to the reconciling activity of God revealed in the actions of Christ—healing, forgiving, reconciling, and working to realize God's reign.

7

Is Religious Diversity a Problem to Be Solved? Not Particularly

with Ernest W. Durbin II

*True universalism requires fidelity to
the particularities of Christian revelation and existence.*
—*J. A. Di Noia, O.P.*

UNDERSTANDING RELIGIOUS DIVERSITY CAN BE SEEN AS EITHER PROBLEM or promise for the Christian community. Inclusivist and pluralist positions tend to view religious diversity as a theological problem to be resolved. However, some Christian theologians, authorities, and believers find these theological efforts confused or misleading. As well intentioned as inclusivists and pluralists may be, it is not clear that the answers they provide resolve problems. Their theological approaches may even intensify the problems.

The particularist model was developed partly in response to perceived inadequacies in inclusivist and pluralist positions (Knitter 2002, 173).[1] Whereas inclusivists (e.g., Rahner) and pluralists (e.g., Hick) tend to be foundationalists, the particularists discussed in this chapter are nonfoundationalists. Their reply to the reality of religious diversity provides an alternative to the other models we have studied. Particularists find religious differences to be deeply significant to individuals and communities. Each tradition shapes participants' lives in particular ways so as to enable them to reach the unique ultimate goal of human life that the tradition discerns. Particularists find that inclusivist and pluralist accounts take these differences too lightly.

Christian particularists do not regard religious diversity as a challenge to their essential beliefs. Diversity, rather, promises an opportunity for dialogue

110

and witness to the distinctive beliefs and values of Christianity. Particularists are interested in constructive conversation with peoples of other faiths, as well as corrective conversation with members of the Christian tradition. They focus less on issues concerning the salvation of non-Christians and more on questions of religious truth.

In going beyond inclusivism and pluralism, they share some characteristics with Paul Knitter's mutualism. Like mutualism, particularism is a "second-generation" theory, developed in response to perceived inadequacies in earlier theories. Second-generation theories focus on a different aspect of the problem of religious diversity from earlier theories concerned with salvation—for mutualism, justice; for particularism, truth. Particularists do, however, have some problems with Knitter's view, as we shall see more explicitly in chapter 8 where we discuss a particular form of particularism.

Particularists can be found throughout the Christian spectrum. We focus on two Roman Catholic scholars: Joseph Augustine Di Noia and Paul J. Griffiths. Di Noia currently works in the Vatican as undersecretary of the Congregation for the Doctrine of the Faith (CDF). Prior to his appointment to this position by Pope John Paul II, Di Noia served as the director of the Intercultural Forum for Studies in Faith and Culture at the Pope John Paul II Cultural Center in Washington, D.C. He earned a doctorate from Yale University. Griffiths is the Schmitt Professor of Catholic Studies at the University of Illinois, Chicago. Griffiths was educated at Oxford prior to receiving a doctorate in Buddhist Studies from the University of Wisconsin, Madison. Formerly Anglican, Griffiths and his immediate family were received into the Catholic Church in 1996. Though steeped in classic Catholic philosophy and theology, they are also influenced by Anglo-American forms of analytical philosophy far more than other scholars who work on religious diversity (except D'Costa, whose affinities with particularism were noted in chapter 6).

Three common themes link particularist positions. First, religious differences are fundamentally important and should be taken seriously. Second, the reality of religious diversity does not require abandoning essential Christian beliefs. Third, interreligious dialogue provides opportunity for intellectual growth and the defense of Christian religious claims.

Religious Differences Are Serious

On the surface the claim that religious differences are to be taken seriously seems almost trite. In the course of interreligious dialogue, even without theological impetus, common courtesy alone should command that participants take their differences seriously. Yet particularists argue that inclusivism and pluralism denigrate religious differences and reduce their importance in the daily lives of individuals. In this section we will examine the primacy of religious practice and the way it shapes the lives of its participants. A basic claim of particularism is that the theories discussed so far in this book underestimate religious difference.

Griffiths has developed a functional definition of religion in an effort to provide a philosophical groundwork for his work on religious diversity (Griffiths 2001b, 7). Religion is "a form of life that seems to those who inhabit it to be comprehensive, incapable of abandonment, and of central importance" (Griffiths 2001b, 7). A "form of life" is "a pattern of activity that seems to those who belong to it to have boundaries and particular actions proper or intrinsic to it" (ibid.). Particular activities give an identity to a form of life. Some practices are clearly central to the form of life, and others are identified as outside the form of life (Griffiths 2001b, 8).[2] One can imagine a Buddhist meditator, but not a Buddhist butcher. One can imagine a Baptist street preacher, but not a Baptist bootlegger. Practices engaged in and avoided by participants show the distinct shapes of forms of life.

Individuals may participate in numerous forms of life. There may also be subsets or particular practices included in a more encompassing form of life. For example, both living faithfully with a spouse and parenting children can be considered distinct forms of life, each with particular actions in which one participates (or avoids). Yet both of these could fall under the greater category and form of life of marriage (Griffiths 2001b, 8). Obviously, as our oxymoronic examples above show, some forms of life are incompatible because their practices are incompatible.

What makes a religion distinctive as a form of life is the addition of three other characteristics: it is comprehensive, incapable of abandonment, and of central importance (Griffiths 2001b, 9).[3] A form of life is comprehensive if it can "take account of and be relevant to everything" (ibid., 9; 1997, 2–3). Nothing falls outside of or is irrelevant to a comprehensive form of life (2001b, 10). A form of life is considered incapable of abandonment when it is so definitive and constitutive that those living in it would view it as "impossible to leave without also leaving themselves" (ibid.). Finally, religious forms of life "address the questions of paramount importance" to the ordering of life (2001b, 11). A religious form of life provides its members a basic orientation by prescribing how we relate to other people, the nonhuman order, and ourselves (1997, 4). That a secular ideology such as one expressed in committed membership in the Communist Party (in its heyday) could be construed as a "religious" form of life, on Griffiths's account, simply shows how powerful ideological communities and institutions are in shaping participants' lives.

J. A. Di Noia is also convinced that religious differences are a serious matter. He addressed these concerns most directly in his discussion of religious aims and patterns of life. He began with the supposition that religious communities disagree as to what constitutes the true aim in life (1998, 58, 66; 1992, 35). This seems obvious. Buddhists aim for Nirvana; Christians for heaven. Nirvana is an emptiness, sometimes imaged as the blowing out of a candle. Heaven is the fullness of communion with the triune God, sometimes imaged as life so abundant as to be joy beyond our wildest dreams. Di Noia contended that each religious community teaches its members how to cultivate a pattern of life with its distinctive religious aim in mind (1992, 7; 1990a, 122; 1990b, 256). It follows that individual "lives come to be shaped by the ultimate aims that are sought"; what is comprehensively important orients the whole of life (1998, 60; 1995b, 28). Buddha is the pathfinder who shows the way Buddhists are to live and thus can be seen as a unique revealer of the Dharma (law) that comprises all that concerns Nirvana and its attainment. Jesus Christ is regarded by Christians as the unique revealer and mediator of salvation. Each of these ultimate religious aims requires Buddhists and Christians to walk different paths. The Christian does not wish to follow the Eightfold Path to Nirvana, nor does the Buddhist wish to be a disciple of Christ following the way(s) Jesus commanded (see Di Noia 1998, 59–60; 1995a, 40–41; 1995b, 25–26; 1992, 1–8; 1982, 365). In short, the terrestrial paths and the ultimate destinies constituent of different religious forms of life are irreducibly different.

Different doctrines help shape these particular patterns of different forms of life. (Di Noia 1992, 2–3). Religious communities, in fact, "place great emphasis in their practical doctrines on the acquisition and development of appropriate dispositions for enjoying the true aim of life" (1990a, 123). Di Noia remarked that the Torah, Gospel, and Dharma all "designate patterns of thinking and acting" that form and equip members of religious communities for all of life's engagements, interests, and occasions (1992, 56). Doctrinal differences are too significant for life as lived in these traditions for any theory that reduces their distinctiveness to be credible.

The point of such practical doctrines is a comprehensive shaping of participants' lives as a whole (Di Noia 1990a, 256). Religious people perceive themselves in possession of what is "ultimately important in life." This knowledge results in an orientation and a direction to their life (Di Noia 1998, 66; 1995b, 28). "What is ultimate, whether it be a transcendent agent or an as-yet unrealized state of being, invades life at every moment and summons the community's members to order in shape their lives in view of the aim" (Di Noia 1998, 60). The echoes here of Griffiths's "centrality of importance" are clear.

Di Noia developed his argument in contrast to classic inclusivism and pluralism. Neither takes religious differences seriously enough. He wrote that "inclusivists are those who espouse some version of the view that all religious communities implicitly aim at the salvation which the Christian community most adequately commends, while pluralists contend that all religious communities aim at salvation under the variety of descriptions enshrined by their traditions" (1990b, 250). Di Noia's principal disagreement with both these models is that they fail to give enough weight to the specificity and distinctiveness of religious aims (1995b, 25).

Inclusivists fail to notice the distinctiveness of other faiths because they tend to reinterpret non-Christian patterns and aims in Christian terms (1998, 59). Inclusivist theologians claim that non-Christians attain "salvation" as Christians understand it, that is, as eternal fellowship with the divine Trinity, established uniquely through Jesus Christ (Di Noia 1990b, 250). Theological inclusivism in effect erases the particularities of other traditions by viewing them in the Christian scheme (Di Noia 1993, 83). The concept of non-Christian "anonymity" of religious experience does not take the unique and distinct differences of that experience seriously. Christian reinterpretation of the ultimate aims of non-Christian religions overtly belittles those aims and subsequently devalues their distinct differences.

Pluralism "does not so much explain the differences and disagreements between religious beliefs as to explain them away" (Di Noia 1998, 66). Rather than trying to incorporate religious differences within the Christian scheme, as inclusivists do, pluralists modify their "existing particularities" (Di Noia 1992, 53) by claiming that in one way or another all religions aim at "salvation." Salvation, however, is not understood in Christian or any other particular religion's terms, but in terms of a move from "self-centeredness" to "Reality-centeredness," to use John Hick's terms (Di Noia 1995b, 24; 1990a, 128). No particular religious tradition centers on "reality." Each tradition gives its participants a particular aim. If religious aims are ultimately diverse, then pluralism is at best confused or at worst disdainful of religious particularity.

Religious Diversity and Essential Christian Beliefs

Both Di Noia and Griffiths affirmed the universal salvific will of God and the unique mediatorship of Jesus Christ inside that will.

For Griffiths the position of Jesus Christ as the unique mediator of salvation is "non-negotiable" (1997, 9). He took this essential feature of the Christian form of life as the claim that salvation is available only through Christ—the "only" in this claim being in contrast to contemporary inclusivists and mutualists. It is "entirely correct that Christian orthodoxy, which is constitutively trinitarian, requires as a fundamental grammatical principle the claim that God is fully present in Jesus, present in Jesus, therefore, in a unique and unparalleled way" (2003, 23). Nor can Christians claim that other traditions are on a par with or complementary to Christianity. He affirmed the axiom "outside the church there is no salvation." For Christians, the "discussion of salvation cannot be separated from either christology or ecclesiology" (1997, 9). Griffiths acknowledged that these orthodox declarations about Jesus Christ as central to salvation require that we think hard about the salvation of religious aliens, that is, those who live in and live out other faith traditions (1998, 157), but he did not cite Sullivan's magisterial work on this topic (1992).

Griffiths does not find that these principles entail the denial of salvation to non-Christians. He did not claim that everyone must have, in the short period of one's life, "explicit knowledge of and assent to teachings of Jesus of Nazareth" (1997, 10). Knowledge of and assent to Jesus of Nazareth is of "inestimable advantage for humans." The point is not to judge people. Even if we can say in a formal way what is necessary and sufficient for salvation, "these conditions include facts about the hearts of people that in principle we cannot know" (ibid.). The knowledge available to make such judgments resides only with God. We do not know whether any person or group is saved. Griffiths does not rule out the possibility of anyone's salvation; however, he explicitly indicates that salvation is not guaranteed for all and that eternal separation from God, known as damnation, is possible. We would call his position an "open exclusivism" with regard to salvation: "exclusivist" in that it proclaims that salvation comes only through Jesus Christ and participation in the life of Christianity; "open" in that Griffiths remains properly agnostic about who God regards as inside the saved community.

Griffiths found that theories about who can be saved and how God saves them have, at best, a very low probability of being true. We should not "waste much time on them" because they do not form part of "the essential structure of Christian belief." They "are of interest principally as a defense against the charge that Christians cannot coherently assert the kind of christocentrism about salvation that we must assert" (Griffiths 1997, 10). His approach demands a robust proclamation of the undiluted gospel, tempered with a vigorous charity, which is the practical outworking of agnosticism about God's will for people other than Christians.

Di Noia is more explicit than Griffiths about the universal availability of salvation. He noted, "the Christian scheme is ordinarily understood to include doctrines about the universality of salvation" (Di Noia 1992, 70; but see Griffiths 2001b, 9–10, 140). In addition, Di Noia found no theology of religions fully consistent with central Christian doctrines that do not strongly affirm the universality of salvation, at least as a possibility (Di Noia 1992, 70). Like Griffiths, Di Noia warned about the implausibility of overly detailed accounts in explaining how God's universal salvific will is actuated (Di Noia 1982, 108). Di Noia, utilizing the concept of the providential diversity of religious aims, regarded his view as "compatible with a strong Christian affirmation of the universality of salvation" (1992, 72).

The concept of the providential diversity of religions is the cornerstone of Di Noia's account. In light of the serious differences among religious traditions, the problem is to see how their different aims foster development in their members of dispositions toward what Christians believe is the true aim in life, fellowship with the blessed Trinity (Di Noia 1992, 67). Di Noia's premise is that in spite of the fact that we cannot state that other religious communities aim at salvation as we see it, we can and must affirm that their members are not excluded from sharing fully in salvation (ibid.). He seeks to balance the distinctive aims of life of other faith traditions with the unique value of the Christian community as vehicle of universal salvation by ascribing an "indirect or providential value to other religious communities" (ibid.). God could provide a real, although unspecified, role for other faith traditions in the economy of salvation. Christianity bears a unique and specific witness to that plan but may not be the only way God realizes the divine plan for the world (ibid.). We can value other religions not because they are "channels of grace or means of salvation," but rather because we can affirm that they play a role in God's divine plan, even though we cannot comprehend what that role might be (Di Noia 1992, 91; 1982, 387). Other religions can "foster social climates supportive of Christian values" and assist their members in developing dispositions in the direction of "the attainment and enjoyment of salvation" (Di Noia 1982, 387; 1992, 69).

Di Noia's understanding of the function of other religious traditions is eschatological. He found that "God wills that other religions perform functions in his plan for humankind which is now only dimly perceived and which will be fully disclosed only at the end of time" (Di Noia 1982, 387). Di Noia's view is that God can (and will) somehow ultimately reshape others who aim at other ultimate destinies such as Nirvana into creatures fit for communion with the Trinity. We cannot now see how others are saved, but we may understand it when we are finally saved. Hence, we can have confidence in affirming "the possibility of salvation for non-Christians . . . . [I]t by no means follows from the particular and unique role ascribed to Jesus Christ in central Christian doctrines that those who do not now acknowledge him will be permanently excluded from sharing in the salvation he both signifies and effects" (Di Noia 1992, 104, 107). Di Noia termed this a form of "prospective salvation" (1992, 94).

One advantage of this understanding of God's salvific plan is that Christians can avoid "implausible descriptions" of the present state of the members of other communities. It frees Christians from speculating about how those communities have or do not have salvific value or how the dispositions and conduct they cultivate contribute to God's plan (Di Noia 1992, 103). In effect, Di Noia advocates a confident faith in God with a healthy agnosticism about just how God provides for all the creatures of the world.

Di Noia affirmed a nonexclusive particularity for Jesus Christ. He argued that "true universalism requires fidelity to the particularities of Christian revelation and existence" (1992, 84). Di Noia poetically described God as "squeezing" into the particularity of history. Despite being infinite, God is accessible, specifiable, and identifiable personally in the finite and particular. The divine entrance into an "obscure corner of humankind" does not mean that God's presence is limited to that particular group (1992, 85). Salvation in Christ is intended for all human beings. To become accessible to us required that God take the form of a particular person, "one whom we can encounter, touch, hear, and speak to" (1993, 54). If God is to "squeeze" into actual human form, God must begin the divine mission of salvation at a particular time, incarnate in a particular person who is part of a particular tradition. God does not become enfleshed to save believers alone, but to bring salvation to the whole of humanity.

Given particularists' stances regarding Jesus Christ, the salvation uniquely wrought in and through him, and the substantial differences between religious traditions and forms of life, a practical question arises. How are Christians to interact with members of other faith traditions?

Interreligious Dialogue: Opportunity for Intellectual Growth and Defense

The CDF declaration *Dominus Iesus* states that Catholic theologians cannot take other faith traditions as complementary to Christianity. Griffiths argued that this is correct with regard to religious complementarity. However, it would be unfortunate to think that this claim might imply that other faith traditions might not be *epistemologically* complementary to Christianity. Griffiths cogently argued that to say "that *the revelation of God in Christ is complete* (which must be said) is not the same as and does not imply the claim [that] *the truth about God explicitly known and taught by the church is complete*" (2003, 23; *italics original*). The church needs to learn from other traditions to help the church more definitively "understand the revelation" that God has given the church (ibid.). Interreligious dialogue does not give the church new truths about God, but can provide the Christian community with new *insights* into God's revelation.

Griffiths advocated what he called an "open inclusivism" on the question of alien truth. He sees the possibility of Christian appropriation of non-Christian insights about God as important to the future work of theologians (2001a, 166). Citing examples such as Augustine's use of Plato as well as Aquinas's of Aristotle, Griffiths argued that many of "the greatest advances in Christian thinking have come when serious Christian thinkers have paid close attention to alien particularity" (ibid.). In so doing, he shifts the focus of "inclusivism" from issues of salvation to questions of truth. Open inclusivism "affirms the possibility of the existence of alien truth that Christians need to learn." Hence, studying other traditions is an imperative (2001a, 168; 2001b, 60).

Griffiths contrasted open inclusivism with closed inclusivism. Closed inclusivism allows recognizing and embracing alien truths wherever they are found, but denies that any alien truth is not already known to Christians (2001a, 168; 2001b, 59). For closed inclusivism, we learn what we already know; for open inclusivism, we learn what we have, but don't yet know. Griffiths recommended that we humbly listen for what Dupuis called the *logos asarkos,* the "logos spermatikos, traces of the divine word sown in all human hearts" (Griffiths 1997, 11).

Christians do not yet comprehend the depths of the riches of their own tradition. Our access to the tradition is necessarily limited by time and ability. Our access to other traditions is similarly limited, and we are challenged to understand them as well. Hence, modesty is appropriate in interreligious dialogue, especially when making judgments about particular non-Christian accounts (Griffiths 1997, 8). We may have God's definitive revelation, but we don't possess all God wants us to know yet.

J. A. Di Noia is also concerned with humility, mutual respect, and esteem in interreligious dialogue. He advocated that the Christian community respect others as fellow seekers after religious truth. Christians should learn from their proposals, claims, aims, and arguments (Di Noia 1992, 31). Di Noia may stop short of Griffiths's open inclusivism (on truth), noting in one of his more recent writings that the knowledge of God and revelation is "the distinctive possession of Christianity" (Di Noia and Walls 1998, 39). Nonetheless, Di Noia found that Christians can learn from others: "Christians should be open to possible developments of their own doctrines that might be suggested in the course of their study of other religions and in dialogue with their adherents" (Di Noia 1992, 31). Like Griffiths, Di Noia finds that we can learn more deeply what we already know. While it is not clear that other traditions give us truths, they can and do provide the context for new Christian insights.

Griffiths admits to frustration with much contemporary interreligious dialogue. Interreligious dialogue as it is often practiced minimizes authentic engagements between religious communities. Typical interreligious dialogue fosters "a morally dubious kind of syncretism" where the goal is never to be argumentative but rather always to be understanding (1994, 32–33). Confrontation is avoided, particularly those "awkward questions about truth and about the universalistic aspirations of most religious communities" (Griffiths 1994, 33). Interreligious dialogue that does not also take religious differences and oppositions between religions seriously cannot finally be serious.

Hence, Griffiths proposed a reintroduction of "apologetics" to the Christian community. Apologetics is traditionally understood in the religious community as "reasoned argument in defense of what one takes to be true" (1994, 35). Religious communities have a "moral and intellectual duty" to engage in apologetics. When faced with religious others who do not believe what they do, they must argue for the truth that they believe to be profoundly important to all human persons (ibid.). If believers are not willing to argue for their claims, why should anyone hold them? Withholding a truth of vital eternal importance to others or refusing to argue with others is akin to refusing to offer help or correction to a person whose beliefs and practices are leading him to "dire physical danger" (ibid.). "I must, therefore, if I am to behave with moral integrity, engage my interlocutor" (ibid.). If one is engaged intellectually with another and thinks that the other is wrong in belief or practice, one is obliged to show the other a better way if one can.

Besides the moral obligations Griffiths indicated, apologetics in interreligious dialogue can have other benefits as well. One might become convinced by the other. Or one might learn more about one's own tradition from the arguments of the other. Interreligious dialogue structured as apologetics can lead to "important discoveries about the inner logic of religious belief-systems" (Griffiths 1994, 36) and even to conversion. The minimal result of apologetic engagement should be that each comes to understand the subject much better than before the meeting.

Griffiths's introduction of apologetics into interreligious dialogue runs against the current that favors finding common ground. Not shy of controversy, Griffiths has written on the nature of proselytism and tolerance (Elshtain and Griffiths 2002). In this article Griffiths compares and contrasts the two practices, finding the grammar and syntax of proselytism to be "conceptually superior" to that of toleration. Toleration is "enduring" or "bearing something unpleasant." It means "putting up with or permitting or letting be some pattern of action or belief found by those practicing toleration to be false or improper." Griffiths argued that toleration is a "concept of the moral order." Both proselytism and toleration imply judgments about the alien. Either the aliens' beliefs are false or their practices are improper. While proselytizers want to transform the alien, practitioners of tolerance leave the alien in error (Elshtain and Griffiths 2002, 30–32).

Proselytizers act to create proselytes. They want to "turn the alien into kin" because it would be good for them. A proselyte "leaves an old community, whether of belief or practice and enters a new one" (Elshtain and Griffiths 2002, 30). Proselytizers find that we are morally obliged to work to bring the mistaken aliens into the fold. To tolerate those wallowing in error regarding the most important issues in life is not to respect them but to neglect them.

Griffiths found that virtually everyone proselytizes on behalf of something. The question is not whether, but for what, one proselytizes. Griffiths in effect argued for proselytizing for rich and thick religious commitment, not for indifferent tolerance or a liberal pluralism that excludes the possibility that any tradition actually is true. He claimed that advocates of tolerance will inevitably become proselytizers for something, likely tolerance. Proselytism's aspiration to find truth and correct error prohibits it from becoming a species of toleration of error. Thus, when religious people engage in interreligious dialogue, the point is to argue for one's own tradition in an effort to convert the other. Tolerant understanding is not the point; finding the truth is.

Di Noia also has advocated defending primary Christian claims in the course of interreligious dialogue. Interreligious dialogue begins with "readiness to take the distinctive features of other religious traditions seriously" (Di Noia 1993, 87). Once one recognizes the diversity of religious aims, one should not be surprised at or offended by the diversity of religious claims (Di Noia 1995b, 26). Indeed, there should be an expectation in interreligious dialogue that participants from varied religious communities each consistently and seriously teach about the aim of life they propose and the means to reach it (Di Noia 1982, 381).

In interreligious dialogue, Christians should be serious and consistent about their message. Di Noia argues that "the Christian hope for salvation, in all its aspects, rests on convictions about the reliability of the divine undertakings about which the Christian community must bear witness" (1982, 389). Such witness does not require Christians to "remain silent about the church's doctrines in the presence of non-members." Rather, they are to "bear witness to their convictions and hope about the salvation which God promises" (Di Noia 1993, 86). Witness in word and deed is vital to a vigorous Christian mission concerned with "the particular hope and the universal scope of the salvation to which Christians are charged to bear witness" (Di Noia 1993, 88).

Both Di Noia and Griffiths have demarcated interreligious dialogue as an arena of praxis for their particularist approaches. Both take particular differences among traditions seriously. They approach interreligious dialogue as a way for us to develop new insights about the truth God has revealed as well as a way to understand religious aliens, to defend primary Christian claims, and to convince others that Christianity contains, even if it cannot express perfectly, the truth God has given in Jesus.

Does Particularism Fit Catholic Principles?

Given that both advocates of particularism studied here are staunch Catholics, committed to the teaching of the church, this question may seem silly. Our discussion above shows that they clearly fulfill the second and third principles. The question is how, if at all, they fit the first and fourth rules. Di Noia can be passed over quickly regarding the first rule. His prolific written endorsement of the universal salvific will of God, combined with his developed theories of provincial diversity and prospective salvation, demonstrates his faithfulness to this rule.

Paul Griffiths's work requires a little more analysis. Griffiths makes statements about the universal salvific will of God that are not very reassuring. To say that God does not rule out the possibility of anyone's salvation is certainly not as strong as affirming God's will that all be saved. Yet he points out that while probability and possibility are two different things, it is possibility that counts here. It is possible that God can save everyone. We just cannot assert its actuality or say much, if anything, about whether or how God might do it. Griffiths may need to be more precise about God's universal salvific will, but he does not deny the doctrine.

Specific references to the church and its position in the economy of salvation are sparse in the particularists' work. As noted above, Griffiths affirms the difficult motto *extra ecclesiam nulla salus*. However, this ought not be surprising. Both particularists do not find speculative theories about how God saves of interest. Rather, they are concerned with issues of truth and truthfulness. Throughout their work, they simply assume the necessity of the church as witness to and proclaimer of the truth about human life, including its origin, course, and destiny. The church is necessary for salvation because God has chosen the church to be the agent or sacrament and herald of salvation. Although they do not reflect extensively on the church in their work on the diversity of religions—which given their commitment to the church, one might find odd— that particularists fit this rule seems obvious.

Do particularists affirm the dignity of each and all human persons? This rule both challenges and reveals a real strength of the particularist model. The importance of religious differences discussed in the first section above attests to the dignity of each and every human person. In dubbing this approach "the acceptance model," Paul Knitter—in many ways their friendly opponent—recognized the fact that they accept religious differences because they accept the other as other-than-us, not as a pale reflection of us (2002, 218). Recognizing that no historical and temporal language or experience can encompass the infinite and succeed at being totally comprehensive, Knitter asked some leading questions of the particularists:

> Are we at a state in the religious history of humankind in which all religious can admit this [finiteness of their perspectives]? In which all religions can make universal claims without making absolute claims? In which, yes, there will be need of *apologetics* (that is, disagreement, efforts to convince and persuade each other), but there will also be room—much greater room—for *dialogue* (that is, expanding or clarifying or correcting one's own grasp of truth through dialogue with others)? (2002, 228–29)

For the acceptance model to be preferable to the mutuality model, the answers to these questions must be yes. Particularists would answer yes.

Nonetheless, implicit in Di Noia's view of prospective salvation and openly on display in Griffiths's proselytism are issues about human dignity. On the surface, Di Noia's prospective on salvation appears as a potential windfall for non-Christians, above all those who never have been exposed to the gospel. It suggests that they have a place in God's plan and can benefit from the unique mediatorship of Jesus Christ. What does "prospective salvation" say about their personal human dignity? If they are formed for one end, does God undermine their particular personhood by reshaping them for communion with the Trinity? Di Noia is very careful to say that non-Christian religious aims should be respected and esteemed. One of his chief complaints with inclusivism is that it submerges the distinctive soteriological programs of other religions under the Christian scheme of salvation (Di Noia 1992, 48). Yet Di Noia has admitted that the notion of prospective salvation is "some form of inclusivism" (1992, 166). Inside the theory of prospective salvation is the proclamation, in essence, "that every knee shall bow and every tongue confess that Jesus Christ is Lord." It would seem that this assertion, applying even in the afterlife, has questionable implications for human dignity. Insofar as Di Noia's approach is inclusivist, it runs the risk of devaluing the particularity of all persons in their particularity and the fact that not every person wants Christian salvation.

Griffiths's desire to engage in apologetics and proselytism is not an affront to human dignity. All are entitled to argue on behalf of their unique and specific religious aims. Griffiths pays others the compliment of confronting them as they are, different from "us," not as somehow disguised versions of "us." Griffiths finds honest confrontation a moral and intellectual duty. While confrontation may make dialogue less comfortable, working through authentic disagreements respectfully and carefully does not imply disrespect for the dignity of the other. Quite the opposite. Griffiths's arguments about proselytism and tolerance may raise alarms about respecting human dignity, but are properly understood as an authentic expression of respect.

Griffiths makes the point that we all proselytize on behalf of something, or someone. The act of proselytizing, as he defines it, is acting in the best interests of the person being proselytized. Certainly convincing someone to quit smoking or bar hopping is in the best interest of the other. Yet does this apply to religious forms of life? Elements of the religious form of life include it being "incapable of abandonment." People could not leave it "without also leaving themselves" (Griffiths 2001b, 10). For a proselyte to "leave an old community" and enter a new one (Elshtain and Griffiths 2002, 30), the proselyte truly has to abandon his or her very self. This places quite a heavy moral demand on apologists. If one does not have sufficient reason to think that one has the one way, truth, and life, then one may be inviting others to give themselves up to what one does not have sufficient reason to believe to be true. In short, if Griffiths is wrong about the rightness of the Christian form of life, his proselytism is morally repugnant; if he is right about it, it is morally praiseworthy. However, the variety of religious forms of life and the relative epistemic parity of their claims (formally considered) means that it is not clear that one could justify either assessment. Griffiths's approach leads to a moral dilemma.

There is also a tension in Griffiths's work between an open exclusivism with regard to salvation and an open inclusivism with regard to truth. Perhaps this tension is just an illusion conjured up by the use of Race's (1983) inadequate trifold categorical scheme of exclusivism-inclusivism-pluralism. However, if the Logos of God has engendered truths in other faith traditions, it is not clear why the Logos of God could not have also used those traditions to provide paths to salvation as well. Perhaps this imbalance is due to Griffiths's having a very rigorist understanding of *extra ecclesiam nulla salus* (in contrast to Sullivan 1992) and an intellectual and personal recognition of how much Christians have to learn about their own tradition from other traditions. Griffiths may need to explain more clearly how we can overcome or why we should accept this tension.

Griffiths's attack on toleration is directed at a straw figure. Certainly, the tolerance of which he speaks is "bare tolerance." No one serious about her or his religion can subscribe to it except as an excuse for inaction. The "live option" is the sort of active engagement Robert Wuthnow calls "reflective pluralism." Reflective pluralists are active, not passive. They are interested in what others believe about particular issues, study others' views and understand why they hold them, work to show the strengths of active acceptance in a diverse society, respect others by taking their views seriously, and are willing to consider compromises to live with others in peace (Wuthnow 2005, 289–92). They join in with other groups in campaigns to support specific, shared, particular goals. Reflective pluralism is supported by "the goodwill and shared concern for basic human dignity that can be mobilized among the various religious traditions" (Wuthnow 2005, 294). It does not preclude apologetics or witness, but it requires that one see one's opponents, even in religious matters, as friends, not enemies. None of this is incompatible with Griffiths's views, but it is not clear that he has considered such an approach as a live option. His approach intends to respect the distinctiveness of the religious alien, but he does not develop a rationale for proselytism as preferable to other good, nonproselytizing options for engaging in interreligious interaction. His argument defeats only a straw figure representing the most vapid forms of liberal indifferentism. Active engagement and witness may proselytize without argument, avoid the moral dilemma of proselytizing, and respond constructively to the insipidity of bare tolerance.

Is religious diversity a problem or a promise? Unlike other models that seek to find theological solutions to the problem of religious diversity, particularism regards religious diversity as a promise. Particularists recognize and respect the real diversity in the ultimate aims of various religious traditions.

They resist homogenization of the traditions, intellectual imperialism, and indifferentism. In avoiding these traps that the other models may more easily succumb to, particularists do not find religious diversity a problem to be solved but a reality filled with promise for dialogue.

That the particularist approach may be more successful than other approaches in living out the four principles is not shown. Indeed, given that they focus on issues of truth rather than salvation makes it clear that the approaches are not directly comparable. Each has a different conception of the issues and a different proposal. That there are problems with the particularist approach backing its opponents into uncomfortable corners is clear. That it is at least as viable an approach for mainstream Christianity in general and Catholicism in particular seems obvious.

As mutualism is an offshoot of pluralism, so particularism has generated an interesting and important offshoot, an even more radical understanding of diversity. Chapter 8 explores the radical particularism of S. Mark Heim.

8

Many Salvations

Does God Offer Humanity Many Destinies?

with W. Coleman Fannin

Since Christ died for all,
and since all human beings are in fact called to one and the same destiny,
which is divine,
we must hold that the Holy Spirit offers to all
the possibility of being associated, in a way known to God,
to the paschal mystery.
—Gaudium et Spes § 22

UNITED STATES BAPTIST THEOLOGIAN S. MARK HEIM HAS DEVELOPED A fascinating and unique response to the historical and social reality of religious diversity: the world's religious traditions are so different that their differences extend to a real diversity of actual religious ends. In brief, he has argued that there are *many salvations,* each constituted as the distinct ultimate end to which particular historic forms of life point. Heim thus radicalizes the particularist position discussed in chapter 7. Like the particularists studied above, his work is influenced strongly by Anglo-American patterns in philosophy. Unlike them, however, his work is concerned more with issues of salvation than with issues of truth.

As well as being a seminary professor and an ordained Baptist minister, Heim claims expertise in both Indian religious movements (he has both taught and studied in India) and Asian Christianity. He has participated extensively in ecumenical dialogue and served as chair of the American Baptists' Committee on Christian Unity. He has represented the American Baptists on the Faith and Order Commissions of both the National Council and the World Council of Churches. Thus, like the other the theologians we have considered, his response to religious diversity can be understood as an attempt to answer the difficult professional and personal questions that have arisen in the course of his life and work.

Heim has addressed religious diversity in an "unanticipated trilogy" of books. In *Is Christ the Only Way?*, he tentatively sketched the concept of "ultimate pluralism," in which "God allows, and has even established . . . the eternal right of choice and interpretation" for each person. That is, God may give us precisely the ultimate ends we desire (Heim 2001, 11; 1985, 144–50). In *Salvations* and *The Depth of the Riches*, respectively, Heim developed the two sides of this hypothesis: the philosophical side, which seeks "the widest scope for religious particulars to be recognized for what they are," and the theological side, which seeks "the most integrated understanding possible of their relations" by focusing on the particulars of a single tradition; in his case, Christianity (Heim 1995, 222, 209, 9; 2001, 7–8).

Although Heim has claimed to be a "convinced inclusivist," his work also displays characteristics usually associated with pluralism and exclusivism in arguing for a "true religious pluralism" that also maintains the "superiority" of Christianity (2001, 8; 1995, 7). Heim astutely noted, however, that the exclusivist-inclusivist-pluralist typology "is fully coherent only on the assumption that salvation is an unequivocal, single reality" (1995, 4). He has rejected that assumption, as we have, so it is no wonder that his work does not fit that categorical scheme. The strength of Heim's proposal is clearest in his interrelated responses to pluralism.

The Confusions of Pluralistic Philosophy

Heim found that pluralist theologies have a hidden paradox: "The most insistent voices calling for the affirmation of religious pluralism seem equally insistent in denying that, in properly religious terms, there is or should be any fundamental diversity at all" (1995, 2–3). Such theologies are essentially attempts to hold together two fundamental elements of the major world religions: that they are vehicles of salvation and that they make truth claims. As Heim noted, "The key to reconciling the two is to find some shared cognitive content and a way of interpreting the apparent contradictions" (1995, 21). The only way to accomplish this is to locate a neutral, value-free conceptual space from which to interpret religious phenomena, the possibility of which is a presupposition of the liberal rationalism of the Enlightenment. However, "There are no neutral meta-theories that offer a different order of knowledge about the religions" (1995, 10). Rather, liberal theories like John Hick's do not float neutrally "above" the religious traditions, but are theologies in competition with them.

Heim first challenged pluralists on their own (self-proclaimed) philosophical ground of dialogue. We have explored and critiqued several prominent examples of pluralist and mutualist theology in chapter 6, but Heim's analysis offered a fundamental challenge. He claimed that pluralists each develop some universal criterion (e.g., the Real, justice) for evaluating religious traditions. These criteria are *external to the traditions*. They are formulated without explicit reference to specific religious traditions, and at least some traditions do not recognize the validity of the criteria. The pluralists then rule out of the game of interreligious interaction any who do not accept their criteria. Pluralists thus engage in a new form of exclusivism. They draw boundaries as hard as religious exclusivists, though at different points. They find dialogue crucial, but exclude some traditions from dialogue on grounds that those traditions cannot or do not recognize as valid.

Heim's opposition to pluralism has received substantial support, most notably from Paul Griffiths. Central to Griffiths's understanding of religious claims is their relationship to the property of *being true* (Griffiths 2001b, 21). Two opposed religious claims can be *contradictory* in their claims to truth. This means that at least one must be false. For example, "God is pure and only spirit" and "God is both spirit and body" cannot both be true. They are contradictory. More often, however, religious claims are simply *contrary*. Contrary claims may both be true if they are properly understood. For example, "God is spirit" and "God is body" may seem contradictory, but may only be contrary. Both can be true if "body" includes "spirit" and "spirit" includes "body." The Christian affirmation that Jesus Christ is fully human and fully divine may appear contradictory, but cannot be contradictory (that is, necessarily false) if a traditional christology can be possibly true. The point is that claims that appear contradictory may actually be contrary. Both may be possibly true (that is, "compossible"). Before one can judge whether apparently contradictory terms are contradictory, one must analyze them and exclude their "compossibility."

Opposing religious claims are *noncompossible* "if each prescribes a course of action and it is impossible for a single person to perform both." For example, it would be impossible for someone to both "read the Bible as if it were the most important book in the world" and "read the Qur'an as if it were the most important book in the world." If religious traditions make claims ("The Bible/the Qur'an is the most important book in the world") and prescribe courses of action ("You must read the most important book in the world as if it is so"), and those actions cannot be coherently executed by a single person, then the claims and the injunctions are noncompossible. This point could be extended beyond Judaism and Islam. Since religions are comprehensive, seem incapable of abandonment, and of central importance, "no one can inhabit more than one form of religious life at a time" (Griffiths 2001b, 7, 32–34; Heim 2001, 1–4; the challenge to the proponents of multiple belonging discussed in chapter 10 below is obvious; their possible responses will be discussed there).

Although the boundaries of forms of life are often fuzzy, incompatibilities (both contradictions and noncompossible prescriptions and proscriptions) among religious claims remain. What is the proper response to this situation? Griffiths claimed, "Incompatibilities of this sort, it seems to most who have not been corrupted by philosophy, suggest difference with respect to truth" (2001b, 36). The problem with pluralist accounts is that they refuse "to make distinctions among religious claims with respect to their truth, saying instead that all religious claims are on a par in this respect" (ibid.). Pluralists construe particular religious claims as partly true (at best) or as containing truths. Pluralists then typically attempt to locate a subset of claims—the heart or essence—that *are* held by all (major) religions and thus likely are true. This abstraction of an essential likeness warrants the pluralists' finding that particular traditions really do "say the same thing" or at least point to the same Ultimate Reality, even if misleadingly.

The pluralist position depends not only on eighteenth-century philosopher Immanuel Kant's distinction between *phenomena* and *noumena* but also on his argument about the relationship of pure *religious faith* and *historical faith*. For Kant, pure religious faith is the source of the claim "All moral duties are given by God." Kant argues that this claim is discoverable by reason independent of revelation or tradition. Historic traditions are valuable only insofar as they aid individuals in recognizing the fundamental, rational religious claim. The particular revelations or practices of historical religions are not necessary for the discovery or justification of what is essential to true "religion." Their variety (and incompatibility) is thus irrelevant to the heart of religious truth (see Griffiths 2001b, 38–40; Heim 1995, 32).

John Hick's pluralistic hypothesis postulates "an infinite Real" as the true noumenal object of all phenomenal religious practice and belief. Following Kant, Hick found that the transcendent divine (the noumenal) cannot appear "as it is in itself," but only as it is perceived (the phenomenal) in the various, inevitably distorting, historic traditions. The philosopher who stands beyond any particular religious tradition then can *infer* from the phenomena in the world what the noumenal must be like.

Heim found this Kantian philosophical approach dismissive of all particular religious traditions. Since the pluralist model relies on it, it is a devastating flaw in the model. It also arrogates to the philosopher—interesting that this argument is made by a philosopher—a position superior to any believer in understanding what the really Real, or the noumenal, is.

As noted in chapter 6, Paul Knitter has moved away from this Kantian plu-

ralism and sought to ground pluralism in *soteriocentrism,* "the struggle to realize an immanent order of justice." Heim argued, however, that Knitter's position
is no real improvement on Hick's in that the abstract notion of justice is no
more defensible than the abstract notion of the real. Justice in itself, like the
Real in itself, must be beyond all historical traditions. However, there is no warrant for showing what real justice is in itself beyond the various claims that say
what justice appears like—the claims about justice made in the various traditions. Yet it is these particular claims about justice that are at issue in the real
world. As Heim put it:

> In the real world, the claim that "justice" is absolute must translate into
> the claim that some definitions of justice are wrong and others are
> right. To suppose that such claims can prove compelling to significant
> numbers of people without some grounding in an account of the
> nature of humanity, the causes of suffering and conflict, a cosmic order,
> goes against all historical precedent. (1995, 93)

"Justice" is no improvement over "the Real" as a foundation for understanding
the diversity of religions or for engaging in interreligious dialogue.

Pluralists fail to recognize, as philosopher Ludwig Wittgenstein has, the
ways in which religious claims are *really different* from scientific claims in
respect to truth. Religious forms of life apply the predicate *is true* "only to claims
taken by those who assent to them as absolute, non-negotiable, and insulated
from evidence or argument" (Griffiths 2001b, 46). Religious people tend to be
confident that their tradition's claims are true; indeed, "The conviction that one
follows the most inclusive true religion, the superior true religion, with a distinctive fulfillment, is not only defensible but inescapable" for believers (Heim
1995, 227). While this may be so, as argued above (pp. 122–23), this may leave
us in a dilemma if we want to proselytize others.

The Kantian understanding—in Hickian or Knitterian forms—so plays
down the *religious* quality of the commitment to religious truth that the pluralist
understanding is incompatible with the forms of life that constitute the particular traditions. If pluralists say, "treat all fundamental religious claims as partly
true," and religious commitment requires that I "treat my fundamental religious claims as really true," then the pluralist rule and the religious rule are
noncomposible. Yet Knitter and Hick are both Christians. Heim implies that,
to be consistent, they must give up either their religious commitment to their
tradition or their pluralist philosophy.[1]

Heim employed Nicholas Rescher's "orientational pluralism" to describe a
way out of this dilemma. Heim argued that philosophy (and theology) requires
a fundamental commitment to a particular perspective. Orientational pluralism accepts this. It explains the diversity of views not as all of them being

partially true and partially false or as referring to different realities or as being partial historical perceptions of an ultimate eternal truth. Rather, Rescher found that each claim is *tenable* given the perspective of the viewer. Each particular claim is *warranted* in that orientation, not by the object it refers to. Hence, the dispute is not over different truths, but different warrants grounded in different orientations.

Consider the old stories of the blind men touching various parts of the elephant (ear, trunk, side, belly, leg). Each comes up with a different description of the elephant. On Rescher's account, they are not coming up with partial truths about the one elephant. Rather, their different descriptions are all valid, but only limitedly warranted or justified. The warrants are limited by the blind men's orientation to the elephant. Each had different experiences of the elephant. These limited perspectives—and all human perspectives are limited—mean that our *warrants* are not universal but perspectival. This does not imply that our claims are not true. Each claim may be simply true, but the grounds on which one warrants it and thus legitimately asserts it are limited by and to one's perspective.

Another way of putting this is to consider the narrator's place in fiction. Some narrators are omniscient; they know everything that is going on in every character's mind. Some stories are narrated by one or more characters in the story; they only know what they can see from their perspective. We are not omniscient narrators, but characters in the story. What any character may say at any time may be simply and totally true. But it is a perspectivally warranted truth, not universally warranted. No one has a God's-eye view. The point is that we do not need to deny the *truth* of our claims, or postulate multiple realities, or cut reality into unknowable noumenal and comprehensible phenomenal realms. Human limitations give limited range to the *warrants* or *justification* for our claims, not to the scope or the truth of our claims.

In short, pluralists have misidentified both the problem and its solution. The problem is not diverse truths but diverse truth *claims*. The solution is not to move to a Kantian metatheory that finds each claim partly true, partly false (as if the philosopher has the sight to know what the elephant was really like while all the rest of us religious folk are blind). Rather, it is to recognize that each claim is relatively well justified or is not well justified within a particular perspective. Such perspectives may be broad by being shared with others or as narrow as one's own individual view. In any event, philosophers possess no perch on high to scan the religious claims below. Rather, they are also seeking to justify their claims from a particular (broad or narrow) perspective; they are as sighted or as blind as the rest of us. Hence, the justification offered by a philosopher or theologian may be limited by its perspective, but that does not mean that the claims they make cannot be universal in scope and possibly simply true (Heim 1995, 136–37). Even nonomniscient narrators sometimes get their claims precisely right.

Accepting orientational pluralism "involves the rejection of pluralism and its hopes. Any attempt to judge all religious phenomena from a religion-free place will necessarily fail" (Griffiths 1996, 51). A pluralist move "beyond inclusivism" turns out to be impossible because "We can only pursue *the* truth by cultivating *our* truth" (Heim 1995, 222; Rescher 1985, 199). The "place" from which we judge religious phenomena cannot be religiously neutral or philosophically privileged; the questions are about how inclusive our orientation is, how broad is the perspective that we share, how skilled we are at perceiving what there is. Our perspective can never be universally broad, at least this side of the grave. Hence, pluralism is plagued not only with confusion but also with the arrogance of assuming the omniscient narrator's perspective with regard to the Real. The postulation of a One beyond the many and of One Ultimate Destiny of the various religious paths is rooted in a problem-plagued theory.

Rescher's orientational pluralism is open to rational persuasion. One philosopher might convince another to change her or his intellectual orientation. Yet the challenge to particularists is different. It requires warranting the claim that working for another's moral and religious conversion to one's own position is better for the other person. A change of orientation is not necessarily a change in a form of life; a religious conversion is the abandoning of a self and the taking up of a new self in a new form of life. That particularists like Griffiths have warranted the legitimacy of this practice is not clear; people may believe they have the "true religion," but it is not at all clear that they can sufficiently warrant that belief so it can be shown to be morally correct to persuade others to reshape their lives to the "true view." Heim's radical particularism, by recognizing that there may be many truths about the ends of humanity, may avoid the dilemma that arises for Griffiths of proselytizing for a limitedly warranted truth claim.

Heim's acceptance of orientational pluralism also warranted his challenge to inclusivism. Like contemporary Yale professor emeritus and Lutheran theologian George Lindbeck, Heim recognized that religious traditions have distinct cultural-linguistic shapes that may result in incommensurable forms of life. By "incommensurable" Lindbeck meant that there is no single common standard or criterion for measuring them. For example, if one wanted to measure various religious traditions on their "effectiveness of bringing folk to the authentic human end," one has to spell out what that "end" is. Buddhism construes that "end" as Nirvana and Christianity as heaven. How could one measure their effectiveness without presupposing that one was right and the other wrong about the human end—and thus decide the outcome of the measurement before the measurement was taken. The faith traditions of the world are not only different, but finally incommensurable.[2]

Heim also agreed with J. A. Di Noia that both inclusivism and pluralism "fail to account for the connection between the particular aims of life com-

mended by religious communities and the specific sets of dispositions they foster to promote the attainment and enjoyment of those aims," thus divorcing
"what in most religious traditions are understood to be inseparable" (Di Noia
1992, 55). However, Heim disagreed with Di Noia's contention that a new theology of religions can honor this connection while continuing to assume that
there is a single ultimate destiny. Instead, Heim crucially argued, the world's
religions are so different that engaging them requires acknowledging not only
that they are really different here on earth but also that they propose really different ends for their inhabitants, and that each of those ends may be real.

Heim's second main challenge is related to his first in that pluralists assume
that all religious traditions have the same goal—*salvation*—and that there could
be only one such fulfillment; this assumption enables them to group and order
these traditions. Because their opponents—exclusivists and inclusivists—
believe salvation is solely in and through Jesus Christ, "pluralists are required
to broaden considerably the meaning of the word *salvation*" (Fredericks 1999,
7). The pluralists' central claim that they take the religions seriously on their
own terms is undermined by redefining salvation so as to "regard all the distinctive qualities that are precious to each one as essentially irrelevant in terms
of religious fulfillment" (Heim 1995, 102–3; 2001, 18). As Di Noia noted, this
ignores both the diversity of ultimate ends sought by religious communities
and the one thing they seem formally to agree on, "that the possibility of obtain-
ing and enjoying the goal of life in the future depends upon the shape that life
in the present takes" (Di Noia 1992, 7). Rather, a faithful representation of a
religious tradition must attend to its distinct end or aim, which is "defined by
a set of practices, images, stories, and concepts." This set "provides material for
a thorough pattern of life," is "understood to be *constitutive* of final human fulfillment and/or to be the sole means of achieving that fulfillment," and "is in
practice exclusive of at least some alternative options" (Heim 2001, 21). The
only way a pluralist understanding of salvation is possible is by abstracting it
from any and every religious form of life that gives meaning to what life is ultimately for—and thus vitiating it. By using such an abstract measure, the odd
result is that Christianity and Buddhism are both terribly wrong about the final
end of humanity, but offer equally good paths for getting there.

Because he shares the pluralists' goal of authentic interreligious dialogue,
Heim sought an understanding of salvation that enables Christians (and others) both to learn from other traditions and to challenge them on areas of difference *using the categories of their particular tradition*. The hypothesis of
multiple religious ends "allows us to affirm, as religiously significant, a much
larger proportion of the *distinctive* testimony of the various faith traditions."
Further, it may be that "a very high proportion of what each tradition affirms
may be true and valid, in very much the terms that the tradition claims" (Heim
2001, 20). In short, rather than disparaging the particularities of the faith tra-

ditions as pluralists do, a radical particularist finds that faith traditions truly do direct their adherents to the end that each identifies.

The presence of much truth in differing traditions again raises the question of what is meant by "true." According to Heim, the apparent contrariness of some religious claims may be illusory. For example, the statements "The ascetic life is the only path to salvation" and "The sensual life is the only path to salvation" appear to be in conflict, but this is due to the ambiguity of the term "salvation." If salvation has a different meaning (i.e., if it refers to a different concrete end in each case), then there is no conflict: "To say the two paths both lead to 'salvation' then is only to say they lead to *some* type of desired end, not necessarily the identical one" (Heim 2001, 4). "Different," then, does not necessarily mean "contradictory." "Nirvana and communion with God are contradictory only if we assume that one or the other must be the sole fate for all human beings" (Heim 1995, 149). For Heim, it seems that truth is as orientationally loaded a term as warrant is; truth also seems to be "perspectivally limited."

Many Mansions

Heim bypassed the usual questions of if and how persons of other religious traditions attain salvation as understood in the Christian tradition. The universe has some ultimate character or order. A particular religious tradition may describe this order more fully or more accurately than another. However, the model of multiple salvations "requires only that the nature of reality be such as to allow humans to phenomenally realize varied religious ends" (Heim 2001, 24). It does not specify precisely what the nature of reality actually is.[3]

Heim argued that the hypothesis of multiple religious ends "can be interpreted and defended on Christian grounds" (Heim 1995, 184). These different religious ends do not correspond to different "heavens," with Christians in one, Buddhists in another, and so on. Rather, these ends can be "ordered," leaving open the possibility that one tradition may contain the "best approximate representation" of religious fulfillment as well as the possibility that all traditions eventually converge. Although such a convergence is not required, "The fact that this unity has been manifested to us in Christ . . . means that Christians will look for such a convergence" (Heim 2001, 269).

This opened Heim to an important charge. According to Knitter, "Heim is as interested in the future *integration* of religions as he is in their incorrigible *distinctions*." Yet Knitter observed that the "vision of future integration, if found, will come from one particular viewpoint" (Knitter 2002, 200). Heim referred to the process of discovering this vision as a "competition":

> To put it another way, the question is whether one faith's sense of the ultimate is such as to allow it to recognize that real (if limited or less than full) relation to that ultimate exists in another tradition, *in terms largely consistent with the distinctive testimony from that tradition itself.* The faith that proves able to do this for the widest possible range of compelling elements from other traditions will not only be enriched itself, but will offer strong warrants for its own truth. (2001, 128)

Heim's Christian viewpoint, of course, construed Christianity as the faith that correctly recognizes that members of other traditions come to "ends" less in full relation with the living and true God than do Christians.

As a Christian, Heim cannot but claim that Christianity *is* the "best approximate representation." A Christian radical particularist must find that realizing "something other than communion with the triune God and with other creatures through Christ . . . is to achieve a lesser good." Lesser goods might be "some measure of what Christian tradition regards as loss or damnation." However, he also argued that the afterlife can be seen as more complex than the usual "ultimate eschatological visions" of annihilation or universal salvation (Heim 2001, 44, 182, 118–19). Catholics familiar with the doctrine of purgatory and the now-discarded concept of limbo should not find such a vision of eschatological complexity surprising.

Heim envisioned four types of human destiny: Christian salvation, the fulfillments of other religious traditions, "fixation on a created good," and "the negation of the created self" (hell); he offers two striking illustrations of this vision. The first image is like the three-level cosmology of Dante's *Divine Comedy*, which reveals that Christians have long affirmed degrees of relation with God. The second image is related to the first. Heim redescribed Dante's picture of purgatory not as a mountain but as a mountain *range* stretching across heaven with each mountain representing a different "penultimate religious fulfillment," each of which "grasps some dimension of the triune life and its economic manifestations, and makes it the ground for a definitive human end." The Christian mountain is not "higher." Rather, looking out enables one to appreciate the diversity of the trinitarian life in God and in God's relationship with all God's creatures (Heim 2001, 272, 277–79).

Heim speculated that "there is a 'hierarchy' between full communion with the triune God and lesser, restricted participations" (2001, 179). Less clear is whether Christians at the "top" of this hierarchy will have a "greater" experience of God than those of other religions. According to Heim, however, "There is loss or deficiency in this picture only when some ends are compared with [Christian] salvation," and there is no reason to expect those experiencing other ("lesser") fulfillments to make such comparisons. In the end, "There is no evil in such [divine] plenitude"; multiple ends are God's way of honoring "the freedom of persons to relate to God as they choose, to value the dimensions of divinity on their own terms, and to select the human end they wish" (2001, 264, 255). In sum, God gives each as much fulfillment as possible for each person—shaped by a particular tradition for a particular end that the person reaches. The fulfillments are not commensurable. Each gets what each wants and deserves.

The implication of this approach is that God affirms our choices eternally, even against the divine will (which is for full communion with God for all). God's "choices themselves may contain within them true elements of God's intent, including profound relations with God. When humans choose less than all God offers, it does not mean they choose nothing God desires. This is the extraordinary mystery and wonder of the divine providence." This assertion "rests on the conviction that the most emphatic no of the human creature to the end of loving communion with God meets always some variation of God's merciful yes to creation" (Heim 2001, 269; 1995, 163). God allows and affirms the choices of those humans who have chosen lesser goods.

Even with these qualifications, Heim recognized that the hypothesis of multiple religious ends "does not fit easily into traditional Christian theological frameworks" (1995, 228). Lest his critics question whether it fits the frameworks at all, Heim argued that his hypothesis is reflected in the doctrine of the Trinity. As he put it:

> Trinity provides a particular ground for affirming the truth and reality of what is different. Trinitarian conviction rules out the view that among all the possible claimed manifestations of God, one narrow strand alone is authentic. Trinitarian conviction would rule out as well the view that all or most of these manifestations could be reduced to a single pure type underlying them. A simple exclusivism and a simple pluralism are untenable. There is an irreducible variety in what is ultimately true or of greatest significance. Christians can find validity in other religions because of the conviction that the Trinity represents a universal truth about the way the world and God actually are. (2001, 127)

Heim built on the work of Orthodox theologian John Zizioulas. Zizioulas inverted the typical Western approach to God, which tends to make understanding the being of the one God prior to understanding the persons of the triune God. This leads to an assumption that God's being is in some way prior to God's personhood. Zizioulas argued that God's being a Trinity of persons is prior to God's being as God. Heim further argued that differences among religions—now and in the future—reflect the understanding that in God, *being* is not prior to *personhood*: "God's nature is to be a person constituted by the communion of persons. . . . There is no more basic source of divine being than person and communion" (2001, 171–72). Knitter noted that to affirm this "social" view "is to also affirm that all beings must draw their existence and life from differences that give rise to relationship" (2002, 195). Just as there are a variety of relations within "the complex nature of God," so there is "the possibility of a variety of distinct relations with God" (Heim 2001, 179). It is therefore reasonable to expect that people will find distinct forms in which to live out these relations, that these forms may endure into the afterlife, and that God may well have *willed* this complexity.

Heim also utilized Raimundo Panikkar's description of three "spiritualities" in religion—synthesized in the Trinity—to reimagine the trinitarian "persons" as "dimensions": *impersonal transcendence* (the Father), the *personal icon* (the Son), and *impersonal immanence* (the Spirit) (Heim 2001, 132, 148–55). He insisted that other religious ends, not just Christian salvation, are also grounded in these dimensions: "They become separate ends by virtue of isolation and limitation, but this does not compromise their reality" (Heim 2001, 9). He then offered examples from other world religions: the Nirvana of Theravada Buddhism corresponds with divine impersonality, Islam's vision of heaven with encounter between persons, and Christian salvation with divine communion. Although they have a particular affinity with the Son, "Christians hold that the richest human end is a communion with God that encompasses all these dimensions" (Heim 2001, 198).

Heim did not employ the category of communion in relation to other religious traditions but saw it "as the balancing function that establishes all three persons as equality in difference" (D'Costa 2002, 138). Heim pushed his argument further by suggesting that trinitarian theology *requires* acceptance of religious difference:

> If Trinity is real, then many of the *specific* religious claims and ends must also be real. If they were all false, then Christianity could not be true. The universal and exclusive quality of Christian confession is the claim to allow the fullest assimilation of permanently co-existing truths. The Trinity is a map that finds room for, indeed requires, concrete truth in other religions. (2001, 167)

Heim's emphasizing of the Trinity corresponds to a deemphasizing of the significance of Jesus Christ for those who are not Christians. Because God always saves in particular, the salvation effected by Christ is always and *only* particular; in fact, it is the uniqueness of Christ that necessitates the recognition of other fulfillments: "The decisive and universal significance of Christ is for Christians *both* the necessary ground for particularistic witness *and* the basis for recognizing in other religious traditions their own particularistic integrity" (Heim 1995, 226).

Although the doctrine of the Trinity "teaches us that Jesus Christ cannot be an exhaustive or exclusive source for knowledge of God nor the exhaustive and exclusive act of God to save us," it is also "unavoidably Christocentric in at least two senses." First, it is through Christ that we came to know God as triune. Second, it is also through Christ that we see the particularity of revelation. The three dimensions of the Trinity and the corresponding relations with these dimensions that we noted above "are each embodied in Christ." Still, because the "ordinary function" of each religion "is to attain its own religious end, not the Christian one," Jesus is the "constitutive cause" for Christians only (Heim 2001, 134, 200, 269).

Heim's understanding of the role of Christ stemmed from his understanding of *revelation* and *experience*. For Heim, "Human knowledge and experience are partially constituted by the contexts and categories we bring to them. This includes the experience of religious fulfillment, both now and in the ultimate future." Because people come from very different contexts (or cultures) and have very different categories (or personalities), "We cannot posit some event that would be experienced as having the identical content and the identical meaning" for each of them. The Christian tradition typically views the incarnation—the life, death, and resurrection of Jesus Christ—as just this sort of "blinding revelation." According to Heim, however, "Any revelation consistent with humanity as we know it will condescend to the conditions of our knowing (even if stretching those conditions), not violate them" (2001, 30–31). Although religious ends may be transcendent and not causally dependent on these categories, they will always reflect them in particular ways. That religious experiences are diverse is no reason to question their validity; rather, it is reasonable to "preserve the highest degree of concrete validity in the largest number of them" (2001, 42).

Heim is concerned with supporting dialogue among the world's religious traditions. Christians universalistic claims may actually be true, but have only limited warrant. Other religious traditions may also make universal claims, also with limited warrant. In this situation, Heim found that "it is appropriate then for each to argue for and from its own universal view, so long as the diversity and actuality of religious ends are recognized" (1995, 143, 215). Authentic dialogue involves both witness to others and openness to the witness of others. Such openness requires one to be "a learner before superior wisdom . . . [that] extends not only to historical knowledge of the other religious tradition and its practices, but to aspects of the divine life, to truths hidden or never expressed to Christianity" (1995, 222; 2001, 294). Recognizing the "fact" of orientational pluralism opens us up to learning from those who have different orientations.

Radical Particularism Assessed

Heim's hypothesis of multiple religious ends is comprehensive. He has worked hard to overcome the double take it engenders on first glance. As he acknowledged, "Many people find it self-evident that there can be only one real religious end" (Heim 2001, 33). This common-sense belief is, of course, also the teaching of most, if not all, of the religious traditions of which he speaks, including the Christian tradition.

Griffiths, for one, thinks this hypothesis "stands a chance of being both coherent and acceptable to Christians" (Griffiths 2001b, 50). However, Griffiths's understanding of religious forms of life undermines this finding: "If a form of life seems to those who belong to it to be comprehensive, then it seems to them to take account of and be relevant to everything—not only to the particulars of all the forms of life they live in, but to everything in the strict sense." Such forms of life "do not stand easily alongside other forms," excluding or ignoring them; "instead, they englobe or contain these others, providing a frame within which they have their being and meaning" (Griffiths 2001b, 9–10). Not only do most religions believe in a single end *for everyone*, this is often the most important question there is: "It is existentially important because it has to do with the proper end of the life of the person asking it, with what that life is most fundamentally and comprehensively for. And it is conceptually and ethically important because it has to do with the proper ends of all people, including not only one's religious kin but also the religious alien" (2001b, 140). How Griffiths can hold this view and still find a hypothesis of multiple ends coherent and potentially legitimate for Christianity is perplexing.

Heim could cite the fullness of God's graciousness, the plenitude that God offers in giving people what their lives have shaped them for. He would then have to admit that he is an inclusivist in a much more robust sense than he seems to want. Nonetheless, Griffiths's main point remains a challenge: Christians think that salvation is union with the Trinity or the beatific vision, not something else. Buddhists think that the ultimate goal of our lives is the bliss of emptiness that is Nirvana. How can we rejoice in the awarding of second prizes, much less fifty-seventh prizes, if not booby prizes, for people we allegedly value, kin and alien, and whom we say God loves?

Heim fails to account fully for the real diversity of religious forms of life or the complexity of the identities of religious (and nonreligious) persons. It is appropriate to speak of the comprehensiveness prescribed by religious traditions and to make some generalizations about them, for, as we noted above, "no one can inhabit more than one form of religious life at a time." Yet the boundaries of religious traditions are permeable. As the spiritual shoppers in our commodified culture and the dual belongers discussed in chapter 10 show, hybridity in religious faith is not impossible. The advocates of comparative theologies of religions discussed in chapter 9 have taken better account of this hybridity (the focus of Hill Fletcher 2005).

Heim has focused almost exclusively on the so-called world religions to the neglect of minor traditions and sects as well as agnostics and atheists. However, the belief that people can be easily sorted into one religion or another is a modern fiction: "Christians did not, before the modern period, have the idea that there is a type called *religion* of which there are many tokens or instances"—for example, Christianity, Islam, or Theravada Buddhism (or Mormonism or Scientology). Religious forms of life "are not to be found only within the so-called world religions; neither are all the forms of life found there properly religious" (Griffiths 2001b, 4, 15). In reality, religious people are formed by a variety of communities and languages, some of them rather shabby on most Christian accounts. Could God fulfill people shaped in such traditions to want the ends all those traditions prescribe?

Heim implied that in the afterlife people will be able to survey the various "mountains" or "mansions" and make such a choice among them. Yet he spent little effort on analyzing the possibility that religious traditions may be wrong about the ends they prescribe or that the ends imagined (or not imagined) by some persons are not compatible with his proposal. For example, Leo Lefebure asks, "What would become of those who practice a religious tradition while remaining skeptical and suspending judgment concerning the afterlife? . . . Would their judgment continue to be suspended?" (1996, 237). If a religious tradition were to collapse in the afterlife, would this mean the end assumed by all its adherents was illusory or inadequate? Heim cannot have it both ways: if people could know about other ends so as to "survey" them as live options, how could Heim affirm that an end that they had achieved less than communion with God could fully satisfy them? If such surveying is possible, even in the afterlife, how can the ends be incommensurable? Heim cannot have it both ways: his position cannot simultaneously be radically particularist and salvifically inclusivist.

Although Heim admits the speculative character of his hypothesis, he also calls it "a fact to which the existence of diverse religions testifies." Applying Occam's razor (that is, the rule that the simplest explanation is likely the correct one) to the problem of religious diversity, he declared that because "pluralism looks real . . . the best explanation for this appearance turns out to be that it is real" (Heim 2001, 33). Heim recognized the problems with both making unified universal claims *and* presuming that many traditions could be wrong about their fulfillments. Yet he also appears uneasy with his *own* hypothesis as he recognized a possibility of a single, ultimate end beyond the particular ends of the religious traditions. In short, Heim is trapped; as a Christian he must declare that other religious traditions are *both right and wrong*—right about achieving their religious ends, but wrong about those ends being the only ends and ultimate or universal—or as a philosopher he must admit ignorance about the ends of humanity and the possibility that all may be right or wrong.

This problem is analogous to the pluralists' problems with truth. This is not a claim about warrant or justification that can be remedied by orientational pluralism, but a claim about "partial truth" in the traditions. Thus, Heim's view has the very problem that he found in the pluralists.

Heim also displays a deep confusion when he speaks of "many absolutes." As Knitter put it, "An absolute is a one-time production. Therefore, to suggest that there are many absolute expressions of truth is to imply that there are no absolute expressions of truth" (Knitter 2002, 234). Heim appears wary of truth claims on the one hand, but shows no reluctance in making or ordering such claims on the other. Although he tried to avoid doing so, he followed exclusivists and inclusivists in seeing religions other than Christianity as somehow lesser. Indeed, as Hick suggested, this hypothesis could be construed as offering "a bleaker future for most of humanity than traditional inclusivism," which *necessarily* brings all persons into the fullness of Christian salvation (Hick 2001, 412, 414).

Heim also followed pluralists in making what Knitter calls an imperialist judgment about the ends described by religious traditions: "Most religions would agree with each other that there is only one goal for all humanity, even though they may disagree on how to get there. To ask the religions to accept that there are multiple salvations, multiple and very different ultimate goals, for humans and their religions would be, for most religions, a strange if not heretical belief" (Knitter 2002, 231).

In sum, it is not clear that Heim escapes the difficulties he attempts to avoid in pluralist and classic and contemporary inclusivist positions.

Can Catholics Accept Radical Particularism?

Although Heim is a Baptist and therefore not subject to the Roman Catholic Church's magisterium, he is intimately familiar with the Catholic conversation about religious diversity and in many ways is an important part of it. His position is challenged less often on his fidelity to the tradition than on its internal coherence. Heim is directly or indirectly concerned with the principles we have developed in chapter 3, and, charitably read, does not intend to violate any of them. However, it is not clear that his position comports with them.

Heim's position clearly is in tension with the first rule. The Catholic tradition has always understood that because there is one God ("I am"), there is but one final destination (Christian salvation) at which God's salvific will aims. As Knitter indicated, Heim's reimaging of the Trinity goes "only half-circle" in this respect. The Trinity does reveal that diversity is part of God's nature, but God is also one; therefore "the three divine persons . . . have something in common that enables them to transcend their differences without doing away with them." Inasmuch as we are related to the triune God, we are united, and this calls us to affirm "a common ground that recognizes different paths, but not different final goals" (Knitter 2002, 231). Dupuis also found that the Trinity itself necessitates convergence: "The expansiveness of God's inner life overflowing outside the Godhead is . . . the root-cause for the existence in human history of *convergent paths*, leading to a unique common goal: the absolute mystery of the Godhead which draws all paths to itself, even as in the first place it launches them into existence" (Dupuis 1997, 209). While Heim invoked the divine plenitude to make a case for multiple destinies, it is hard to see just why Christians should think God has provided lesser goals as *ultimate* ends for those who walk other paths.

Dupuis also questioned whether the idea of orientational pluralism can be sustained by an appeal to divine communion. Although D'Costa, on whom Heim relied, is correct in arguing that "the Trinity provides the deep Christian grammar for relating particularity and universality," he did so to create a place for other religious traditions "in God's providential plan for humankind," not to imply the possibility of multiple religious ends within that plan (Heim 1995, 167; Dupuis 1997, 312–13). Kathryn Tanner has wondered if Heim may be inadvertently "replacing the traditional importance of the three persons of the Trinity in Christian accounts of God's relations with the world," so much so that there may be nothing "distinctly Christian" or "specifically trinitarian" remaining (Tanner 2003, 290).

Heim also claimed to be a "convinced inclusivist" and has maintained the "superiority" of Christianity (Heim 2001, 8; 1995, 7). He ordered hierarchically the particular goals of the particular traditions. Hence, it is possible that one tradition best approximates ultimate fulfillment for human beings and that all traditions eventually converge. It is not clear that Christians who can "look for . . . a convergence" (Heim 2001, 269) of religious ends ultimately cannot but affirm that God can make it so. This seems to involve the denial of the particularity of ends. Such inclusivism would fit better with God's universal salvific will than a radical particularism, but if the position is inclusivist, then why speculate on the ultimacy of particular ends? The tensions in Heim's work make it hard to see whether his position conforms to or violates the first principle. If his position is inclusivist, it likely conforms. If his position is radically particularist, he seems to deny the universality of the salvific will of God. It is not clear how to understand his position.

One of the central convictions of Christianity (and Judaism) has been trust in God's fidelity to his covenants, and for Christians, one culminating in Jesus Christ. The Catholic tradition holds that God's revelation in Jesus Christ sometimes (but not always) invalidates or overcomes the "mediating structures" of our cultures and personalities. The unity of salvation history and revelation requires that "the only adequate foundation on which the singular uniqueness of Jesus Christ can be based is his personal identity as the Son of God made man, as God's incarnate Word. No other Christology can, in the last analysis, account persuasively for Christ's universal mediatorship in the order of salvation" (Dupuis 1997, 191). Heim's position restricts Christ's salvation and mediatorship to Christians. Heim's position is at least in tension with the second rule. How it could fit with this rule is not at all clear, short of a hierarchical account of the relationships of ultimate ends—which would reduce this position to another form of inclusivism that denied the ultimacy of the ends proffered by other traditions. Again, reading Heim as espousing a very complex form of inclusivism may make his view fit this rule; if his view is radically particularist, it would not fit this rule at all, but question the validity of the rule.

Although Heim rarely mentions the church, what little he says indicates that, as Christ's body, it is also important for Christians only (Heim 2001, 63–64). If one considers salvation narrowly, his view fits the third rule. Only Christians are saved and they are saved in their connection with the church. This conception of the church's mission falls short. Heim would not deny the need for the church to proclaim the salvation wrought in Jesus Christ to the world, but it remains unclear why the church would be necessary for others' salvation.[4]

The apparent strength of Heim's view is its support of the dignity of each and every human person. That he is concerned to respect others as other is not in doubt; he affirms that each person has access to truth, that each tradition has something to teach us, and that each person's religious fulfillment must be one that does not violate his or her dignity. However, there is little reason to conclude that other approaches to religious diversity do not also honor this dignity, and further, there are reasons to question whether Heim's hypothesis actually *does* honor it.

Frank Clooney, for one, wondered if theologians in other traditions "will be able, on their own (and nontrinitarian) grounds, to embrace the attitude to which Heim now invites Christian theologians" (Clooney 2001b, 330). Gavin D'Costa questioned whether Heim's attempt to read all religions through the trinitarian category of relation does not negate his goal of accepting them "in terms of their own self-description." For example, D'Costa noted, "It is difficult to see the *telos* of Advaita being eternally preserved within a trinitarian framework" (D'Costa 2002, 139). Hick concluded that, in the end, "only Christians . . . can be helped by the doctrine of the Trinity" (Hick 2001, 414). Further, as Dupuis noted, "The unassailable rights of every human person are based on the equal dignity of all human beings before God." Positing distinctions between different ultimate ends assigned *by God* risks "unwittingly fostering discrimination or a covert exclusivism" (Dupuis 1997, 312). Why would God designate some people—Christians—for "greater" fulfillment? Does according them the right to be inferior in the end really support their dignity?

For other theologians, the diversity of religions ends with death. Hence, we ought to work to minimize or end this diversity (of the traditions themselves, if not of their adherents) in the present through evangelism in dialogue, witness, and proclamation. Heim's view that any final sorting of religious claims in the afterlife may not be an antidote to bland tolerance (except, perhaps, for the exclusivists, who are fundamentally intolerant). In the end, despite its creativity, the hypothesis of multiple religious ends may be too speculative, include too many anomalies, and remain too much in tension with the principles guiding mainstream Christian approaches in general and Catholic approaches in particular to religious diversity. It reflects, as much as anything we have discussed thus far, the dangers of a speculative approach to the problems of religious diversity.

Still, there is much we can learn from this hypothesis, particularly its concern for understanding the all-encompassing character of religious claims. More importantly, as Clooney and Fredericks pointed out, it opens a door through which we can more fully consider the possibilities of comparative theology (Clooney 2001b, 330; Fredericks 1997, 642), though if it is a foundation, it is shaky.

9

Dialogue before Theory?

The Practice of Comparative Theology

with Lora M. Robinson

> Before Christians can fully understand themselves
> and the role of their religion in the history of the world's many religions,
> we must first learn about non-Christians. . . .
> After learning about non-Christians and their religions,
> we will then be ready to learn from them.
> —James Fredericks

LIKE ADVOCATES OF THE MUTUALIST MODEL, COMPARATIVE THEOLOGIANS move beyond beginning with theory and advocate beginning in action. Like the particularists, they have moved beyond foundationalism, the assumption that one needs a theory to legitimate practices. The practice they advocate, however, is different from the mutualists' or the particularists' approaches. They begin as Christians interacting with the members and texts of other religions to see what they have to say to and about Christianity. They do not attempt to cooperate in solving the world's problems or accept differences as incommensurable. They engage in the practice of examining texts, beliefs, and practices, and let both insights and theory emerge from their work.[1]

Comparative theologians advocate "dialogue before theology," respectfully dialoguing with other religions to gain understanding of other traditions and Christianity in light of those traditions. Rather than starting with the Christian tradition, as most theologies of religion do, comparative theology starts with dialogue. Comparative theologians presume that the theologian knows his or her own tradition thoroughly. Yet they also find that we should theologize about how we can respond to and account for other religions in light of one's own only after we have come to know and understand the other tradition in its own context.

Comparative theology starts with the practice of dialogue because "the information on religions now available to us is far too complex and far too concretely situated to be accounted for justly by one or another of these theories and because, by extension, there is, in fact, no universal position from which one could adequately articulate such a theory" (Clooney 1991, 483). Comparative theology is Christian theology. Comparative theologians "look on the teachings and practices of other religious traditions as resources for enriching Christian self understanding" (Fredericks 2004, 28). Christian principles are not to be diluted in the name of courtesy or political correctness (Fredericks 1999, 125, 127; 2005b, 14–15). They are to be enhanced by the comparativists' work.

Comparative theologians call for a "moratorium on theologies of religions." However, the reality of religious diversity demands not that there be a "moratorium on reflection on pluralism" and diversity (Clooney 2003c, 324), but only that theologians should stop "trying to promote grand narratives about the others" (Fredericks 2004, 28) as theologies of religions typically do. Indeed, some that we have placed in the mutualist and particularist camps in this book also engage in comparative theology, although they do not eschew "doing theory."

Comparative Theology

Comparative theology is "the attempt to understand the meaning of Christian faith by exploring it in the light of the teachings of other religious traditions." So claims a leading comparative theologian, James Fredericks, who works primarily in Buddhist-Christian dialogues (Fredericks 1999, 139).[2] The goal is to have a better understanding of one's own faith (Fredericks 1999, 139–40). Comparative theologians find the texts and practices of other religions valuable enough that Christians' own faith might benefit from learning from other religions. Similarities with the other may allow friendships to grow. Finding differences may fill gaps in our own faith or help us to articulate our own faith better. Thus "'by using the insights of non-Christian religions as a resource,' he [Fredericks] has been enabled to 'embrace his own cherished beliefs in a new way . . . at a deeper level'" (Knitter 2002, 206).

Theology is interreligious, comparative, dialogical, and confessional work. So claims Francis X. Clooney, S.J., another leading comparative theologian, who specializes in Hindu-Christian dialogue (Clooney 2001a, 7–11, 164–81). Theology is interreligious in that theology is not restricted to a certain group in a certain place; all can theologize and all can hear and respond to a theology. Theology is comparative in that one can learn more about what is unique in one's own beliefs by comparing and contrasting them with the beliefs of others. In fact, theology has "always been an inherently comparative discipline"

(Renard 1998, 3). The "full meaning" of the faith cannot be determined within the limited context of one religious tradition. Theology is dialogical because people from different religious traditions comparing and contrasting their religions leads to a fuller understanding of each (Clooney 2001a, 10). Finally, theology always remains confessional: theologians remain committed to their home tradition.

Comparative theology starts by sharing one's own religious beliefs with others and listening to others' religious beliefs in a conversation that is a "mutual search for truth" (Fredericks 2004, 108). Thus comparative theology is a "constructive" theology. It is built *after* the interaction between members of two religious traditions (though the comparativist remains rooted in one tradition). Comparative theologians build on the insights developed in interreligious dialogue "rather than simply on themes or methods already articulated prior to the comparative practice" (Clooney 1995, 522; 1993, 7).

Six Characteristics of Comparative Theology

Six characteristics are common to the practice of comparative theology: focusing on specifics, honoring both similarities and differences, responding to the *real* other, being open to transformation, balancing the tension between loyalty and vulnerability, and engaging in interreligious friendships.

Comparative theology focuses on specifics. Clooney has argued that it is impossible to make general comparisons between religions, given the amount of information available about other religions (1991, 483). Rather than sweeping, general comparisons, a comparativist studies "a specific text, concrete ritual, focused beliefs, particular theologians, limited contexts, or historical periods," and this limited vision will provide deeper comprehension (Knitter 2002, 207; see also Clooney 2000, 118; 2001a, 14, 163, 166; 2002c, 253; Fredericks 1995a, 506). Rather than trying to compare and contrast Hinduism and Christianity in general, a comparative theologian compares and contrasts specifics, such as the idea of incarnation in Christianity with the idea of Avatars of Vishnu in Hinduism, not only to understand the similarities and differences of these concepts but also to see if the Hindu concept can be used to help understand the Christian mystery. This focus on specifics helps prevent the mistakes of distorting other religions, domesticating (or playing down) differences, or spinning out grand narratives of religions (Fredericks 2004, 27). Comparative theologians typically do case studies that compare and contrast specific elements or aspects of two traditions.

Comparative theology honors both similarities and differences. To focus too much on either similarities or differences causes problems; one needs to balance both in order to truly learn in a comparative exercise (Clooney 1993,

12; 2001a, 168). Fredericks, as Griffiths noted (see chapter 8), found that too often theologies of religions focus on the similarities at the expense of difference. He challenged the comparativist to go beyond tolerance to a place where differences are seen as "valuable opportunities for deepening our own religious commitments in conversation with other religious believers" (Fredericks 1999, 172). For these "differences can be as illuminating and as useful as the similarities that link religions," and so the differences must also be "recognized and respected" (Fredericks 1999, 158, 163). Clooney agreed that it is the differences between texts that provide the most "important and interesting" insights (1993, 165). Comparative theology should really be called comparative and contrasting theology, for it seeks to do both. (In what follows, "comparing" includes both exploring similarities and contrasting differences.)

Comparative theology works to respond to an *actual* other, not a projected or theorized one. Comparative theologians talk with members of other religions and read the other religions' texts (Fredericks 1995b, 86; Clooney 1993, 7; 2001a, 91, 160, 173; Lefebure 1989, 5). Comparativists start their constructive work by developing their knowledge of other religions on their own terms and in their own contexts. At best, they learn the target tradition as they have learned their own, by learning its practices and beliefs from skilled and thoughtful practitioners (Fredericks 2004, 110–11). This knowledge is necessary because "before Christians can fully understand themselves and the role of their religion in the history of the world's many religions, we must first learn about non-Christians. . . . After learning *about* non-Christians and their religions, we will then be ready to learn *from* them" (Fredericks 1999, 9). Developing a deep understanding of another religious tradition takes a long time—decades may not be enough (Clooney 1993, 10, 197, 201; 2001a, 164).

In responding to an actual other, one must not abstract a belief or practice from its context in the target tradition. It can be tempting when making specific comparisons to forget the broader context of the religion from which these specifics flow (Clooney 1993, 167; 1996, 297; 2000, 120; 2002a, 46–48). Clooney emphasized that one must understand the tradition in its own context *before* moving on to speak of the implications for one's own faith or universal significance (Clooney 1995, 528). Abstracting a specific item from its home context runs the risk of distorting the significance of the text or practice.

Responding to an actual other also means that comparative theology is a truly "located" or "sited" theology. Because one encounters real people in real locations, comparative theology in Japan is different from comparative theology in India (Fredericks 2004, 110; Clooney 2003c, 324). The religious tradition of the dialogue partner matters: a dialogue with a Buddhist or a Jew will result in different conversations (Fredericks 2004, 110). For comparative theologians, concrete particulars are significant.

One must be open to the possibility that other religious traditions have worthwhile insights that may or may not already exist within one's home tradition (Clooney 1993, 196). This opens up the possibility—comparative theologians would argue the certainty—of transformation. One cannot "truly encounter the central texts of another tradition and dismiss them while one's own views remain unaltered" (Renard 1998, 9). When one is truly open to encountering another religion, the comparativist risks finding the other religion preferable to the old. One may find a new way or lose "one's way in the presence of that other" (Clooney 1996, 304). This prospect can be and should be frightening; it may even entail a loss of self, as Griffiths has argued (2001b, 10; Elshtain and Griffiths 2002, 30). The transformation that results from interaction, however, does not have to be a conversion to another religion. The practice can lead to understanding Christianity in new ways (Fredericks 1995a, 520; 1999, 176; Clooney 1996, 304).

For example, imagine hearing the Gospel read at a Catholic Mass. The lector begins, "There was a man who had two sons. The younger one said to his father, 'Father, give me my share of the estate.' So he divided his property between them." At this point the Catholic thinks, "Oh, the parable of the Prodigal Son. I've heard this one before," and then does not listen to the rest of the reading. By reading the religious texts of other traditions, and then bringing that insight back to Christian texts, one can see a familiar story in a nonfamiliar way that would otherwise have been impossible without the insight from another religious tradition (as we will see below in the section on methodology). Leo Lefebure, a priest-professor of theology specializing in Buddhist-Christian dialogue, echoed this point: in "listening to Buddhist voices Christians can re-hear our own Scriptures and re-cognize images of our own tradition with greater awareness and appreciation" (1989, 6).

Knowledge "of other religious traditions does not detract from Christian faith" (Clooney 2002c, 249–50). Knowing other religions can deepen one's commitment to one's own faith. It is one thing to grow up and know only the faith in which you have been raised. However, if one is exposed to and comes to understand several traditions, then one must *choose* to convert or to remain in the home tradition (Clooney 2002c, 245; compare Wolfe 2003, 242). Understanding multiple traditions puts one in position to explain *why* one is committed to one particular faith rather than another. Clooney "paradoxically envisions a way of deepening Catholic identity by radically expanding the context in which that identity takes place" (Schmalz 2003, 134; see also Clooney 2000, 122). Willingness to learn from other traditions enables comparative theologians to be open to listening to what other traditions have to teach them. Dialogue partners from other traditions can even help one develop the understanding of the faith of the home tradition.

Comparative theology is both open and confessional (Clooney 2001a, 21, 26). This leads us to the fifth characteristic: balancing the tension—being both vulnerable and loyal. Comparative theology is a demanding practice. Learning from another tradition runs the risk of disturbing the inquirer's faith. One must balance openness to understanding another tradition as its members understand it with steadfastness in one's own tradition (Clooney 1993, 4–6; see also Clooney 2000, 103–32). Though the tension can be uncomfortable, we must "resist the temptation to overcome this tension" (Fredericks 1999, 170; 2004, 97). Creative tension is inherent in comparative theological work.

The sixth and final characteristic of comparative theology provides a way to deal with this tension: through interreligious friendship. Comparative theology advocates interaction with the actual members of other faiths. Interreligious friendship brings the meeting of religions from the confines of books to the "actual lives of Christian believers" (Fredericks 1999, 176). The risks and benefits of comparative theological work are shaped by these characteristic emphases.

Comparative Theology: Methodology

Since comparative theology is a relatively new practice, the methods are still developing (Knitter 2002, 206–7). The approaches each theologian takes are different. This section unpacks some of the methods. Each exercise is an example, not an illustration, of a "perfect(ed) theory" (Clooney 1993, 155). Nonetheless, the examples of comparative theologians' approaches show a general pattern in the practice of comparative theology.

Comparative theology requires "crossing over into the world of another religious believer and learning the truths that animate the life of that believer," but it also means "coming back to Christianity transformed by these truths, now able to ask new questions about Christian faith and its meaning for today" (Fredericks 2004, xii). Thus the process of comparative theology is to "allow our minds and imaginations to be stirred and sharpened by stories outside our religion," and then to "return to our own stories and images with new eyes and ears" (Fredericks 1999, 139–61; see reference in Knitter 2002, 209; Lefebure 1989, 5). The method Fredericks advocates requires both crossing over and coming back (see Clooney 2002d for a similar method.)

Clooney, the most prolific writer in the field of comparative theology, has suggested five patterns of practice for doing comparative theology: coordination, superimposition, comparative conversation, comparative tension, and collage (Clooney 1993, 168–75). Coordination allows the comparativist to take two texts together looking for similarities in terms, themes, and structures without melding the two texts into one. Superimposition imposes "one reality—idea, person, thing, word—on another, for the purpose of an enhanced meditation on the latter" (Clooney 1993, 169; the "dual belongers" discussed in the next chapter exemplify a radical form of this practice). Clooney drew this insight from the eighth-century Hindu theologian Sankara. The superimposition of higher reality on a lower one is temporary and for the purposes of comparison. Superimposition occurs when the comparativist "superimposes a text from another tradition upon one from his or her own" (Clooney 1993, 170). This comparison is not neutral, but there is "no reason to perform comparisons exclusively from a strictly neutral position" as is the case in comparative religion. Comparative theology is a practice of believers, not "neutral" observers (Clooney 1993, 170).

Comparative conversation is a position promoted by David Tracy's reflections on the work of Hans-Georg Gadamer (Clooney 1993, 170). It initiates a conversation between the reader and the text, between one religion and another. It requires following the questions encountered wherever they may go, noting that the conversation is extremely unpredictable. Furthermore, this method works only when both sides are allowed to both speak and to listen (Clooney 1993, 171). Comparative tension is a method whereby comparing the texts leads to insights more profound than those generated by either text alone (Clooney 1993, 175).

Clooney also noted the influence of literary theorist Philip Wheelwright on this method: using juxtaposition by placing two texts side by side, reading them together, and discovering new meanings. Placing two works from different contexts creates a tension: "they come to mean differently, though only insofar as they also maintain their own meanings" (Clooney 1993, 172; see also Clooney 1990, 70–71). As a metaphor, which juxtaposes two items that are not like each other to evoke a new insight (e.g., "Juliet is the sun" from the balcony scene in Shakespeare's *Romeo and Juliet*), so juxtaposing two texts can evoke insight. In both cases, the significance of the terms juxtaposed is not changed, but the juxtaposition creates insight.

The final practice, collage, is borrowed from the visual arts. Just as an artist cuts out various pictures and then pastes them together to create a collage, the comparative theologian cuts up texts from two religious traditions and then pastes them together to create a textual collage. The texts are uprooted from the context of their tradition and placed with uprooted texts from the other tradition, resulting in new insight and meanings. Taking the texts outside their context (a technique usually frowned upon by comparative theologians) can lead to new insights (Clooney 1993, 174), but not to a deeper understanding of the texts as texts of a particular tradition. The best way to evaluate the effectiveness of all of these practices is to engage in them to see what results from the work (Clooney 1993, 174–75). Done well, comparative theology enhances the understanding of the home tradition by these comparative practices.

A final suggestion in method from Clooney is pedagogical. One begins with the familiar—a theme or issue in the Christian tradition—and then provides examples related to that theme from other traditions. The point is to allow people to examine the familiar theme in light of the insights of the other tradition (Clooney 2002c, 253–55). Clooney used this method in teaching classes on interreligious issues. Good methods codify successful practice; they are not the "foundation" for engaging in practices.

John Renard, a theologian specializing in Islamic-Christian dialogue, displays a slightly different approach to comparative theology (Renard 1998, 3–18). An "intertextual" practice tells how "one community reads another's texts." Reading the texts of another tradition is of value in itself. Reading another tradition's texts may seriously affect the reader (Renard 1998, 9). A "phenomenological/thematic" method shows "how theologians can clarify their understanding of their own traditions by observing parallels in others" (1998, 12). This approach can shed light on doctrines in the comparativist's own tradition by comparing particular, analogous theological concepts in different religions (ibid.). An intertextual hermeneutic focuses on "how a theologian today can profit from reading another's sacred text without resorting to polemics" (13). Every religious text contains something worth studying. One can and should "respect the religious integrity of another scripture while interrogating it from the perspective of one's own tradition" (ibid.). Renard warned that one understand the integrity and message of the text in its own religious context and not "read into the text signs of Christianity by another name." Rather, one "focuses on the specific theological issues discussed or implicit in the other tradition's text as stimulus for reflection on Christian issues." Renard used Clooney's work as a case study of this method (ibid.).

Most of the literature in comparative theology consists of specific examples or experiments. Thus, the best way to understand comparative theology is through a specific example. The example here is drawn from Fredericks's work (see 1999, 140–41).

Fredericks starts by telling the story of Krishna and the milkmaids from the beloved Hindu text *Bhagavad Gita*. Krishna is an Avatar or bodily manifestation of the Hindu God Vishnu. Krishna is a lover of the *gopis* (milkmaids). One night he plays enchanting music on his flute and calls all the milkmaids to come and dance in the forest with him (Fredericks 1999, 140). The *gopis* begin to get jealous of one another because each one wants to dance with Krishna alone. They begin to compete for Krishna's affection. He disappears from their midst only to reappear. He has multiplied himself so that each one of the *gopis* can dance alone with him.

Fredericks summarized a traditional Hindu interpretation of the story: "those who try to possess divine love for themselves succeed only in making it disappear from their life . . . divine love cannot be hoarded, but it is infinitely skillful in offering itself to us" (1999, 141). He then turned to the Christian parable of the prodigal son. A man has two sons. The younger one takes his inheritance and squanders it in reckless living, while the older one stays home and works for his father. After hitting rock bottom, the younger son "comes to his senses" and returns home to his father. His father holds a party in celebration of the return of his younger son. The elder son is upset because he feels it is unjust for the younger brother who was irresponsible to be rewarded, while the older son who has been responsible has never been rewarded. The father consoles him. Fredericks next recapitulated the traditional Christian interpretation of the story that emphasizes "the father's joy over the repentance of the younger son" (1999, 143).

Fredericks applied the insight from the story of Krishna and the *gopis* in its own context to the parable of the prodigal son. The story of Krishna can help "Christians to see aspects of Jesus' parable which otherwise go unnoticed" (1999, 143). Rather than focus on the issue of justice and repentance in the story, the Hindu story suggests a focus on the issue of love. Fredericks's interpretation is that just as Krishna divided himself to be with each of the *gopis*, God poured out the divine "love on the dutiful and the irresponsible alike" (144). The parable is not about the prodigal son but about the father's love for both his sons.[3] Fredericks concluded that "the more we insist that God does not love those who are less moral or less faithful or less dutiful than ourselves, the more divine love disappears from our own lives, like Krishna disappearing from the midst of his selfish *gopis*" (ibid.). By reading a parable of Jesus in light of an episode from the *Bhagavad Gita*, Fredericks developed a new insight into a key text of his own tradition. Comparative theologians accept what another tradition teaches and bring home insights into their own tradition.

Responses to Comparative Theology

Catherine Cornille, a theologian specializing in theologies of religions and interreligious dialogue, argued that Fredericks's aim to move beyond the theology of religions fails because his comparative theology is "on a crucial point, implicitly pluralistic" and comparative theology can better be done "from an inclusivists' perspective. . . . [C]omparative theology does not render the theology of religions superfluous but, on the contrary, requires and even presupposes it" (Cornille 2001, 132). Perry Schmidt-Leukel, a University of Glasgow professor who specializes in theologies of religions, interfaith dialogue, and especially Buddhist-Christian dialogue, argued that the comparative theologians throw the baby out with the bathwater by discarding theologies of religion temporarily or for good (2005, 18). Both Cornille and Schmidt-Leukel claimed that a theology of religions is necessary for the encounter of religions. Furthermore, Stephen Duffy, professor of systematic theology at Loyola University, New Orleans, claimed that comparative theology cannot start from a blank slate but needs the theologies of religions to help provide a foundation and pre-understanding (2000, 125–26). Theologies of religions provide both a starting point for dialogue and help provide boundaries to ensure fidelity to the home religious tradition (Duffy 1999a, 34). In a critique of comparative religion, Raimon Pannikar, an interreligious theologian whom we discuss in the next chapter, agreed that theologies of religions build on one another: "theology of religion is only made possible by a previous theology of religions" (Pannikar 1973a, 132). Duffy claimed that theologies of religions *and* comparative theology are intertwined and are both needed for successful interreligious dialogue (1999a, 37, *emphasis added*; see also 33; 1999b, 105–15). Responding to the discussion between himself and Clooney as to what should come first and what should come second, theologies of religion or comparative theology, Paul Knitter concluded both are needed and "there is no 'first this, then that'" (1997, 292).

Most of these criticisms presume that practices require foundations. Yet postmodern and postliberal nonfoundationalists claim not only that practices do not require foundations, but that searching for them is confused. A practice is not to be defended by finding intellectual permission to engage in it but by pointing to its results when it is done well. The test of practice is pragmatic. Clooney maintained that "sequence is important" and that the theology of religions can commence only after reading the texts of another religion (1990, 66). The practice gives rise to the theology, not vice versa. Comparative theology does not need a theology of religions as a foundation any more than bicycling or worship requires a theory to be articulated either to make sense of engaging in the practice or to provide a priori criteria for successful engagement. What the critics tend not to note is that comparative theologians are on the nonfoundationalist side of the argument between foundationalism and nonfoundationalism in theology (see Thiel 1994, passim). The critics' arguments presuppose that foundationalism is necessary, a point that the comparative theologians do not and should not concede.

Several theologians have argued that Fredericks's comparative theology ignored the basic questions of theology of religions such as revelation, mediators, salvation, and truth claims of religions (Cornille 2001, 132; Cheetham 2000, 359; Schmidt-Leukel 2005, 27; Knitter 2002, 236–37). Such questions are not even on the table in comparative theology; theologizing about them is not necessary as a foundation for practice. To place these issues on the table is to place a Christian argument on the table, rather than to attempt to compare beliefs and practices of two religions. One cannot address such large questions without a thorough knowledge of other religions (Clooney 2000, 123). Thus, one cannot even begin to discuss such issues or make a choice between two competing truth claims until one understands both claims within their religious tradition, something that could take a lifetime (Clooney 1993, 189–93).[4]

The first step in doing comparative theology is to encounter the other tradition in its own context without preemptively using one's home religion's theology as an interpretive matrix. Yet one is also supposed to maintain the tension between being open and being loyal by remaining rooted in one's own religious tradition the entire time (Clooney 1995, 522; 1993, 7). How does one remain rooted in one's own religious tradition without allowing it to influence the way one approaches another religion? It is impossible to completely abandon one's own religion when examining another. As John Renard put it, "under no circumstances do I presume that any investigator can be free of bias" (1998, 16). One could respond that the comparative theologian might not be aware of this bias: "theological suppositions might be implicitly influencing what he [Fredericks] sees in other religions" (Knitter 2001, 874). However, this applies to all theologians. The comparative theologian must be aware of this possibility as an ineradicable part of the method. Of course, Clooney claimed that one cannot study another religion apart from the lens of one's own tradition (1990, 64, 66, 74–75; 2003a, 220; see also Duffy 1999a, 36; Knitter 2002, 212–13). Yet well-educated comparative theologians can be so aware of the shape of their religious lenses that they can correct for the ways it bends the light from other traditions as they do their work.

Comparative theologians do not attempt to hide their faith (see Clooney 1993, xv). Many theologians, including comparative theologians and the writers of this book, agree that one cannot discard one's theological commitments and work as if one were a theological tabula rasa. However, if one is aware of them, one can discern possible distortions they might introduce as well as insights they can provide into other traditions.

Therefore, comparative theology requires one to possess a deep understanding of one's own tradition in order to engage in working with another tradition (Clooney 1993, 198–207). That a vast number of Christians in America today do not possess extensive knowledge of their own religion, much less any other tradition, seems obvious (a point we return to in chapter 11). There are few people with the thorough knowledge of Catholicism and another tradition, along with the capacity to read texts in other languages fluently (Duffy 1999b, 114). Thus there is a danger of elitism. Clooney agreed that comparative theology will fail if it is done only by specialists (1995, 536). He attempted to address this problem by writing a book for a nonspecialist audience (1998). These issues of believers' knowledge and the danger of elitism are challenges to comparative theology; but the same challenges apply to theologians who work in other areas as well.

Matthew Schmalz, professor of theology at the College of the Holy Cross, found some issues still remain more complicated than they seem in the works of the theologians (2003, 133). Comparative theology not only takes a specially trained person with the means and opportunity to study another religion intensely, but it also requires decades of work . Who can take the time to learn to do comparative theology? What institutions will support those who do? These social questions remain significant.

Fredericks's idea of interreligious friendship provides a possible solution to the danger of elitism. In America today, one need only look to one's neighbor or coworker to find a member of another religious tradition. By fostering such interreligious friendships, ordinary parishioners can begin to learn about other religions. However, the fact that the ordinary parishioner will certainly not be trained to do comparative theology points to the fact that this is a problem for further reflection. Wuthnow has chided religious educators for the shallowness of their treatment of others' traditions (2005, 96–104). That comparative theology is reserved to an elite is due in part to the denominations' refusing to educate their own members about other traditions; hence, those who do learn about others' traditions cannot but be an elite.

Comparative theology is an example of one of four forms of dialogue discussed in the International Theological Commission document *Dialogue and Proclamation* (1991). Comparative theology can be seen as a dialogue of theological exchange, where "*specialists* seek to *deepen their understanding* of their respective religious heritages and to appreciate each other's spiritual values" or a dialogue of religious experience "where persons, *rooted in their own religious traditions, share* their spiritual riches" (*Dialogue and Proclamation* § 42; *emphasis added*). Two other forms of dialogue remain: the dialogue of life and the dialogue of action. Comparative theology is part of the work, not the whole. It may be legitimately the work of qualified specialists, just as the practices of law and medicine are specialized.[5] Comparative theologians' work is a significant part of dialogue.

Comparative Theology: A Catholic Approach?

In some ways, it is difficult to evaluate comparative theology using the principles developed in chapter 3. Generally speaking, comparative theologians as nonfoundationalists do not have a theology in the sense that pluralists or inclusivists do. They tend to take the rules for granted. Nonetheless, we can tease out some indicators of their standing regarding these rules. Fredericks, for example, has explicitly argued that Christians cannot deny God's universal salvific will. Observing this rule is one of the two necessary aspects for being faithful to the Christian tradition, a criterion Fredericks uses in evaluating theologies of religion. One does not water down one's tradition to engage in the dialogue (Fredericks 1999, 125, 127; 2005b, 14–15).

The claims each tradition makes are warranted within each tradition's context. The point of orientational pluralism is that warranting is perspective specific or, in the present context, tradition specific. Yet it is wrong to say, as Knitter does, that "the truth of what the Christian is saying and the truth of what the Hindu is saying can only be understood and then assessed within their own cultures and systems" (Knitter 2002, 213). Assessment is not limited to originating traditions, but can be done when items from different traditions are brought together to produce insights. Moreover, comparative theologians work in a context wider than any single tradition. Knitter's critique presumes that cultures and systems are unchanging wholes, a presumption that cannot be sustained (see Tanner 1997). An approach that compares and contrasts texts or practices from different traditions in effect expands the perspective in which claims are or can be warranted. Hence, warranting Christian claims about revelation or salvation is a much more difficult business because the interreligious context is more complex. One's warrants have to be valid not only in one's own tradition, but also at the point where traditions meet and, at least at a particular time and place, fuse.

Comparative theologians such as Clooney suggest that we cannot say which faith tradition, if any, has better warrant. We should not try to answer questions of truth and justification until we have made a "long, patient effort at understanding those claims in their own language and context. And that is precisely what comparative theology is all about" (Clooney 1993, 187–93; see Knitter 2002, 214). Comparative theologians *believe in* their tradition. If they did not, they would have to abandon it. The process of *justifying* specific beliefs is another matter, especially in dialogue with others who also believe that the universal claims their traditions make are true and that their beliefs, as well as Christians', have some justification.

Catholicism affirms the value of other religions. Even *Dominus Iesus* states that the texts of other religions "direct and nourish the existence of goodness and grace which they contain," and that God "does not fail to make himself present in many ways, not only to individuals, but also to entire peoples though their spiritual riches" (§ 8; Clooney 2002b, 159). *Lumen Gentium* states that grace is also found in the "rites and customs" of other religions (§17; Fredericks 2005b, 6). If other religions, texts, rites, and customs contain grace and result in some way from the presence of the Holy Spirit, then Christians can certainly learn from other religions and comparative theology is a useful exercise. Insofar as Christians get new insights from other traditions, they may or may not learn new truths; but they should be in a better position to justify their claims as a result of understanding others' views.

Comparative theology finds value in the texts of other religious traditions and believes that it is beneficial to use these texts as a resource for Christian theology. Thus, comparativists see theology not as "the practice of thinking *about* the non-Christians" but rather "the practice of 'thinking Christianly' with assets or resources that include non-Christian elements" (Clooney 1991, 488). There is good reason to do this, for "almost all of what counts as theological thinking is shared across religious boundaries" (Clooney 2001a, 165). Other religious texts provide more resources for a "creative revision" of one's religious tradition (Fredericks 1995a, 506). This gives even more weight to comparative theology's reading of the texts of other religions in order to see one's own tradition in a new way.

Comparative theologians explicitly address the second rule, "thou shalt not deny the sufficiency of God's salvation in and through Jesus Christ." Fredericks "takes for granted that Christian convictions and claims about Jesus as the unique, real, and historical incarnation of God in human history are part of the *identity* that Christians bring to the task of comparative theology and dialogue with others" (Knitter 2002, 211). Dialogue partners don't want you to lie about or dilute your faith; they want to hear how Christians really view Jesus and how Christians really view them (Fredericks 1999, 125, 127; 2005b, 14–15). Comparative theologians start with recognizing the salvation that comes in Jesus (Knitter 2002, 212).

Clooney agreed with *Dominus Iesus* that "we do no good for others or ourselves if we fall silent about Jesus, or mention him merely in passing, as if he were optional, not the center of our lives" (Clooney 2005a, 14). Clooney also affirmed the Catholic Church's claim to the truth found in *Dominus Iesus*. It is normal for a religion to claim that its own content is true, and that it is not just true for believers of that tradition, but for all (Clooney 2002b, 160–61). Dialogue partners from other traditions do the same thing (Clooney 2003a, 221, 223; 2002b, 160–61; 2003b, 306–33). "There is no reason for Catholics to become diffident or halting in their confession of the Lordship of Jesus" (Clooney 2002b, 166). Clooney found in his work that an honest sharing of one's beliefs serves to deepen dialogue rather than prevent it. All religions make exclusive and unique claims as part of their religion, a point emphasized by Gavin D'Costa in his more recent work (see pp. 85–87 above). Comparative theology fits with the Catholic Church's desire to speak boldly concerning Jesus.

Fredericks claimed that one must hold to Jesus' uniqueness because not to do so is not to talk about Christianity: "to be committed to Jesus as God's unique Son does not reduce Christians' vulnerability to other religions or their readiness to be shaken up and transformed by other texts and symbols" (Knitter 2002, 211, quoting Fredericks). Comparative theology can "affirm the salvific presence of God in non-Christian religions while still maintaining that Christ is the definitive and authoritative revelation of God" (Clooney 1990, 73, quoting D'Costa; see Knitter 2002, 212).

With regard to the necessity of the church, Stephen Duffy noted that "in our pluralistic era Christians can no longer proclaim their truth in isolation" (2000, 126). Duffy argued that the Catholic Church must respond to the reality of religious diversity and the necessity of dialogue (2000, 126). Comparative theology is an appropriate response because "the goal of comparative theology is the goal of all theology, viz. the good of the church and of individual believers" (2000, 124). Comparative theology must be a necessary and central part of Catholic theology today in order for the church to be truly catholic: "ours is a world where comparative work for the good of the church must increasingly become an intrinsic dimension of all theological work" (Duffy 1999a, 33; 2000, 126). Fredericks stated that "comparative theology, like all theology, is part of the life of the Christian community, the church" (1999, 179). Comparative theology can help the church because "doing theology comparatively presumes that Christian doctrine continues to develop . . . comparative theology does not envision the abandonment of Christian belief, but rather its slow and careful transformation. In this respect, comparative theology must be seen as a form of Christian hope" (Fredericks 1999, 178).

Like S. Mark Heim, comparative theologians do not dwell on the necessity of the church, but presume it. Without the church, there would be no tradition to work in and from. In assessing comparative theology, we might find that the comparative theologians need to pay more attention to the work of the church as community and institution, but there is no indication in their theologies that they violate this principle.

The affirmation of the dignity of each and every human person is at the heart of comparative theology. *Dominus Iesus* declared that dialogue is necessary, as is respect for the dialogue partner (Clooney 2003c, 320). John Paul II taught that "human dignity is realized in community" and that interdependence should be "embraced" in order to uphold the "dignity of each and every human being and the common good of the human community" (Fredericks 2005a, 9). Thus, through interaction with members of other traditions comparative theologians embrace interdependence and uphold the dignity of their interlocutors.

By beginning in dialogue, comparative theologians uphold the dignity of other traditions by making them partners through conversation in a "mutual search for truth" (Fredericks 2004, 108). Comparative theologians hold that the members and texts of other religions, as well as the religions in general, have something to teach us; they advocate learning *about* and learning *from* other religions (Fredericks 1999, 9). The acknowledgment that other traditions contain insight that may or may not already exist within the Christian tradition is another illustration of upholding the dignity of believers of other religious traditions (Clooney 1993, 196). The desire to study other religions in depth, in their own context, and remain open to the probability that they will transform the comparativist also shows respect for the dignity of other religious traditions and their members. This transformation has positive consequences: "If a Christian reads a Hindu verse and ponders it according to the traditions of Hindu learning, this eventually has an effect—salutary I suggest—on how he or she thinks and reads, contemplates and encounters Jesus of Nazareth, who even today wishes to encounter us" (Clooney 2002a, 57).

Furthermore, comparative theology advocates interreligious friendships, and these friendships promote dignity through personal encounter and reciprocal sharing and listening with honesty and respect.

This chapter began by noting the fundamental move that comparative theology shares with the particularists and other postmodern and postliberal theologians: the reversal of the priority of theory and practice. Most of the critics have simply taken foundationalism for granted. That presumption is no longer warranted. Our assessment is that comparative theology is an appropriate and effective response for Christians to the reality of religious diversity. Clooney has claimed that he and his fellow comparative theologians are simply starting the conversation (Clooney 2001a, 183). They are hopeful that others will continue what they have started, for by meditating "on the particularities of other traditions, learning from what they say and feel, how they pray and serve" Christians can come to deeper and fuller appreciations of Christianity (Clooney 2005b, 19). Comparative theologians would agree with the phrase "two heads are better than one." Christian comparative theologians will enjoy a deeper understanding of Christianity from the insight gained in studying another religion. There are dangers in comparative work, but any worthwhile theological work can be dangerous to the faith of a complacent worker.

However, some people stay in that expanded context "between" religious traditions. While comparative theologians, at best, have an adherent's understanding of the practices and beliefs of the tradition they study, they usually do not also consider themselves as belonging to that tradition. They may engage in the practices of the target tradition, but do so more as "visitors" or "resident aliens" than as "citizens." Yet some do have a "dual citizenship." Chapter 10 discusses the practices of "multiple religious belonging."

10

Multiple Religious Belonging

Can a Christian Belong to Other Traditions Too?

with Louis T. Albarran

Christ is the only mediator, but he is not the monopoly of Christians and, in fact, he is present and effective in any authentic religion, whatever the form or the name.
—*Raimundo Pannikar*

COMPARATIVE THEOLOGIANS ENGAGE IN DIALOGUE WITH PERSONS AND texts from other traditions. In contrast, it seems that those who belong to multiple traditions make that dialogue not merely interreligious, but internally interreligious. The practice of multiple religious belonging is a serious business. Some would find it dangerous to a person's faith and personality. This pattern of "dual citizenship" or "dual allegiance" is not to be undertaken lightly.

Yet walking through any local bookstore seems to suggest otherwise. At least for the past half century, the number of books on religions other than Christianity and Judaism has grown immensely. Spiritual shoppers buy into non-Christian religions and traditions in an increasingly globalized marketplace. That people are aware of diverse traditions is a good thing. But when commodification makes access to "other" traditions seem easy, the serious demands and dangers of multiple religious belonging may be swamped by a tidal wave of comfortable, optional, and sometimes bogus spiritualities. As we noted in chapter 2, contemporary consumerism leads us to treat religions as commodities for purchase, exchangeable for cash and a bit of time, not an investment of a whole self. If religions are commodities to be easily bought and sold at the local bookstore or over the Internet, then it seems easy to dip into another religion. This is not multiple religious belonging. The level of commitment needed for multiple religious belonging risks the whole self.

People who sincerely engage other religious traditions, to the extent that they claim to belong to multiple traditions, know that belonging to a religion is not as easy as our culture might lead us to believe. Reading *Zen and the Art of Motorcycle Maintenance* on a Sunday afternoon, after having attended a Catholic mass that morning, or engaging in Zen meditation or yoga during a Christian retreat does not constitute multiple religious belonging. Rather, multiple religious belonging may even be a source of confusion and suffering (Cornille 2003, 48).

Multiple religious belonging is a technical term applied by theologians to describe a person who lives "within or between more than one religious practice" (Knitter 2002, 28) or someone who is a member of two or more "particular systems of beliefs and practices within bounded communities" (Phan 2003b, 498). We have used the metaphor of dual citizenship. This chapter explores how and why people find themselves or choose to exist in this space between religions. After discussing its more theoretical aspects and assumptions, it explores texts written by and about people who actually practice multiple religious belonging. It concludes by assessing multiple religious belonging as scholars see it and evaluating it as a legitimate way for Catholic Christians to respond to the promise of religious diversity.

Multiple Religious Belonging: Assumptions and Theoretical Aspects

The idea of belonging to dual or even multiple religions may be new to the West since the advent of Christianity, but it has been a characteristic of Asian religious cultures for centuries. Catherine Cornille noted that "in the wider history of religion, multiple religious belonging may have been the rule rather than the exception" (Cornille 2002, 1). Peter C. Phan also found that what appears to us as multiple religious belonging is not only common but has a very different cultural context than in the contemporary West. He claimed that "the very expression 'multiple religious belonging' as understood in the West . . . is a misnomer in Asia where religions are considered not as mutually exclusive religious organizations but as having specialized functions responding, according to a division of labor as it were, to the different needs and circumstances in the course of a person's life" (2003b, 498). Unlike the "Western" presumption, exemplified by Paul Griffiths's notion that one can belong only to one religious tradition because it is "a form of life which seems to those who inhabit it to be comprehensive, incapable of abandonment and of central importance" (2001b, 7), the "Eastern" presumption is that religions or religious practices are "useful means."

The possibility of belonging to multiple religions remains a theological problem for the Western monotheistic traditions, Judaism, Christianity, and Islam. These traditions do demand an absolute and exclusive commitment to their respective faiths (Phan 2003b, 498). Perhaps that is why, as Cornille pointed out, Westerners who attempt multiple religious belonging commonly approach an Eastern religion such as Buddhism first (Cornille 2003, 43; 2002, 1) which can be embraced, in some of its forms, with minimal or no "doctrinal" commitments that conflict with the expectations that Judaism, Christianity, and Islam place on their adherents.

The argument for living the hybrid existence that is characteristic of multiple religious belonging need not be as shocking to Christians as one might first think. The Catholic-Hindu-Buddhist theologian, Catholic priest, and comparative philosopher Raimundo Panikkar has argued that in many ways Christianity is already a hybrid. He wrote that "history might teach us a mighty lesson by reminding us how Jewish, Greek, Zoroastrian and other 'dogmas' seeped into the Christian mind, making themselves part of what we nowadays call the common Christian heritage" (1978, 17). Christianity is not a "pure" religion, but one that has been affected by and has incorporated elements of other traditions.

Hill Fletcher has also noted that hybridity is not new for Christians. She observed that "the 'Christian' identity of the earliest Christians was often informed also by their Jewish identity or Greek identity. They were simultaneously family members and socially related to their respective Jewish or Greek communities" (Hill Fletcher 2005, 89). Christian identities in antiquity emerged not only in conversation with the religious traditions of Judaism, Greece, and Rome, but "possibly even Buddhism and Hinduism" (Hill Fletcher 2005, 96). The ascetic practices of early monastic communities were Stoic practices. Phan took the point further, claiming that "it must be acknowledged that historically, double religious belonging was the common form of life of the earliest Christians" (2003b, 504). He refers to Acts 3:46 to warrant his claim: "they went to the temple area together every day, while in their homes they broke bread." Multiple religious belonging is one intense response to situations in which embracing hybridity is unavoidable.

Multiple belongers today tend to be religious geniuses rather than ordinary participants. Pannikar noted that "most of [humankind's] great religious geniuses did not create or found new forms of religiousness out of nothing; rather they fused more than one religious stream, moulding them with their own prophetic gifts" (1978, 68). Understanding multiple religious belonging begins with the recognition that "one can have an authentic internal religious experience in more than one religious tradition without betraying any of them" (ibid.). This is neither common nor easy. A person "cannot experiment with religions as if they were rats or plants, but one can believe in them as authentic paths and try to understand and eventually to integrate more than one religious tradition" (Panikkar 1978, 68). Spiritual shoppers tend to experiment with religions; multiple religious belongers do not merely buy into the traditions, but give themselves over to the traditions.

Cornille suggested why some might attempt simultaneously to explore the great questions of life in multiple traditions. However, the question is "why search for answers to the fundamental questions of life in only one religion when so many alternative proposals by time-honored traditions are readily available?" (Cornille 2002, 1). For someone aware of those traditions, the answer is not obvious at all. A person usually enters into multiple religious belonging as the result of participating in a sincere encounter between two or more religious traditions that are in dialogue with each other. The positive results from this encounter can occur on two levels, what John S. Dunne refers to as a "passing over" and "returning" experience on the one hand, and the practice of remaining in the space between both traditions and participating in both, rather than simply returning to one's own, on the other.

Dunne defined "passing over" as "a shifting of standpoint, a going over to the standpoint of another culture, another way of life, another religion" (1972, ix). As Lawrence Cunningham noted, for Dunne "these transits are not exercises in information gathering as if one wanted to 'store up' knowledge or experiences to enrich the cultural and intellectual horizons of a person" (Cunningham 1988, 194). Rather, something more profound occurs. In Dunne's sense of the term, passing over is "a way that one learns from, and experiences, [other] traditions in a genuinely empathetic manner, and then return[s] again to one's tradition enriched and deepened by that experience" (ibid.). "[Passing over] is followed by an equal and opposite process we might call 'coming back,' coming back with new insight to one's own culture, one's own way of life, one's own religion" (Dunne 1972, ix). For Dunne, this may not be only a mental or spiritual exercise but can also involve physically moving to another place and then later returning home.

One cannot just prepare to pass over; one must also prepare to come back. This means establishing a strong foundation before embarking on the passing-over experience in the first place, or else risk jeopardizing the essence of the experience altogether. Cunningham noted that "one cannot 'pass over' . . . in Dunne's sense of the term unless one has a deep experiential center that serves as an anchored reference point. Otherwise 'passing over' loses the sense in which Dunne intends for it and becomes a kind of dabbling in religious experience(s); a kind of spiritual tourism" (Cunningham 1988, 194). Passing over requires exercising a dual commitment to both the home ground and the host tradition; to be committed only to one makes the experience shallow.

Cornille called such passing over and returning a "deliberate and growthful experience." She argued, however, that "the experience of profound identification with one religion without losing one's attachment and commitment to another seems to be more often than not deeply confusing and spiritually unsettling." This is the second sort of experience, the experience of multiple religious belonging or life "between" and "within" the two traditions. Passing over is spiritually unsettling because, sometimes, there is "no 'coming back' from a deep identification with another religious tradition." In that case the subject finds him/herself "in between traditions, unwilling to renounce the tradition of origin and unable to deny the truth discovered in the other tradition." As Cornille put it, "it is here that we may speak of multiple religious belonging in the full and most dramatic sense of the term" (Cornille 2002, 4). Passing over and returning can lead to multiple religious belonging if the "return" is not definite or stable.

Phan has argued that Christians who engage in multiple religious belonging must make a fundamental assumption, that "it is possible and even necessary not only to accept in theory this or that doctrine or practice of other religions and to incorporate them, perhaps in a modified form, into Christianity but also to adopt and live the beliefs, moral rules, rituals, and monastic practices of religious traditions other than those of Christianity, perhaps even in the midst of the community of the devotees of other religions" (2003b, 497).

Multiple religious belonging is the limit case of what Jeannine Hill Fletcher recognized as hybridity. We are all hybrids because we all participate in multiple communities. She wrote that "our very understanding of the religious dimension of our identity is informed by the diverse features of our location and experience. There is no 'Christian' identity, only Christian identities impacted by race, gender, class, ethnicity, profession, and so on" (Hill Fletcher 2005, 88). Christian identity is also impacted by other ways of faith. Multiple religious belonging internalizes this in an exceptional way.

For someone who truly believes they belong to multiple religions, the moment of truth appears when absolute claims from the respective traditions are irreconcilable. Irreconcilable absolute truth claims pose a challenge, because a person engaged in sincere multiple religious belonging refuses the luxury of bracketing religious convictions. One response is to confront the criticism head on.

In chapter 8, we noted Paul Griffiths's point that religious injunctions may be *noncompossible* "if each prescribes a course of action and it is impossible for a single person to perform both," since such actions cannot be performed by a single person. Hence, "no one can inhabit more than one form of religious life at a time" (Griffiths 2001b, 32–34; Heim, 2001, 1–4). Multiple religious belongers can respond that they do inhabit one form of life, but at different times. In fact, some oscillate between traditions. Griffiths's view is simply a Western prejudice.

A second response is to challenge the notion that religious traditions can be isolated from one another as clearly as Griffiths implies. The examples cited above show that the boundaries are fluid and permeable. Hence, it is not clear that one cannot inhabit the liminal space between religious traditions. Certainly some Jews in the earliest Christian movements in Judaism did just that. Beyond the ancient patterns, today's "Jews for Jesus" and other groups show that hybridity can create new spaces "between" the established traditions. Multiple religious belongers do not take the pluralist way out that Griffiths effectively blocked, but find spaces that he has not seen—admittedly "deviant" from established traditions.

A third response is to recognize a kind of complementarity. Roger Corless struggled to express a vision in which Christianity and Buddhism both fit reality. He wrote that

> what Buddhists experience epistemologically as Emptiness is experienced ontologically by Christians as Christ, and that to understand the mind of Christ we need to understand Emptiness, and in order to understand Emptiness we need to understand the actions of Christ. . . . [T]he mind of Christ and Emptiness, that is to say the Gospel and the Dharma, are complementary to each other, not as yin and yang which imply each other, but perichoretically, or co-inherently, such that each is autonomous and without need of the other, but each can somehow illuminate each other so as to establish the other on a surer foundation. (1990a, 89–90)

Such a vision must originate in a mind that has belonged to both traditions. Yet it is not a fusion of what cannot be combined, two different traditions. It may be "ambiguous" (Foster 1990, 100) or "more provocative than clear" (Corless 1990b, 2), but it suggests that one might inhabit two incommensurable realms simultaneously. Here, a very dynamic image of dual citizenship applies.

A fourth response is to order one's commitments. At the entry level of interreligious dialogue, "one religion remains the primary object of religious identification, and the norm or criterion through which elements from a different religious tradition may be recognized as true or valuable" (Cornille 2003, 46). At a more complicated level, one religion undergoes a radical reformulation "according to the worldview and philosophical categories of another" (Cornille 2003, 47). This shift approaches multiple religious belonging. A famous example of someone who attempted this was the French Benedictine monk Henri Le Saux.

After failing to found an Indian Christian monastic community, Le Saux immersed himself in Hinduism and, while remaining Catholic, he used the Hindu mystical tradition of *Advaita* along with the category *saccidananda* to reformulate traditional Christian notions such as the Trinity and the Christian view of human beings in a personal dialogue with God according to Hinduism (Cornille 2003, 47; Dupuis 2002, 71). *Advaita* is the tradition of nonduality. Ultimately, all the universe is one, and the diversity we see is destined to be united in the Ultimate Unity. *Saccidananda* is the union of being, knowledge, and bliss in God, a union that is echoed in each human being. Like Fr. Bede Griffiths, also known as Swami Dayananda ("the joy of compassion") and the founder of a monastic community called *Saccidananda*, Le Saux never remained only within the Hindu tradition or only within the Christian tradition. He remains a paradigm of multiple religious belonging. He stood in that "space" between Hinduism and Christianity created by the hope for an ultimate convergence of the religious traditions (see Dupuis 1997, 278–79).

A fifth response is to deny that the truth that characterizes faith traditions is propositional. Griffiths presumes that the truth of a tradition can be formulated in propositions. These may be contradictory or contrary, compatible or incompatible, commensurable or incommensurable. Yet Sallie B. King, professor of religion at James Madison University and a committed Quaker-Buddhist, challenged this presumption. Her claim has been that religious truth is not doctrinal or dogmatic (that is, propositional) but experiential. As a Quaker, she follows George Fox in allowing that the "authority of religious experience, that is, the Inner Light, to be superior to that of scripture" (King 2005, 93). She has claimed that the same point is to be found in Buddhism. She quotes contemporary Zen teacher Thich Nhat Hanh: "Do not be idolatrous about or bound to any doctrine, theory, or ideology, even Buddhist ones. All systems of thought are guiding means; they are not absolute truths" (King 2005, 96). Just as one may know two languages fluently, so one may come to know and accept two (or more) faith traditions. Raimundo Panikkar has made a similar claim in arguing that the nine sutras he develops from the experience of encountering Christ are not theses to be defended but "condensations of experiences lived (and often suffered) within the framework of tradition" (Pannikar 2004, 143).

Multiple religious belonging, living in multiple religious spaces, may lead to a person losing a clear sense of one's primary religious commitment. Cornille put it this way:

> The loss of one's original or primary religious commitment may also lead to a genuinely intermediate position in which one tradition is normative in certain areas of belief and practice and another tradition in other areas. Buddhism may thus be believed to be true and normative in certain fundamental questions and Christianity in others, or one may submit to the absolute authority of a Buddhist teacher on some issues and to a Christian teacher on others. It is here that one might

rightly speak of an experience of double religious belonging. (Cornille 2003, 46)

Peter Phan noted that at the heart of multiple religious belonging, the primacy that is granted to one religious tradition over another "is not a matter that is settled once and for all but continually fluctuates, depending on the circumstances" (2003b, 510). It also may be that one gets lost in a maze that has no exit.

In theory, then, multiple religious belonging occupies a precarious place. In tension with the accepted patterns of the traditions they seek to inhabit, the multiple religious belongers inhabit a space that may undermine their faith commitments in the name of an illusory hope for convergence. *Pace* Griffiths, multiple religious belonging is not impossible. Yet Cornille and others are quite right to point out its instabilities.

Multiple Religious Belonging in Practice

Multiple religious belonging is "a lived drama of tension, never fully resolved on the theoretical level, but affirmed at the existential plane" (Phan 2003b, 513). The only way to engage multiple religious belonging, then, is through practice. Sallie King has had a "double identity" as a Quaker and a Buddhist for two decades (King 2005, 88). As she stated about her own life, "[doing] these practices and engaging them with seriousness and commitment are what mark me as a Buddhist and a Quaker" (King 1994, 158). Panikkar argued that in the engagement "[one] must be prepared to stake everything he is and believes . . . because the venture hazards—or to be more precise, let us say makes possible—a conversion so thoroughgoing that the convictions and beliefs he had hitherto held may vanish or undergo a far-reaching change." In short, one's engagement must be so sincere that "you gamble your life" (Panikkar 1978, 13)—not quite the price the spiritual shopper pays.

Roger Corless, a Catholic-Buddhist, and King provide contemporary examples of people engaging multiple religious belonging. They have both written personal accounts of their experience with multiple religious belonging and published these articles in *Buddhist-Christian Studies*. Their accounts illumine multiple religious belonging for the reader on a very intimate level, and, in the case of Corless, should the reader choose to engage his proposal, experience it first hand.

In "A Form for Buddhist-Christian Coinherent Meditation" (1994), Roger Corless, emeritus professor of religion at Duke University, presented a very personal, reflective, and thought-provoking description of his own attempts to practice both Buddhism and Christianity in one prayerful, meditative experience. He began by acknowledging the fact that indeed certain truths in Buddhism and Christianity may contradict each other, but that does not force him to abandon his project. To allow for multiple religious belonging he employs a distinctively Christian concept of coinherence, used at the Council of Nicaea (325 C.E.) to clarify seemingly contradictory christological claims. As Corless explained, the council applied the concept of coinherence to state "that the divinity and the humanity of Christ each enclose the other totally yet without blending or interfering with each other" (1994, 139). In general, then, Corless uses coinherence as a model to allow for "the full and equal mutual presence of contradictory entities" (ibid.). For Corless, this means that his Buddhism will remain Buddhist and his Christianity will remain Christian in his meditation. So what's the point? Corless states: "the main purpose of the meditation is the acknowledgment of Buddhism and Christianity as two Absolute Systems coinhering on the same planet (in humanity as a whole) and in your own consciousness. What these systems will then do is not your concern" (ibid.).

After his introductory statements and clarifications, Corless walked the reader through an account of how one might practice a Buddhist-Christian meditation. He started with a thick description of the elements he uses during his meditations, then explained the invocations and mantras he used, and concluded by visualizing specific symbols from the respective traditions coinhering.

Items needed for the meditation are (1) a shrine, (2) rosary or other prayer beads, and (3) an icon of Buddhist-Christian coinherence. Each item has a crucial significance. Corless did not outline any specific requirements for assembling a shrine, except that it ought to contain "items illustrative of, or important to, your spiritual autobiography, items which speak to your Deep Self" (Corless 1994, 139). "Your Deep Self is to be recognized as a microcosm of Gaia, the planet earth considered as a living and conscious being, the womb from which both Buddhism and Christianity (and, indeed, all religions, philosophies, and ideologies whatsoever) have sprung and the common matrix that they now coinhabit (139–40). A rosary is an aide "in the recitation of the suggested mantras" (140). The icon of Buddhist-Christian coinherence is needed for the all-important visualization component. His is basically two concentric, eight-spoked wheels.

With the previous items in place, one is ready to begin the meditation. First, there is the invocation of the Gaia, "calling to mind the arising of Buddhism and Christianity out of Mother Gaia" (Corless 1994, 140). The series of words for this part are a variation of something like: "Praise to you, GAIA! Mother from whose belly we all come." Then, there is the invocation of the Dharma and the Gospel. In this one calls to mind "the enlightenment of Sakyamuni Tathagata under the Bodhi Tree," with words similar to "Come, our Refuge, venerable Buddhas." The mantra "*OM-AH-HUM*" is repeated ninety-nine times, for all the Buddhas of the past, while visualizing "the Triple Treasure in front of you, in the form of three blazing, wish-fulfilling jewels," recalling the three jewels of the Buddhist tradition, "I take refuge in the dharma, I take refuge in the buddha, I take refuge in the samgha (the monastic community)." After a short silence, one calls to mind Jesus Christ's crucifixion and resurrection saying, "Come, God our Father and Mother; Come, God the Word; Come, God the Holy Spirit; Come!" Then, the practitioner repeats the mantra "MARANA-THA" ninety-nine times, "symbolizing the coming of Christ into the world (1 Cor 16:22)," while visualizing the Trinity "in the form of three interlocking circles of light." After that, there is another short period of silence (Corless 1994, 140–42).

The last major part allows the two religions to meet. One calls to mind both God and the Buddhas saying, "Come, Holy Trinity! Come, Holy Triple Treasure! Come!" The final mantra and the visualization for this meditation is a most important part: One is to repeat the mantra "MARANA-THA OM-AH-HUM" ninety-nine times while visualizing a chalice, "above which there is, on one side, the Triple Treasure and on the other side, the Trinity." Then, at the one-hundredth recitation, one is to say the syllable "MAH (a sound contained in, and therefore symbolizing the coinherence of, the mantras MARANA-THA and OM-AH-HUM)," while visualizing "the symbols of the Trinity and the Triple Treasure moving toward each other, dropping into the bowl of the chalice, and, when they reach the node of the chalice, transforming into the coinherence symbol (two concentric, eight-spoked wheels)." At this point, one allows the "energies" and "realities" of Buddhism and Christianity "to sit and marvel at each other." The important thing to remember is Corless's disclaimer from the beginning of the meditation: "what these systems will then do is not your concern" (Corless 1994, 142).

Crucial to appreciating Corless's practice is understanding that it is rooted not only in a profound religious commitment but also in decades of study. Corless is not suggesting that one just start "doing it" without learning about the faith traditions involved. Rather, the ritual practice deepens the understanding and the understanding guides the practice. Nor does the sort of ritual Corless describes preclude one from participating in Catholic sacraments or Buddhist meditation. The combination, however, may well change the ways one participates in those practices.

Sallie B. King offered her own reflections on how to understand multiple religious belonging in "Religion as Practice: A Zen-Quaker Internal Dialogue." King emphasized that these insights came to her through Quaker practice. She reported that "the gist of these thoughts came to me one Sunday morning as I sat in silent Quaker meeting for worship. I do not offer these remarks in any normative sense as suggestions to anyone as to how one should understand religious identity, but as a simple report of my own views, offered in the spirit of dialogue" (1994, 157). In fact, her whole notion of multiple religious belonging stems from the fact that she is drawn to the practices of both traditions. As she put it,

> I am a Quaker because I am drawn to Quaker practice, specifically to the unprogrammed, largely silent meeting for worship with spontaneous verbal ministry from any of those assembled; to corporate decision making "in the Light," as Quakers say, at the monthly business meetings; to lay ministry in a community of equals; to the challenge of spiritual social activism inherent in Quakerism; and to the community life of Quakers. I am also a Buddhist because I am drawn to Buddhist practice, specifically to a variety of meditation and mindfulness practices; to the discipline and self-expression of the five lay precepts; to the challenge of spiritual social activism inherent in the Buddhist group of which I am a member; and to the community life of Buddhists. Wanting to do these practices and engaging in them with seriousness and commitment are what mark me as a Buddhist and a Quaker. (1994, 157–58)

King noted, however, that it is not as if a person can just randomly belong to multiple religions. There is the basic requirement of time and effort; something King refers to as "caring energy."

> I could do more things, religious and otherwise, than I do now, but I could not do them with care. That is, I could not give myself to them with any seriousness; I could not call up the energy to concentrate and bore into them in any depth. The same limitation applies to a sequential monogamy of religious affiliations. As in interpersonal relationships, whether marriage or friendship, so also in religious practice one can only attend with care to a small number of serious affiliations in a human lifetime. Long-term commitment and the expenditure of lavish amounts of caring energy are required in order to enjoy and benefit from the relationship. (1994, 158)

King's writing shows the intensity of the commitment demanded of the authentic dual belonger.

King's approach is different from Corless's in that she is not as concerned with bringing the two religions together. As she put it, "The value of being both a Quaker and a Buddhist to me is the ways in which the practices of each are unlike the other. I have nothing against synthetic practices, but I am not looking for them, either. I want to do both Buddhist and Quaker practices, rather than a synthesis of the two" (1994, 161). Her reason for keeping the two religions separate rather than creating a synthesis of the two is practical. King has recognized that each religion "has strengths which the other lacks and for me the strengths of each complement what is comparatively weak in the other" (ibid.).

In Corless and King we see two patterns for practicing multiple religious belonging. Corless, like Le Saux and Griffiths, looks for a future convergence anticipated in present practice. King, like Pannikar, finds mutual enrichment in the different practices. Neither is much worried about doctrine for the sake of doctrine.

Why Belong to Multiple Religious Traditions?

Raimundo Panikkar has stressed the need to go beyond our common understanding of interreligious dialogue and to consider "the often-neglected notion of an *intrareligious* dialogue" (Panikkar 1978, 40), which we have above called "internal interreligious dialogue." He fears that interreligious dialogue does not become actual dialogue because of our concern with the phenomenological epoche—"the bracketing of one's 'faith' as the necessary condition for fruitful 'interfaith dialogue'" (1978, 41). Intrareligious dialogue is "an inner dialogue within myself, an encounter in the depth of my personal religiousness, having met another religious experience on that very intimate level" (Panikkar 1978, 40). Intrareligious dialogue, then, assumes multiple religious belonging because the two religious traditions meet not in a "dialectical arena that leaves both [religions] untouched but in a self that besides being myself is also shared by the other" (1978, 40–41). This level of dialogue allows for a more authentic and fruitful experience of other religious traditions than does an external dialogue.

At its best, multiple religious belonging, in the form of intrareligious dialogue rooted in diverse religious practice, allows a member from one religion to experience the other religion not as "other" but from "within" the religion. This has two positive effects. Multiple religious belonging can become a means to reconciliation, and it can also serve as an opportunity to enrich the religion of origin. Methodist theologian and process philosopher John B. Cobb, Jr., an emeritus professor from Claremont Graduate School, argued that true multiple religious belongers ought also to confront the failings of the different religious traditions as well as their benefits. Multiple belongers can be in a position to utilize the encounter with the other religion as a means to enrich the religion of origin and reconcile the people of different traditions who have insulted or injured others. As Cobb suggested regarding Christianity's relationship with Judaism, "we must transform both our teaching and our practice to embrace our elder brothers and sisters in the Abrahamic faith. We must learn from them about who and what we have been and also about ways in which we can incorporate elements of their wisdom into our lives" (Cobb 2002, 25). He suggested a similar encounter with Muslims, Indians, and Native Americans.

Why should those of us who are "monotraditional" appreciate multiple belongers? The fact is that they have much to teach us about our own tradition as well as others'. Cornille commented that Cobb understands that "the sins and injustices committed against other peoples and religions can only be understood from within those traditions, [and] it takes individuals versed in both religions to bring about the insights and awareness necessary to promote peace" (Cornille 2002, 4). If multiple belongers can aid in that task, monotraditionalists can be grateful to them.

Catholic Principles and Multiple Belonging

It is impossible to apply the four principles developed in chapter 3 directly to the claims of multiple religious belongers. Each of them is a doctrinal principle. As we have seen, multiple religious belongers are far more centered on experience and practice than doctrine. Some of them reject the doctrinal approach. However, we can consider "The Rules of the Game in the Religious Encounter," as Pannikar titled one of his essays, to show how one multiple belonger considered rules similar to those we developed in chapter 3. Pannikar's reflections, of course, may not be shared by the others discussed above. But the point is to show that someone who engages in this practice has reflected on and has sought to abide by rules like those we found to shape the Catholic tradition and laid out in chapter 3.

Those who practice multiple religious belonging simply presume God's universal salvific will. Although the concept of God implied by someone like Le Saux requires rather different articulation than the traditional approach, that God, however conceived, has provided a world in which so many practices are available for human flourishing. In a move similar to Heim's, considered in chapter 8, some consider the possibility of multiple religious ends; others are more comfortable with a pluralist intuition that there is one fulfillment for all that is better than anyone has yet imagined. Multiple belongers are sympathetic with the notion that "salvation" has wildly diverse meanings. Pannikar makes his conformity to the first rule explicit: "God wills that all men should reach salvation. Here salvation is that which is considered to be the end, goal, destination or destiny of Man, however this may be conceived" (Pannikar 1978, 36).

Multiple religious belonging is not necessarily inconsistent with the second rule. Pannikar found that "Christ is the only mediator, but he is not the monopoly of Christians and, in fact, he is present and effective in any authentic religion, whatever the form or the name" (1978, 36). Jacques Dupuis observed that "while it may be true that there exists a mutual complementarity between Christianity and the other religions, it cannot be said that this mutual complementarity is a symmetrical one" (Dupuis 2002, 66). Pannikar's approach suggests the presence of divine grace in and through the various traditions that can be construed as similar to Dupuis's view. However, Pannikar's approach to complementarity suggests the possibility of more symmetry than Dupuis or other contemporary inclusivists would accept.

The third and fourth rules have a unique relationship within the category of multiple religious belonging. Recall that the third rule is "thou shall not deny the necessity of the church for salvation," while the fourth rule is "thou shalt affirm the dignity of each and all human persons." In multiple religious belonging, the fourth rule is sometimes emphasized over the third rule. This preference fits with the intimate relationships and concerns multiple religious belongers share with and for other religions. However, it need not mean that multiple religious belongers "deny the necessity of the church for salvation." It may simply mean that they conceive of the church the way Panikkar conceives of the church. He states, the "church, as the sociological dimension of religion, is the organism of salvation (by definition); but the Church is not coextensive with the visible Christian Church" (Panikkar 1978, 36). Like many inclusivists and pluralists, Pannikar refuses to identify the people of God—the church—with the Roman Catholic Church. Indeed, it is not a position Catholics ought hold (see Sullivan 2006).

Catherine Cornille has elegantly articulated a warning against regarding multiple religious belonging as an ideal or normal situation. Although critical of the practices, she has conceded "that many of us have benefitted from the experiences and struggles of pioneers or 'liminal figures' who have experimented with double religious belonging. But that does not necessarily mean that it should or could be advocated as an ideal" (2003, 49). Peter Phan sounded another warning. He has noted that the pioneers of multiple religious belonging "were highly competent in the classical languages of these religions and intimately familiar with their sacred texts and even held doctorates in Hinduism and Buddhism. . . . [W]ithout this hard and patient intellectual work, multiple religious belonging runs the risk of shallowness and trendiness" (2003b, 511). Phan properly worries that the "shallowness" is more characteristic of our contemporary situation because the intellectual competence displayed by the early pioneers "seems to be lacking in many contemporary Western practitioners of multiple religious belonging" (2003b, 511). He continued:

> While it [multiple religious belonging] has been made more acceptable by recent theologies of religions, its practice by people, especially the young, who do not possess the necessary qualifications that were present, to an eminent degree, in those pioneers, can easily lead to the "nebulous esoteric mysticism" and "Nietzschean neo-paganism" that we have been warned against. (2003b, 514)

Raimundo Panikkar, one of the pioneers of multiple religious belonging, gave a warning similar to Cornille's and Phan's many years ago:

I need hardly add that not everyone is called to such an undertaking, nor is everyone capable of it. Besides a particular cast of mind, it pre-supposes perhaps a special constellation in one's character and back-ground that enables one to undergo the experience without any taint of exoticism, exhibitionism or simply unremitting intellectualism. (1978, 12)

It is worth noting that for all the warnings and cautions issued about multiple religious belonging, the critics surely recognize, as Panikkar does, that given the complexities of our U.S. site and the fact that we are all hybrids, "one way or another we are all embarked on the venture" (Panikkar 1978, 22).

It is not clear that mainstream Christian traditions ought to encourage mul-tiple religious belonging. Indeed, it is not clear that the belongers themselves would *encourage* any who were not already inclined toward their difficult prac-tices to engage in them. However, it is also not clear that such an esoteric prac-tice should be rejected. Charitably understood, multiple religious belongers may indeed fit the principles that shape the Catholic tradition. That fit may be "loose," but the mystics and other "strange ones" of the tradition whose prac-tices are not "for all" may well show the rest of us possibilities that we had not conceived. In so doing, they serve the life of the tradition and the thriving of the community.

We agree with the nuanced appraisals and warnings collected in this chap-ter. They guard against an overly optimistic view of multiple religious belong-ing. Our response to multiple religious belonging is like that of most of us to sky diving, motorcycle jumping, and piloting spacecraft: we can appreciate the skill of those who engage in the practices, but its dangers and distinctiveness are not, and should not be advocated, for all. We also have some sympathy with critics who find that multiple religious belonging stretches the rules so far that they break.

Pannikar's final caution properly leads us to our final chapter. How can we as theologians working on the U.S. Catholic site assess this variety of ways for dealing with the perils, the problems, and the promise of religious diversity in our world and even in our homes?

11

Theologies of Religious Diversity

A "Site Specific" Evaluation

by the seminar

THE CATHOLIC CHURCH IS EVOLVING RAPIDLY IN THE UNITED STATES. IN addition to a cultural context shaped by continued immigration, religious diversity, political nonestablishment, market-driven commodification, and globalization, generational differences affect the church.

A rapidly dwindling senior cohort came of age religiously before the watershed event of the Second Vatican Council (1962–65). Born before World War II, their church was hierarchically structured, doctrinally rigid, laden with myriad devotional practices, and centered on a Latin mass that was incomprehensible to most, yet internationally unifying because it was celebrated the same way around the globe. Those born in the 1940s and '50s were decisively shaped by the perceived revolution of Vatican II and its aftermath. The unchanging church changed: the church's structure became democratized, and visible female leaders emerged; its authoritative teaching on sexuality, reproduction, and other issues was controverted; its devotional practices were mostly abandoned; and a vernacular Eucharist came to be led by a clerical presider and a host of lay ministers. Those born in the '60s and '70s found a church that encouraged people on their spiritual quests, hoped people would choose to listen to its historic wisdom, and worshiped in a bewildering variety of styles from chanted Latin masses to jazz, folk, and rock Eucharistic celebrations; during this period, while a "conservative backlash" emerged, represented visually by a peripatetic paternal pope who was both scholar and media celebrity featured regularly on secular channels and on Mother Angelica's Eternal Word Television Network. Those born in the '80s and '90s who are now coming of age may be a generation of "evangelical Catholics" who were not given much of a religious identity by their church. They have had to form their own identity by making a decision for the church, just as religiously unformed Protestants may have to respond to an evangelical preacher's altar call to accept Jesus as their personal Lord and Savior (see D'Antonio et al. 2001; Portier 2004).

Generations younger than the senior cohort have had to choose their religious path. Many no longer inherit a tradition definite enough to bother rebelling against. They have become generations of seekers (Roof et al. 1993). Given the increasing influence of commodification, these generations can be lured into seeking salvation in the spiritual marketplace. Given globalization, the religious wares and ways on offer have also multiplied. Globalization and commodification are of increasing importance for evaluating the suitability of theologies or religious diversity for theologizing on the U.S. site.

Beyond differences of generations, gender, economic class, race, ethnicity, and sexual orientation among its members, the church has been rocked by revelations of sexual crimes and perversions among the "celibate" clergy. These revelations also disclosed pathetically inept or corrupt exercises of episcopal oversight. Dioceses have resorted to secular bankruptcy courts to save their assets from being dispersed to pay off successful suits by the victims of unreported sex crimes. The greatest challenge to the church may be to endure its greatest scandal ever in this country. The effect of this crisis relevant here may be that it increases the pressure to "choose" one's path in the face of the crisis. Not only are some seekers likely to search out other paths, but others are also likely to choose aggressively to hold fast even more strongly to the identity markers that give meaning and definition to the tradition that certain members of the church choose to live in and live out.

Those in recent generations who are not well formed in their home traditions have often become spiritual shoppers, not by choice, but by default. In an era that finds mainstream churches losing their appeal while spiritual hunger continues unabated, spiritual shopping may be the only live option. Yet the spiritual shopper may not remain a shopper as Jerry Rubin did (see p. 38 above). Eventually the shopper may bring home the goods and allow them to grow in her and herself to grow in them. After all, many people who date a lot eventually settle down into a monogamous marriage. Although it may be countercultural and counter to commodification, a shopper may lose his life only thus to find it. Whether many spiritual shoppers actually come to give themselves to a faith tradition and stop shopping is unknown; anecdotal evidence supports the claim that this happens, but says nothing about its extent.

Generational difference affect members of all religious traditions. The "Greatest Generation" is succeeded by Baby Boomers, Generation X, and Millennials in a rapidly changing culture that challenges all religious traditions. Intermarriage between people of different ethnicities, religions, and races has become increasingly more common. Late capitalist society has commodified nearly everything, including religious comforts, so that spiritual shopping is no longer the domain of a leisured elite. As the destruction of the World Trade Center towers and the later bombing of buses and trains in London, Madrid, and Mumbai indicate, globalization has not only reshaped the global hyperculture but made it possible for the tribalist reactions occasionally to erupt far from the locales that are their homes.

Given these specific recent complications on the site sketched in chapter 2, how can we evaluate the positions sketched in chapters 3 to 10 for their effectiveness on this site? Perhaps we had best begin with what we cannot do.

First, we cannot evaluate the persons who articulated the positions and practices. Beyond the fact that all are, at least, of sound mind and good heart, most of them are at home in more than one practice. Dupuis, Griffiths, Fredericks, Clooney, Knitter, Heim, Pannikar, and others who have represented various theories and positions here have engaged in interreligious dialogue and comparative theology. Heim, Fredericks, Phan, Clooney, Di Noia, and others may be inclusivist in attitude even if they are not much inclined to inclusivist theories. Knitter's and D'Costa's positions have evolved significantly. The point is to discuss the practices and theories, not the scholars whom we have used to exemplify them.

Second, as noted in the introduction, we cannot simply compare the positions and practices to one another to judge them. They are incommensurable because of their substantial differences. It makes no sense to ask whether nonfoundational practices provide a firm foundation, which practice has the best foundational theory, or how well particularists appreciate the multiple paths to one salvation. We could ask these sorts of questions, but the answers would not be judgments but expressions of prejudices in favor of one position. Nonetheless, we can ask how they deal with specific issues to get a handle on their suitability for those who live on this site.

Third, we cannot discern their utility for every site. We can try to discern their suitability only for this specific site by seeing how each deals with particular issues, opportunities, cultural characteristics, or problems. The conclusions that we reach are not "principled," that is, conclusive judgments made strictly on the basis of applying clear rules. Rather, they are "practical," that is, tentative judgments offered as pro tem assessments in light of their evident suitability for this site. We presume that sites that have similar characteristics may find some use in these judgments.

Fourth, we cannot determine whether any of these patterns should become dominant in religious education. Religious educators need to form their charges, whether young or old, in the ways of their tradition. Yet they must also actively encourage Christians to listen respectfully to those who live in and live out other faith traditions. That we have sometimes, at least, failed to do so is evinced by Wuthnow's reporting that the most important thing others want from Christian communities and individuals is "greater respect and understanding" (Wuthnow 2005, 64). Participants in other faith traditions do not, for the most part, want to convert to Christianity. Nor are they dissatisfied with their own traditions, as some Christians seem to assume. As Wuthnow put it,

> What American Hindus, Buddhists, and Muslims most often say they want from American Christians is simply greater understanding. Some of them would like converts to their religion, but most are interested in gaining respect. They do not mean this only in a politically correct way, but in terms of greater familiarity and knowledge. . . . They do not expect Christians to give up being Christians or Christian leaders to fundamentally alter their teachings. But they realize that they are a presence with which Americans are going to have to come to terms. . . . They believe better understanding would be good for the rest of the population as well. (2005, 72)

The tolerance of indifference is not sufficient. Nor is it sufficient to simply dismiss the religious other as either eternally damned or "not really different." Although the diversity of faith traditions is not something that we can ignore but must respond to positively, it is not clear than any one of the theories analyzed here supports religious and interreligious education better than another. Obviously, we do not advocate dual belonging, especially when so many are unsteady in their understanding of their own traditions. But given that unsteadiness, how religious educators ought to approach the salvific efficacy and the truth claims of other traditions is undecidable on the basis of principles alone.

More positively, we keep in mind something distinctively Catholic. *Dialogue and Proclamation* § 42 identified four practices that are crucial in a situation of religious diversity. First is the practice of living together so as to support one another in the local context of religious diversity (the dialogue of life). Second is the practice of collaboration across faith traditions to work for justice and development for all people (the dialogue of action). Third is the practice of seeking to understand our own heritage and to appreciate others' heritages as well; all can learn from participants in other traditions by listening to and appreciating the testimony and criticism of others (the dialogue of theological exchange). Fourth are the practices that involve sharing spiritual values and practices across traditions, as when Tibetan Buddhist and Western monastics share their traditions and practices or when religious leaders of various traditions prayed with each other at Assisi in 1986 (the dialogue of religious experience). We keep these practices in mind as we engage in our evaluations.

The practices prescribed by *Dialogue and Proclamation* are just the sort of practices needed for the emergence of the "reflective pluralism" that Wuthnow found the key to healthy religious diversity in the United States. Reflective pluralism occurs when people committed to different faith traditions understand, respect, cooperate with, and support those who belong to other faith traditions. Reflective religious "pluralism involves more than the mere coexistence of multiple traditions. At the very minimum, it requires engagement across traditions. And such engagement necessarily challenges preconceived ideas about beliefs and values" (Wuthnow 2005, 104–5). Religiously committed people can meet those challenges, sometimes by standing firm in their beliefs and practices, sometimes by adopting a religiously richer view. We happily conclude that the practices commended in *Dialogue and Proclamation* § 42 are entirely appropriate for the U.S. site and its needs.

Inclusivisms on the U.S. Site

Perhaps the most promising and threatening concept for theologizing on this site remains that of Rahner's anonymous Christian. This concept can help Christians recognize participants in other faith traditions (or of no faith tradition at all) as people who have been touched by divine grace and not rejected it. If Christians are prone to nativist prejudices as new immigrant groups bear their distinctive religious traditions to the United States, then the concept of the anonymous Christian may be beneficial. Rabbi Jonathan Sacks has challenged us, "Can we find, in the human 'thou', a fragment of the Divine 'Thou'? Can we recognize God's image in one who is not in my image? There are times when God meets us in the face of a stranger" (2003, 17). Classic inclusivism provides support for committed Christians to meet the challenge of treating newer immigrants with respect and dignity as people touched and loved by God and who have responded to God's touch, even though they do not acknowledge Jesus.

"Christian identities are always 'hybrid', that is, they are created by intersecting with other categories of identity" (Hill Fletcher 2005, 89). Christians have already incorporated insights and practices from other traditions into their own. Classic inclusivism may encourage complacency. Assuming that God cares for the religious others may seem to imply that we do not need to do so. It also may discourage people from recognizing others as truly different, not merely "like us" in their religious practices and beliefs.

Classic inclusivism also tends to privilege one tradition over others. This attitude may be religiously unavoidable, as Gavin D'Costa argued, but is civically problematic. Rather than being concerned about political establishment, inclusivists have been concerned with more general cultural trends. Rahner saw Europe become increasingly less Christian as Christianity became "culturally disestablished." The majority of Dupuis's work was developed in a minority situation. D'Costa's experience of both India and Europe sets his work in pluralistic situations. As a view generally developed within Christianity as a way to enable Christians to understand their responsibilities with respect to relating to non-Christians, inclusivists have used traditional Christian concepts, but have done so in a situation that is post-Christendom. For inclusivism to be useful, it must be carefully sundered from any notion of cultural hegemony, for such hegemony no longer exists, even if inclusivists cannot but religiously prefer their own tradition's ways.

Commodification has led to spiritual shopping. "Spiritual shopping among a wide variety of religions presupposes exposure to religions other than the faith of one's upbringing" (Wuthnow 2005, 110). The criticism that classic inclusivism is too parochially Christian may be transformed into a boon on the U.S. site. Classic inclusivism works to preserve the meaning of Christian beliefs, symbols, rituals, practices, and attitudes. Anonymous Christianity does not invite Christian to buy into others traditions, but to revere them as God reveres them. Dupuis's argument for inclusive pluralism, recognizing that other traditions may be God's gifts as vehicles of grace, presents an especially apt development of classic inclusivism for the United States. Dupuis claims that faith traditions other than Christianity can be de jure, rather than just de facto, traditions that transmit God's grace. While other traditions are not the same as or complementary to Christianity, inclusive pluralism suggests that the traditions, as well as the people who inhabit them, are to be respected as divinely graced in the concrete circumstances of the diversity of religions and cultures. Properly understood, classic and contemporary inclusivisms should discourage complacency and encourage interaction and mutual support.

Globalization has not just made the world small with regard to communication; it has brought varying cultures into immediate contact and people from diverse cultures and tradition into one another's immediate vicinity. One result of this has been resistance when one culture tends to dominate others. This phenomenon lies behind criticisms of the missionary movement in the United States during the twentieth century, whereby missionaries have been perceived as agents of American culture rather than, or in addition to, the church.

With regard to religious traditions, then, there is also the possibility of domination and resistance. One of the major criticisms of the classical inclusivist approach of Rahner (and D'Costa in his more recent work), but that is not so relevant to Dupuis's work, is that it does not allow for an understanding of the non-Christian in the context of her own tradition. Wuthnow's statement that "What American Hindus, Buddhists, and Muslims most often report they want from American Christians is simply greater understanding" (2005, 72) shows that mutual respect and dignity are lacking in Christians' practice. Understanding is the desire; domination is the tendency. However, regard for the other through intimate understanding of the meaning of her beliefs, symbols, rituals, practices, and attitudes involves some type of movement into the other's religious culture and is a move distinctive to Dupuis's theory and D'Costa's practice.

Inclusivist theologies clearly improve on traditional Christian exclusivism. Whether the practices of dialogue that Wuthnow called for, that Rabbi Sacks commends, and that *Dialogue and Proclamation* mandate need such a theory is debatable; certainly the nonfoundationalists would think the theory superfluous. Nonetheless, contemporary developments in the inclusivist camp seem better suited for the needs of the U.S. site than classic inclusivism. Preaching this approach on this site could well be a boon for Catholics in particular and Christians in general who live with and support members of other faith traditions in a mutual search for peace and justice—including the justice that comes when religious differences are recognized as divine gifts, not evils to be overcome.

Mutualism and the U.S. Site

The mutualist approach clearly would encourage avoiding nativist elitism. The strength of the position is its commitment to mobilize diverse religious communities against common problems. As noted in chapter 6, both Hick's pluralist view and Knitter's mutualist approach are rooted in their authors' increasing awareness of religious diversity brought about in part by immigration. Hence, pluralist approaches in general are designed to function well in a nation of immigrants, but theoretical pluralism like Hick's is untenable for Catholics on this site. The justice-oriented mutualist variant not only seems to fit (if roughly) Catholic principles, but also fulfills Wuthnow's calls for engagement between persons of different faith traditions.

The nonestablishment of religions in the United States should produce a civic respect for the diversity of religions that is not to be confused with theological pluralism. Theological pluralists who disavow claims of religious superiority also logically support the nonestablishment of religions. The mutualist approach fits exceedingly well with Wuthnow's call for interreligious concern, dialogue, understanding, and cooperation. Perhaps more than any other position under consideration, a mutualist approach supports the cultural need to develop (in Wuthnow's sense) a reflective civic pluralism.

Commodification of religion is a major obstacle to pluralism's usefulness in the U.S. site. A self-aggrandizing consumerist approach to religion is a particular threat to all religious communities in the United States. Pluralism could be suspected of being particularly vulnerable to this malady because of its openness to other faith traditions as either philosophically pointing toward "the same" ultimate reality or mystically generating "the same" silence. A person who subscribed to pluralism might be more likely to dabble in the wisdom and sacred scriptures of other faith traditions.

The mutualist variant on pluralism, however, may provide an antidote to the poison of commodification. Knitter claimed that his focus on *Soteria* allowed a Christian to focus on salvation through Christ with an active role for the church (1987b, 187). Knitter asserted that simply because the kingdom of God is first in his schema it does not imply that the Spirit is second (1996, 131). More importantly, the focus of working for justice is not on the development of a self but on the creation of a just and peaceful society. This approach resists commodification of religious practices and beliefs because of its focus. Working wholeheartedly for the aim of realizing such a society is a practice that shapes the practitioner. Shaping a life worth living is not the goal (as for shoppers) but the effect of living for the goal of justice. Knitter's liberation-based mutualism is less likely to encourage subordination of religious tenets and practices to an abstract concept such as the ultimate reality or to encourage people to distance themselves from their own religious traditions to shop in the religious markets of the world. Thus, Knitter's *Soteria* or concern for human well-being is directly opposed to consumerism and commodification. One can never argue that this threat is ever fully averted within the U.S. site for theology, but mutualism seems a very appropriate theological approach because it respects diversity and encourages cooperation between members of various faith traditions.

A standard criticism is that pluralism is a Western academic view imposed on other traditions. James L. Fredericks has argued that justice-based pluralism placed obstacles for dialogue in front of any religious group not interested in the kind of justice mutualists advocated (1998, 134). Knitter responded by arguing recently that his justice-based pluralism casts a wide net in looking for potential improvements to human welfare and alleviating suffering. He contended that it would be imperialistic to assume that the West had a monopoly on any particular method or goal or understanding of what constitutes justice. He also has argued that acceptance of pluralism in non-Western faith traditions is ample evidence that pluralism is not being imposed by the West (2005b, 38–42).

Wuthnow claimed that lasting and fruitful interreligious undertakings tend to consist of dedicated individuals in local communities working on specific shared concerns (2005, 303). Mutualism supports such effective sustained interreligious dialogue rather than sounding like an abstract imperialistic imposition. Mutualists do not imperialistically impose their own views on others, but allow concrete understandings of peace and justice to emerge from dialogues about the problems that the dialogue partners agree need to be addressed. Pope John Paul II claimed in 2002 that all religions contain within them the desire for peace and that this could become a common project around which meaningful religious dialogue should occur (Baum 2005, 144). As the desire for peace and justice is not the sole property of Christianity or the West, these mutualist goals fit with contemporary Catholic teaching.

While classic forms of pluralism may be unacceptable for anyone subscribing to the principles discussed in chapter 3 and be susceptible to supporting spiritual shopping in a commodified culture, mutualism that is based in the mutual seeking for justice and peace among members of varied religious traditions avoids both those problems.

One major problem mutualists seem to overlook is *traditio*. How can the faith tradition be passed to the next generation? Why ought it? Mutualism simply presumes that the people whom it addresses are sufficiently well formed in a faith tradition both to stand firm in their own tradition and to richly engage members of other traditions in seeking after justice. Given our culture, how can a mutualist approach help preserve a faith tradition? Yet if "justice" is the key, the question arises why one ought form people in a particular tradition. If one says that the traditions are good instruments for producing people concerned with justice, then one makes the faith tradition a useful tool, rather than a comprehensive form of life. If one says that the good worth pursuing is justice, then why bother with religion? Why not work to have people politically engaged without regard to religious faith? Mutualists might respond that livable, thick conceptions of justice can only be formed in communities carrying a rich tradition. But that approach remains to be developed. Although no theory is very attuned to the question of reproducibility, mutualist and pluralist views seem less able to cope with these issues than inclusivist or particularist approaches.

Whether mutualism can sustain the strong commitments of people on this site to particular traditions or meet D'Costa's and Griffiths's challenges on issues of truth claims—that holding a position that entails that contradictory positions that may be held by members of other traditions are false—is less clear. Like inclusivists, mutualists construct good, but not perfect, interreligious practices and theological structures on the U.S. site.

Particularism on the U.S. Site

A key strength of particularism is that it appreciates religious differences appropriate to a culture characterized by repeated immigrations, religious diversity, and political nonestablishment. Rooted in postliberal and postmodern philosophical concerns and focused on issues of truth rather than on questions of the extent of salvation, particularists have little to say about challenges on the U.S. site. Obviously, particularists oppose commodification and encourage respect (although not tolerance). They are concerned with globalization, but for them it seems to be a cultural issue that has few religious implications.

The more radical form of particularism that takes diversity to continue eternally—a "many salvations" approach—differs from other forms of particularism in that it *is* focused on salvation. This position clearly values the importance of acceptance of other religious traditions. That Heim regularly engages in interreligious dialogue indicates that his hypothesis does not exclude a priori the possibilities or motivations necessary for engagement. Still, the logic of the hypothesis raises some serious questions as a fitting theological approach in the United States.

If we are all going to come to satisfying, if different, ultimate destinies, why should we talk to one another now? Presumably there are social and political issues that must be addressed, a point mutualism would support, but there seems little reason for conversation about religious practices, beliefs, or aims in the present. Heim claimed that "to focus on ends is to focus particularly on the perspective of persons living in pluralistic environments" because study of religions "exists primarily in the context of the human religious search, and this search is basically oriented to the ultimate conditions people hope to realize as individuals and communities" (Heim 2001, 23–24). However, Hill Fletcher has argued that this focus creates "all too emphatically a separation between Christians and persons of other faiths . . . [that] does not match the lived experience of persons in a pluralistic context" (2005, 76). Our aims overlap; and given traditions may internally have different aims. For example, some Jews encourage and others discourage belief in life after death. Radical particularism seems too neat to account for the multiple forms of religious diversity and overlap.

Part of the problem, as Heim admits, is that "to frame discussion of religions in terms of 'ends' may appear already slanted toward certain faiths," those with a historical character that recognize the importance of "a transformation or journey" rather than those more concerned with a present religious good (Heim 2001, 23). Although his hypothesis notes this distinction, it "still employs conceptual categories of 'the religions' as discrete wholes that can be set one against the other for comparison." Unfortunately, this undervalues the particular persons who relate to many different communities in distinct and complicated ways, a situation only complicated by globalization. By construing each faith tradition as "radically different," we may lose "the common ground necessary for real engagement" (Hill Fletcher 2005, 80–81).

Particularism of all kinds may accept multiple traditions, but "acceptance and tolerance aren't enough"; communication requires *relationship*, and "in order to 'go further' there has to be . . . some kind of a path, or shared direction, along which religious persons can take these next steps." It is unclear that particularism has a way to help us "understand each other, help each other in reaching their goal, or perhaps confront each other about the value of what they are seeking." Knitter may overstate the case, given that particularists like Griffiths engage in comparative theology, but his point reveals a problem in particularism: It seems that all participants in different traditions "can do is wave at each other as they pass" (Knitter 2002, 229–30).

Certainly, particularism preserves the integrity of religious traditions. This gives particularism an antidote to commodification different from mutualism. It may even give particularists a reason to be more focused on practices that could foster resistance to commodification. However, as we noted in chapter 3, we cannot assume that a distinctive countercultural narrative is sufficient to prevent indifference *or* commodification. The complex stories of religious persons in a pluralistic society that breeds hybridity cannot be reduced to any such narrative or theory; such persons will be formed by influences beyond their religious tradition. Just as the division between church and world is not external to Christian believers but cuts through their minds and hearts, so the differences between religious traditions are also internalized in a pluralistic culture.

Particularists find that any rich ethical concept—justice, for example—makes sense only in the context of a particular tradition. But if this is so, then Heim has what seems an internal contradiction in his work. His account of justice is almost classically pluralist: "Since Jesus sought justice as he understood it, we are truly following Jesus when we pursue justice as we understand it. We are following Jesus in a formal, not a substantive, way and need not primarily derive our understanding of justice from the Christian tradition" (Heim 1995, 92). Not only does this statement stand in stark contrast to traditional Christian discipleship, it also depends on the liberal approach Heim rejected and is the antithesis of other particularists' views. The tradition-specific understanding of concepts such as justice means that a particular tradition's substantial understanding of justice must be the starting point for discovering analogues in other traditions and for evaluating one's own view and others'. People must "start where they are." Christians are shaped by their practices of discipleship, including their practices of justice. Heim's account seems not to countenance this well-founded insight characteristic of postliberal theologies, which are the matrix from which particularism arises.

Particularism also may lend unexpected support to the privatization of religious claims. It does not have a strong antidote for those indifferent to the civil rights of other groups or, conversely, to the lack of a religious tradition (or traditions) substantive enough to resist the encroaching power of the nation-state or the consumerism of its culture. Griffiths has argued that "religious people will understand their religious identity to have direct implications for what the state should do" (2001b, 51, 108). That religious traditions can and do clash in the public square over issues in economics, the welfare of the family, and war is clear. But unless particularists are willing to focus on communicating their views in a pluralist context rather than stating their beliefs and arguing for them in tradition-specific terms, there is no reason to think that a pluralistically constituted state will be convinced to do what they think is right. The arguments have to be convincing in a justice system that, whether it is coherent or not, refuses to come to judgment on matters of ultimate truth debated among religious traditions and on positions based on such single tradition-specific claims. In a plural polity, for better or worse, arguments warranted only on grounds particular to a specific tradition simply cannot work. Narrowly warranted claims may indeed be true, but that may be irrelevant in attempting to argue for what the state should do. Politics is the art of the possible, not the statement of the true.

In general, our verdict regarding particularism is *nihil obstat*: nothing prohibits holding this position. It has the strength of providing resources for opposing commodification. Particularism is committed to strong religious traditions and to avoiding reducing religious claims to the mush of a vague and abstract lowest common multiple. Yet it is not clear how their views support the dialogues of life and actions that are crucial in a situation of religious diversity. Particularism may not be inappropriate for this cultural site, but its strengths may be more supportive of maintaining distinctive religious identities than working with and for others on a culturally plural site.

It is not clear, however, that Heim's particular version of particularism is coherent enough to assess. Read one way, it is an elaborate form of inclusivism. Read another way, it is a dismissive form of exclusivism that awards lesser prizes to those of other faith traditions. Read yet another way, it is a form of pluralism that denies a unity beyond diversity. As inclusivist, Heim's view may fit the site; as exclusivist or pluralist, it is hard to say why we ought accept it.

Comparative Theology on the U.S. Site

Comparative theology embraces diversity. People secure enough in their home tradition are positioned to understand, respect, cooperate with, and support others who belong to different faith traditions. Comparative theology advocates moving beyond tolerance by actually engaging and learning from the other tradition. Comparative theology promotes practices that fill Wuthnow's prescription for the reflective religious pluralism needed on the U.S. site.

James Fredericks has argued that globalization has had a huge impact on doing theology in the modern era (2005a). Isolation is impossible; a person is guaranteed to encounter someone of another religion. Leo Lefebure has argued that "to belong to a religious tradition in a pluralistic world challenges us to accept the *responsibility* of exploring our own heritage in dialogue with the other religious traditions of humankind" (1989, 5; *emphasis added*). The Vatican II document *Nostra Aetate* reflects the need for the church to "examine more closely her relationship to non-Christian religions" (§ 1). Comparative theology carries out that mandate in a pluralistic world and society. A fully developed theology in a diverse context is not only necessarily comparative in shape, but also possibly interreligious at root.

Are seekers shopping the aisles of the spiritual supermarket doing comparative theology? Comparative theology seems quite like religious shopping (Wuthnow 2005, 110–29). Although comparative theologians sometimes write as though they "mine" others' texts for nuggets of wisdom, Clooney noted that the "reduction of the compared texts to mere materials for consumption" is to be avoided (1993, 158). That he made this comment indicates that consumerist temptations can be an issue for comparative theology. However, the practice of comparative theology begins with a committed theologian's respect for and understanding of the other tradition. The point of the practice is not to build a personal spirituality, but to serve one's home faith tradition. That doing comparative theological work affects one's spiritual life seems obvious. That it should be done so as to be a boon for the alien tradition is also obvious. But these are not the *goals* of comparative theology. Comparative theologians are not *seekers* of a self, but *servants* of their home traditions.

The stated goal of comparative theology is to understand one's *home* tradition in a different, deeper way. Comparative theologians do not articulate goals for other traditions. Knitter suggested that comparative theology seems to promote Christians' learning from other traditions in order to benefit their own tradition. Knitter found that unbalanced (2002, 209). However, comparative theology requires reciprocity. If one attempts to do comparative theology without return, then comparative theology can be a form of mining or theft. Christian comparative theologians want to and often do work with scholars committed to other traditions. But the choice to reciprocate is up to others (Fredericks 2002, 254). Clooney argued that "comparative theology can be pursued from within any of the religious traditions of the world" (1995, 521); whether it actually is pursued is not for Christians to decide. In the end, lack of reciprocity and disrespectful mining of other traditions has not been a major problem, in large part because members of other faith traditions seem more than willing to work with comparative theologians (see Fredericks 1999, 162) and with pluralist theorists (see Knitter ed. 2005).

Comparative theology is clearly a practice for a committed elite. Comparative theologians must take the time to learn the language, ideologies, rituals, and ethos of another faith tradition. It contributes directly to the dialogue of theological exchange and promotes other forms of dialogue. The danger is that it be practiced only by Western and Christian academics, not that it is an academic practice that requires substantial training. Spiritual shopping is the antithesis of comparative theology. Comparative theology is a practice that fits the injunctions of *Dialogue and Proclamation* and has an important contribution to make to building a reflective pluralism in a nation where all the religions of the world have a home.

When the dialogue between traditions is no longer a dialogue between two or more people, but is internalized by a person, what can result is multiple religious belonging. The most pressing concern for multiple religious belonging regarding our U.S. site is also commodification. Our culture values choice among commodities and is inclined to treating spirituality as just another choice.

Spiritual shopping does not seem to be the antithesis of multiple religious belonging. The difference is more subtle. The key factor seems to be an attitude of submission to the traditions. Spiritual shoppers spend money and some time in a busy life trying to build a spiritual life that can suit them. Multiple religious belongers dedicate their lives to living in and living out the traditions that command their interest. Admittedly, even professional theologians who practice multiple religious belonging sometimes may place too much emphasis on themselves and not enough on the religions. Terry C. Muck, of Austin Presbyterian Theological Seminary, for example, criticized the work of both Sallie King and Roger Corless on this very point in the same issue of *Buddhist-Christian Studies* that featured their articles discussed in chapter 10. He critiqued King for assuming, perhaps with too much confidence, that a person can freely choose religious practices that suit them, and he took issue with Corless over his notion of a "shrine of the heart." Muck put it this way:

> I may be wrong here, but it seems to me that what one ends up doing if one minimizes the objective content of religion, the content that ordinarily determines the stuff out of which practices are designed, is to begin to design a practice based on personal feeling. Sallie says, "I choose the forms of religious practice that I choose because they feel suitable; they feel like a natural expressions of myself." Roger says that his Shrine of the Heart speaks to *my* Deep Self, not God's.

Muck grants "that religious practice needs to take into account individual experience," but wonders if it is not sometimes done "to the exclusion of God's nature" (1994, 176).

This criticism needs to be unpacked. First, it is not clear that doctrines are a *foundation* for practice, but may well be a *component* of practices. The stress Muck places on doctrine presumes a form of foundationalism that a number of particularists and comparativists would dispute. Second, Muck's criticism takes Corless's and King's language at surface value when they talk of their "selves." In a culture that supports spiritual shopping, their language may be unfortunate. However, the work Corless, King, Pannikar, and others do is not so much a quest for a self as it is a task that life has thrust on them. The point is not to shape a self; the point is that "you gamble your life" (Panikkar 1978, 13)—not the price the spiritual shoppers pay unless they leave the spiritual supermarket to live in and live out a faith tradition they have discovered there. Third, multiple religious belongers generally begin in a home tradition. It is not that they "exclude God's nature" in their work, but that they may be forced to gamble on an understanding of God's nature that goes beyond that in their home tradition.

Our judgment on multiple religious belonging in chapter 10 was that it was an esoteric practice that a few might succeed in embodying, but that is beyond the abilities or interests of most of us. No generalized judgment can be made on the contributions of multiple religious belongers. Their particular essays may display or dispel confusion. Their focus on religious issues may force them to ignore or participate in the shared work for justice or other components of the "dialogue of action." Their paths may open ways of understanding for others in their home traditions to learn from traditions of others. They surely have internalized radically the "dialogue of religious experience." At best, multiple religious belongers can achieve native fluency in two incommensurable languages. In so doing, however, they may provide a way not to translate between the two but, for people who are monolingual and monotraditional, to communicate.

Conclusion

In chapter 1, we foreshadowed this conclusion as a "no necessary theory" approach. We have found that none of the theories either perfectly follows or decisively violates the principles that shape the mainstream Christian and Catholic tradition on religious diversity. Even the warnings issued by the Congregation for the Doctrine of the Faith tend to be clarifications rather than condemnations. If pluralist theories shade off into theoretical (if not practical) indifferentism, then they cannot fit the principles. Those exclusivist theories that destine the vast majority of humanity to eternal separation from the bliss of communion with God also do not fit the principles. But theories from classic inclusivism to mutualism to particularism clearly fit the principles more or less well.

Each of these theories also has strengths and weaknesses as a form of theology that is of use to Christians living in the U.S. cultural context. No theory perfectly fits this site. Most—not all—of the authors of this volume incline to doing theology in a contemporary inclusivist or mutualist manner. Most—not all—of us are more sympathetic to a nonfoundationalist approach than to a foundationalist theory. Most—not all—have significant problems with either understanding or accepting Heim's approach. All of us see that no position is perfect. All of us recognize difficulties in each position, even the one each of us inclines to. One particular theory may indeed be true, but we are not in a position to warrant that judgment. We do not have a God's-eye view. Nor does anyone else.

What these theories do show, however, is that there are defenses for the coherence of the four principles we articulated in chapter 3. As noted in chapter 1 (note 3, pp. 192–93) a defense does not give a particular theory about how a set of propositions or principles fits together but shows that the principles can be understood as not contradicting one another. Each of the theories discussed provides ways to defend such compossibility of the four principles. A religious community can coherently accept all of them, provided that they are understood appropriately. Each theory understands those principles in somewhat different ways. But that the principles are at least roughly compatible with a number of theories indicates again that no theory is necessary to explain the principles, but a number of them may be sufficient to show them compatible.

Hence, we do not find the choice of theory to be a problem amenable to a principled solution. Rather, it requires the exercise of prudential judgment on the part of particular religious folk. Deciding which of the tolerable theories is the *best* construct for this tradition located on this site has to be based on the characteristics of the site and the principles embedded in the tradition, the principles that form a "building code" for theology on this site. The decision calls for an exercise of informed judgment, not a deduction.

Admittedly, defenses like this are not satisfying to theorists who want to find a theoretical answer to these kinds of questions. But they are important to show that some practices that assume these principles make sense. Practitioners may be more satisfied with a "no necessary theory" position than theorists would be.

The practices of comparative theology hold great promise for Christian theologizing on the U.S. site. This is not to deny the perils we have adumbrated in chapter 9 and above in this chapter. Some of us have worked in this area to a small extent and can recognize the profound demands that the practice makes on anyone. To learn to do comparative theology is a life's work. But we recognize that comparative theology is not a practice sufficient for our site. It is a realm for an elite who have a major contribution to make, but other practices are necessary if Catholics and other mainstream Christians are to live out their traditions faithfully while working to develop a reflective pluralism in our culture.

We are more chary of multiple religious belonging as a practice or set of practices. Nonetheless, while it cannot be prescribed for any, it should also not be proscribed for the serious practitioners. If the contributions of comparative theologians are slow to emerge, the gifts that multiple religious belongers have for us may take even longer to accept.

But as a corollary to our "no necessary theory" conclusion, we also offer a "no sufficient practice" conclusion. Each of the practices portrayed in *Dialogue and Proclamation* are at least useful, if not necessary, for developing Christians' contributions to the reflective pluralism needed on the U.S. site. But no one of them is sufficient. And it may be that other practices are necessary as well, practices that have not yet emerged. Perhaps an increase in the number of congregations from different traditions sharing a worship space would be a practice worth advocating. Perhaps further joint political campaigns on particular issues where traditions agree on goals and strategies are appropriate. Certainly an increased commitment to educate members of one tradition about other faith traditions is a real necessity (Wuthnow 2005, 305–6 et passim). Any of these specific practices that emerged would have to be evaluated as well.

Practices take time. A person cannot engage in all of them simply because none of us has the time to do them all well. It takes time to learn them, time that spiritual shoppers may be unable or unwilling to give. If one is asked, "Can you play the oboe?" it would be absurd to answer, "I don't know; I never tried." Such an answer would display incredible ignorance about learning to play a musical instrument. As it takes substantial time to learn even the rudiments of playing an instrument, so it takes time to engage in any of the practices that contribute to Christian approaches to and understandings of reflective pluralism. Just as no one can master all the instruments of an orchestra or all the spiritual practices of a tradition, so no one can "do it all." The practices incorporated in the dialogue of life and the dialogue of action may be necessary for all of us to some degree, but neither of these are sufficient for Christians or those among them who are theologians.

The theoretically inclined may find this conclusion unsatisfying. It is certainly not neat. But given that foundationalists and nonfoundationalists have approaches so different as to be incommensurable, that inclusivists and particularists have different foci, that practitioners and theorists have different concerns, and that many of the workers in this vineyard have listened to others and had to shift their positions as a result of learning from others, the terrain we have surveyed cannot but lead to a map displaying a "messy" conclusion. Yet what else might one expect in a world created by the God we worship—a world that has so much religious diversity? For better or worse, understanding the relationship of faith in God and the reality of multiple religions is an untidy and ongoing task.

Notes

Notes to Chapter One

1. Information on Eric Berne is drawn primarily from http://www.itaa-net.org/ta/bernehist.htm, last accessed July 29, 2006. The primary author also worked as an orderly (many years ago) at a hospital where Berne was an attending physician; his theories and practice were frequently the subject of informal discussion.

2. This sketch ignores relatively uncritical approaches and purely academic types of theology. The uncritical acceptance of current, sometimes unfounded, proclamations of "sure biblical teaching" or "papal teaching" are not on our map. Nor are we concerned with the theological speculations of some postmodern theologies developed in academic contexts unrelated to any religious community or institution. Rather, this sketch seeks to place the present work only in a rough-and-ready way in the context of two patterns for theological construction that have some power in and for religious communities.

3. Two propositions constitute the problem of evil. First, "God is all-good, all-knowing, and all-powerful." Second, "There is genuine evil in the actual world." The problem can then be stated as a question: How can a perfectly good being who knows about the evil in the world (as an omniscient being must) and has the power to do something about it (as an omnipotent being must) allow the evil to exist? One religiously inadequate response is to deny that God was all-good, or all-powerful, or all-knowing. That would solve the problem. Two other solutions, however, were proposed as religiously satisfactory: theodicies and defenses. Constructing theodicies, that is, attempting to provide an explanatory theory of how it was that an all-good, all-powerful, all-knowing God could allow genuine evil in the actual world, created more problems than the theories solved. Hence the title of the book, *The Evils of Theodicy* (Tilley 1991). Yet Christians are not intellectually defenseless in the face of the problem of evil. A defense, that is, a demonstration that the two propositions that constituted the problem of evil were compatible (even though they do not seem compatible with each other), could be constructed without invoking any particular theory that explained how God could allow evil in the world. A defense is a "no-theory" solution to the problem of evil. A logical defense is all Christians needed to show that their engaging in the practices of discipleship is not self-contradictory. And, for a practicing Christian, the point is not to theorize about evil but to work to overcome it.

The fact of religious diversity raises a question analogous to the problem of evil.

Basically there are about four principles necessary to guide Orthodox Christians in this area—the rules developed in chapter 3. A number of theories work fairly well to show that these principles fit together or are "compossible" (see pp. 127–29). The theories can also function as defenses of the consistency of these principles. Even if we cannot finally *say* how all these principles fit together perfectly in theory (for we shall argue that none of them is without some strain in holding our principles together), the theories can *show* that these claims are not an inconsistent set of beliefs.

Notes to Chapter Two

1. We are not claiming that the United States is a homogenous site for doing theology. We highlight regional variations in this chapter. We claim only that the characteristics described in this chapter are distinctive to the U.S. site as a whole, not that they exhaustively characterize this diverse cultural site. That is beyond the scope of this, or perhaps any, book.

2. Doing a cultural survey before the religious survey is not an entirely arbitrary choice. It reveals a bias toward taking a certain understanding of local context as determinative of the range of religious possibilities, as terrains determine the sorts of buildings that can be built on a site or the available dyes determine the sorts of colors that can be found in a tapestry pattern. How a tradition inhabits a site affects how it is lived in and lived out. Although the Roman Catholic Church, for example, tends to present a universal faith, as encapsulated in the *Catechism of the Catholic Church*, the demands of building a theology for this living faith tradition on this site and the inevitable U.S. heritage of some native religious and theological elements not mentioned in the "universal" specifications that are detailed in the *Catechism* introduce some transformations of that "universal," off-site, material that are sometimes subtle, sometimes blatant. The same applies to Islam, Judaism, Buddhism, and all the various religious traditions imported into this site (and even Native American religion is diverse, given the particularities of the site). The particularity of the Catholic tradition is reserved for the next chapter.

Notes to Chapter Three

1. Theologians have often sought philosophical foundations for their work. Yet good theological construction, while it must be philosophically perspicuous, does not require a foundational philosophical grounding to be legitimate. Karen Kilby's (2004) recent analysis of Karl Rahner's theological work is an extended illustration of this point. Kilby claimed that the value of Rahner's theology becomes clearer if it is unmoored from its philosophical pier. Many contemporary critics, Kilby included, find that Rahner relied on philosophical claims, derived from post-Kantian and post-Heideggerian philosophy, that are now seen as dubious at best. However they may have once functioned, these philosophical moves do not provide a foundation for Rahner's theology. These arguments do not warrant specific claims that Rahner makes about the human condition and, especially, its religious components. Kilby showed, however, that Rahner's the-

ology survives quite well without those philosophical moves as a foundation if one takes those key claims as constituents in, rather than independent philosophical foundations for, his religious and theological vision.

2. We recognize that the documents we rely on have different levels of authority. We also rely on Sullivan 1992 and Lane 2006. We do not simply "state" the positions that these documents have taken because the attitudes toward and teaching about members of other faith traditions has developed in various ways, as Sullivan shows. At present, scholars are working to find better accounts for the relationships of Christians and Christianity with those who dwell in other traditions and the traditions themselves. Our procedure has been analogous to Sullivan's. We have tried to analyze and state as clearly as possible the principles we see shaping this tradition. Of course, there may be other rules relevant or better formulas than ours, but we think we have uncovered the key principles relevant to theologies of religious diversity. So we do not propose simply to repeat the content of the documents of the magisterium and the commissions but to analyze the principles that they express. Tilley (1999a; 2006) has analyzed some of these documents and we also presume those analyses here.

The rules we formulate show concerns similar, but not identical to, those of other bodies, such as the World Council of Churches (see Ariarajah 2005). The WCC affirms the "uniqueness and finality of Christ" (similar to our second rule), the mission imperative (discussed in light of our fourth rule), and biblical faith (curiously analogous to our third rule). Ariarajah called these "no-go" areas. That appellation suggests that they can be understood as proscriptions analogous to our own. The first rule does not find a parallel in the Protestant "theological boundaries" that Ariarajah surveys. We suspect that this is due in large part to a fundamental disagreement about this issue among Protestants.

3. The arguments of Thiel (2000) and Tilley (2000) show that the Catholic tradition can and does change its claims on specific issues. Sullivan (1992) argues that the varying applications of the rule *extra ecclesiam nulla salus* indicate a deeper principle. We adapted his work in formulating our third axiom. We also note that there is a difference between a rule calling for treating others as "anonymous Christians" or "separated brethren" and calling them or declaring them to be such. The rule guides our conduct; it does not label the others. The controversy about both these terms can be avoided if we recognize them as constituents of prescriptive rules for how we are to treat others well, not as descriptive labels we apply to them.

4. We have chosen to avoid the linguistic quagmire where proponents battle over jots and titles in christology. These battles have led to convoluted theories of religious diversity that are of purely academic, not practical, interest. Is Jesus Christ "constitutive" or "normative" for salvation? What is the difference? In what sense must we understand the "unicity" of salvation in Christ? Is he unique as savior? In what sense? How is his "finality" compatible with the unabrogated covenant God made with Israel?

The rule that seems to us to underlie these claims is better understood, we believe, by using the philosophical understanding of necessary and sufficient conditions. For our purposes, we can say a condition is necessary if for a state of affairs to obtain, the condition must be actual. We can say a condition is sufficient for a state of affairs just in case if the condition obtains, then the state of affairs obtains. To say that Jesus Christ is sufficient for salvation is to say that the actuality of his person and work brings salvation; we do not say that Jesus Christ is necessary for salvation because that would be an inappropriate constraint on God's power (see Tilley 1999a, 323); for that reason, we say Jesus Christ is unique. Nothing else is needed other than Jesus Christ (sufficiency) and no other sufficient condition obtains (uniqueness).

5. We note that the nature of the church is not settled among the authors of this book. The Catholics among us do not entirely agree on ecclesiology. The Protestants among us have further differences. These disagreements, however, are not severe enough to undermine the point being made in this rule. Just what the church is, whether we ought use the term "sacrament," how the Christian community ought to evangelize, and how it is necessary for salvation are important matters. Nonetheless, each of us can understand the rule in a way that we find acceptable, even if one or more of us would prefer to articulate it differently.

Notes to Chapter Four

1. The categorization of approaches to religious diversity is attributed to Alan Race (1983). The present book distinguishes between categories, models, and forms with regard to theologies of religion. The term "categories" refers specifically to the typology of "pluralism, inclusivism, and exclusivism," which "Alan Race put . . . firmly on the map in his influential book *Christians and Religious Pluralism*" (D'Costa 2000, 20). "Models," on the other hand, refer specifically to general, and primarily chronological, groupings within these categories; this chapter discusses a classic model of inclusivism, the next chapter a contemporary model of inclusivism. Finally, the term "forms" will generally be used to explain our own divisions within models (i.e., between the "Christocentric, theocentric pluralism" of Dupuis and the "Trinitarian exclusivism" of D'Costa, both of which, on our map, fall within the model of contemporary inclusivism), even when their own proponents would not classify them as inclusivist primarily to avoid the possible confusion with what we are calling classic inclusivism.

Tilley (1999a), D'Costa (2000, 19–54), and Di Noia (1992), among others, reject the trifold categorization as inadequate; Schmidt-Leukel's defense (2005, 13–27) unconvincingly attempts to save it. The present only uses it where it helps make comparisons more intelligible than not using it would.

2. Karen Kilby, special lecturer in theology at the University of Nottingham, rendered a valuable response to critiques of Rahner by way of an examination of the relationship between Rahner's philosophy and theology. Rahner's notion of the *Vorgriff* is usually taken as the philosophical foundation for his theological work. Kilby proposes a nonfoundationalist reading of Rahner, which contrasts with the view, common among many commentators on Rahner, that his philosophy provides the foundation for his theology. Kilby grounds her discussion and proposal of a nonfoundationalist reading of Rahner in the question "about the relation of the *Vorgriff* as it is presented and defended in his early philosophical works to the *Vorgriff* as it functions in his subsequent theology" (2002, 129). She suggests that we can understand this pre-apprehension of "being" and therefore of God as a *theological* hypothesis rather than a philosophical claim: "*Vorgriff*, in other words, can be read as a claim that is internal to Christian theology rather than as something which stands outside and founds it" (2002, 130). One of the reasons Kilby proposes a nonfoundationalist reading of Rahner is that if Rahner's theology is grounded in his philosophy, then if his philosophy is undermined, so is his

theology. If the philosophical basis of the *Vorgriff* is unpersuasive, then by default his theological position is also at risk. However, another, perhaps more crucial reason for seeking a nonfoundationalist reading of Rahner is that some find the endeavor to ground Christian belief in something more universal, more basic, independent, more general—something that can be regarded as established prior to and apart from faith—to be very problematic. Many postliberal and postmodern theologians find foundationalism problematic because it makes something other than faith—a philosophical foundation—more universal than the universal claims of Christian faith itself. Kilby's nonfoundationalist reading of Rahner avoids this perplexity. Recasting Rahner's theology as nonfoundationalist insulates his theological insights from critics who reject philosophical foundationalism on principle. While this recasting of Rahner's work is not of direct concern for the present discussion, it shows that the whole understanding of "anonymous Christian" can be construed as rooted in an understanding of Christian faith, not in an independent, foundational phenomenological philosophy.

3. This understanding responds to the mid-twentieth-century debates between French Jesuit Henri de Lubac (1896–1991), who held that the natural and supernatural are integral, as indicated by the deep natural desire for God within each human person, and the papal encyclical *Humani Generis*, which held that Lubac's position failed to account adequately for the distinction between nature and grace (Livingston 2000, 209). For Rahner, as for the medieval Dominican Thomas Aquinas, nature is not an independent realm existing outside of, or beyond the order of, grace. Rahner's view opposed other Thomists of the late nineteenth and early twentieth century who regarded nature and grace as each complete in itself.

4. Rahner is using "cause" language associated with Aristotle and Thomas Aquinas. Aristotle identified four types of causation, which included (1) material causation, having to do with the material from which something comes about (e.g., for a chair, wood); (2) formal causation, relating to the form or archetype that defines what an object is ("chairness"); (3) efficient causation, essentially the primary source or ground of any particular object (the carpenter); and (4) final causation, referring to the end, intention, or sake for which something exists or comes about (chairs are for sitting on); see Aristotle, *Physics II*, trans. R. P. Hardie and R. K. Gaye; available from http://classics.mit.edu/Aristotle/physics.2.ii.html; accessed 14 April 2006.

Notes to Chapter Five

1. According to Gavin D'Costa, one of Rahner's contemporary inclusivist interpreters, Rahner saw Jesus as "the final, not efficient, cause of God's universal salvific will. By this, he means that God's universal love is not brought about (efficient cause) by Jesus' death, but that Jesus' death is the final and irreversible expression of what God has always been doing in history (final cause), which has, up until the incarnation, been obscured by the 'ambivalence of human and divine freedom'" (D'Costa 1986, 101). On our account (see pp. 67–68 above) this may be overdrawn because it seems to minimize the distinctive trinitarian theology of Rahner.

2. In his first book Gavin D'Costa described at some length the three general categories of exclusivism, inclusivism, and pluralism. At that point in his career, D'Costa classified himself as an "inclusivist" in the tradition of Karl Rahner.

In the two decades since that book's publication, however, D'Costa has found that the categories don't work. Like the particularists discussed in chapter 7 below, he is more concerned with truth claims than concerns about how God can save non-Christians. His basic point is that if every theologian believes his or her own theology to be essentially correct, then she or he is an exclusivist. Hence, D'Costa now calls his position "trinitarian exclusivism." But of course, on this understanding, everyone is an exclusivist.

His shift is due, in part, the influence of Alasdair MacIntyre and John Milbank. MacIntyre argued for a "tradition-based" understanding of rationality. There is no such thing as "reason," but only reasoning from a particular intellectual place with a heritage that shapes the questions one asks, the concepts one uses, and the answers one is inclined to find. Milbank's broadside against the foundationalism of theologians like Rahner and Gutiérrez (1990) also shaped D'Costa's thinking (D'Costa 2000, 3–12).

D'Costa's shift does not change his position with regard to our framing of the categories. D'Costa still believes that it is possible for people who are not explicitly Christian to be saved and that Jesus Christ has a normative role in human salvation. And so, by our definition, D'Costa remains not only an inclusivist but a *contemporary* inclusivist.

D'Costa's shift is due more to a basic flaw in the typology than from the shift in his own reasoning. While inclusivism and exclusivism are generally defined in such a way as to consider the question of "who is saved," the category of pluralism is usually defined as the idea that religions are relatively equally valid. This distinguishes the pluralist position of John Hick from the position of "universalism," which might more naturally fit within the first two terms of the typology. However, if a person starts the typology from the general definition of pluralism that "one religion is as good as another," then exclusivism becomes redefined as the contrary position: that "one religion is *not* as good as another."

D'Costa's basic point, then, is that no one really believes that all positions are equally right; the pluralists believe that they are more right than the exclusivists, or else they wouldn't be arguing about it. His point is well made, and it shows why this particular typology is not very useful. If everyone is an exclusivist, as D'Costa ultimately claims, then that definition of exclusivism has ceased to function as an explanatory tool and has merely become tautological. D'Costa also seems to assume that theologians' belief in the truth of their own (material) religious convictions must "exclude" the theologians' accepting the (material) beliefs of other traditions. Whether this assumption also properly applies to theologians' (formal) theories about how actual (material) religious beliefs function and whether seemingly opposed religious doctrines are actually opposed are issues that deserve further examination.

3. Despite Dupuis' vindication, the CDF's notification regarding *Toward a Christian Theology of Religious Pluralism* has been included in all subsequent editions of that work. This notification, among other things, construes Jesus Christ as the "sole and universal mediator of salvation for all humanity," and recognizes the universal salvific action of the Holy Spirit. The notification does not use the term "absolute." Dupuis has insisted that the notification simply provides interpretive guidance to readers who might otherwise misread his position. For an argument that Dupuis' position is compatible with the later CDF declaration, *Dominus Iesus*, see Tilley (2006).

4. Biographical information on D'Costa is taken from the University of Bristol Web site, http://www.bris.ac.uk/thrs/staff/gdc.html, accessed 4 August 2006.

Notes to Chapter Six

1. Knitter's position is so nuanced in comparison to many other pluralists that James L. Fredericks also evaluated it separately from other pluralist theologians. Fredericks contends that Knitter's commitment to social justice helps Knitter avoid religious relativism. Fredericks also claims that Knitter is moving further away from a position of pluralism because not all religious traditions are concerned with the sort of justice that Knitter seeks (Fredericks 1999, 132). Knitter's notion that concerns for ecology and justice can serve as opportunities for interreligious cooperation and dialogue still rings true after Fredericks's critique. However, the notion that Knitter may be using semi-exclusive ethical claims to critique cultural and religious conduct is perhaps valid. The notion that most religious traditions contain an interior concern for suffering caused by patriarchy is a claim that Knitter will need to be able to defend as a non-Western imposition. Knitter has worked diligently to avoid this criticism, and for now his work as editor of *The Myth of Religious Superiority: Multifaith Explorations of Religious Pluralism* serves as evidence that he is more than sensitive to concerns that the pluralist position is only attainable within a Christian context. This work, as already noted, contains essays from authors of various religious traditions who support the pluralist position (Knitter 2005b).

2. Haight is often placed in the pluralist category. If the tripartite "exclusivism, inclusivism, pluralism" category were useful, he might well fit there. As we do not think the categorization works, we do not place him in the category. Haight uses the term "pluralist" to describe his position, but it is not clear that it is significantly more "pluralistic" than Dupuis' contemporary inclusivism or Knitter's mutualism.

3. The notification from the Congregation of the Doctrine of the Faith (2005) regarding errors in Haight's work seems rooted in a view that regards language as fundamentally "signifying" rather than "communicative" (see pp. 32–34 above). In each of the areas that the document declares Haight in error, the fundamental problem it finds is that he does not "represent" the tradition in the traditional language. It is, however, just Haight's point that traditional language cannot communicate in the present context, a context so unlike those in which traditional language developed that the words (or their translations into modern tongues) simply have shifted in meaning; they cannot simply be repeated in the present context to communicate the tradition. While Haight takes controversial positions in his work, for example, advocating a "Spirit christology" rather than a "Logos christology," developing a christology "from below" that seems more akin to some pre-Nicene views than Nicene orthodoxy, using a notion of "symbol" that could be more richly developed, etc., the basic presumption that the CDF notification makes, that Haight is wrong because he fails to repeat the form of words from the "old creeds" to represent the tradition in the postmodern world, is dubious.

4. Haight's notion of causality is more modern than the Aristotelian scheme Rahner used. In that sense, there is some incommensurability with Rahner; their terms are similar but are born in rather different conceptual schemes. Hence, we have made this claim rather gingerly.

5. In contrast to the Catholic mutualist tradition, Stanley J. Samartha, a Protestant theologian raised in India, has challenged the notion of the uniqueness of Jesus. Samartha claims that due to the incarnation God entered history and became relative. Samartha goes on to argue that Christian theologians should be cautious about uni-

versalizing the necessity of Jesus because of his relative status within history (Fredericks 1999, 89–90). Samartha's christology serves as a nice counterpoint to Haight's and Kintter's because he too affirms the need to focus on Jesus' proclamation of the kingdom of God. However, Samartha also claims that any metaphysical description of Jesus precludes the possibility of any interreligious dialogue (Fredericks 1999, 92). This would seem to preclude use of either a Logos or Spirit christology, or practically any "high" christology at all. Samartha's position is incompatible with Catholicism because it cannot fit with the second principle developed in chapter 3.

Notes to Chapter Seven

1. Paul Knitter has called this model the "acceptance" model (Knitter 2002, 173–237). Although it is not his own approach, he recognizes its contributions and its potential. We have dubbed it "particularism" because its proponents focus on the particularity of the traditions. Knitter traces this approach to the cultural-linguistic understanding of religious traditions associated with the New Yale School in general and the influential work of George Lindbeck in particular. That we are sympathetic with this view, and with nonfoundationalist views of theology more generally, should be clear. However, we do not sketch that approach here since Knitter has done so (2002, 173–90).

2. Patterns of action, belief, and attitudes create "forms of life." Griffiths, and many contemporary theologians and philosophers of religion, takes this notion from philosopher Ludwig Wittgenstein (1958, §19, §241, p. 226). Griffiths has espoused versions of this functional definition of religion for some time. Earlier renditions are included in journal articles "One Jesus, Many Christs" (Griffiths 1998) and "The Properly Christian Response to Religious Plurality" (Griffiths 1997). In these articles his nomenclature was slightly different. The concept "form of life" was previously called an "account," and "incapable of abandonment" was rendered as "unsurpassability." Despite these differences, the concepts are essentially the same.

3. 3. It is not clear that this functional definition is free from Western or monotheistic bias. See pp. 161-62.

Notes to Chapter Eight

1. Knitter could respond to this challenge by noting that he does not find justice to be universal, but suffering and a degraded ecology to be earth-wide phenomena. It is these phenomena that create a demand that we work for justice. In practice, work for justice means discerning particular problems and working for particular improvements at particular times and places. For Knitter, "justice" does not have to be the absolute that Heim takes it to be, but can be a heuristic principle whose content is to be worked out in the praxis of working for justice. Of course, there are disagreements about justice; no tradition can claim to have a fully warranted, exhaustive understanding of justice. The disputes about the particular demands justice makes in a particular situation are to be adjudicated conversationally.

Heim presumed that Knitter's approach remains foundationalist, deeply indebted to Hick's theory. However, as argued in chapter 6, Knitter has unmoored his view from Hick's Kantian foundationalism. Heim seems to think that Knitter must be committed to a principle such as "because one *conceives of* particular truth claims in particular relationships, these claims are not or cannot be universal in reach." Knitter is not committed to such a principle. Heim seems to make the unwarranted move from the fact that Knitter recognizes that truth claims are constructed and emergent, to the impossibility of those claims being true. Tilley has shown another way to conceive of this, a "consequential realism," which avoids confusing the particular origin of claims with the impossibility of the universal reach of such claims (2000, 156–70).

Knitter does, however, tend to attribute violence to attachment to exclusive truth claims, a position that the particularists in general would dispute (see Knitter 2006, 270). Heim's arguments make sense against classic pluralists, but it is not clear that Knitter and other proponents of mutualism are vulnerable to his challenges.

2. "Incommensurable" does not imply that the traditions cannot be compared to one another. One can ask about their similarities and differences with regard to particular points. For example, How does Christianity compare with Tibetan Buddhism regarding anger? Christianity has a place for righteous anger as a useful tool for change, but Tibetan Buddhists (and most Buddhists) do not find anger a useful tool in any (except possibly the rarest) circumstances. For an extended example regarding Chinese and Western conceptions of virtue, see Yearley (1990).

3. One wants to ask, Which religious end constitutes the fullest human destiny? and What end shall I seek to realize, and why? These questions have both an *objective* dimension—that is, ends must be actually achievable to be worth seeking—and an *evaluative* dimension—that is, not every end counts as "human realization." Considering that, Heim acknowledges that the traditions have different ends and makes room for the possibility of being transformed by learning about them (Heim 2001, 4–5). As Di Noia explained, the universal claims of Christianity and Buddhism, for example, reflect not arrogance but "the seriousness with which each regards the true aim of life and the means necessary to attain and enjoy it." If a religious community takes its own claims seriously it will offer a similar respect to the claims of other communities, and in developing the doctrines that pertain to these other communities there would then be "compelling reasons" to take their teachings into account (Di Noia 1992, 8, 35). If they all finally point at the same end, why bother with them?

4. Several of Heim's fellow evangelicals argue that he has neglected other important Christian considerations, including sin and atonement. His approach also seems in tension with scripture's claims about Christ, the church, and salvation (McDermott 2004, 10; Stackhouse 2001, 93; Stetson, 1997, 359). According to Dupuis, Heim's argument is "deceptive" because it both gives too much credence to human will and misreads the traditional understanding of limbo, which was "devised as a desperate solution . . . for situations in which the conditions for the possibility of a free acceptance of God's offer of grace and salvation seemed to be irremediably inexistent." In short, neither human will nor purgatory can overcome God's universal salvific will. "What is at stake here for Christian belief is not merely the efficacy of God's will to save. It is, even more profoundly, the unity of the human race both in its origin from God in creation and its destiny in him through salvation" (Dupuis 1997, 311–12).

Notes to Chapter Nine

1. Comparative theology is not a theory but a "process or practice" of learning that starts with dialogue as the "basis, or praxis, of doing theology," rather than starting with theology as a "theoretical basis for dialogue" (Fredericks 2004, 26). Theorizing about religions occurs after and stems from dialogue (Knitter 2002, 205); it is not a foundation for dialogue. The practice needs no foundation. The notion that a religious tradition can be treated as an interrelated set of practices in which theology is an emergent component is a characteristic of nonfoundational theologies. For an overview of nonfoundationalism, see Thiel (1994). Tilley (2000) explores this approach with regard to the Catholic tradition.

2. Comparative *theology* should not be confused with comparative *religion*. Comparative religion seeks to "study religion in general," while comparative theology seeks *not* to "make generalizations about religion" (Fredericks 2004, 97) but to compare particular texts, beliefs, rituals, and other practices. Another reason it is called comparative *theology*, not religious studies, is that the goal is truth—one must see if what is true for the Buddhist is true for the Christian, and if this truth has insight for one's own life (Knitter 2005, 207–8). Furthermore, "unlike the philosophy of religion or comparative religion, comparative theology is carried out *within the context of the Christian tradition as well as the academy*" (Fredericks 1995b, 87). A theologian of comparative religion does not necessarily include a confessional background in his or her studies, whereas comparative theology is "an inquiry carried on by believers who allow their belief to remain an explicit and influential factor in their research, analysis, and writing" (Clooney 1993, 4). Thus the comparative theologian's exercise is not merely academic, but has significant impact on the comparativist's theological understanding, personal faith, and religious practice.

3. Members of the seminar noted that independent of Fredericks's work, this interpretation has become one of the standard interpretations of the parable. Even if the illustration is not completely cogent in asserting the source of new insight in general, it may reveal how Fredericks reinterpreted the story, and it does illustrate the point he is making.

4. In a later work, Clooney said that "there must be room for judgments, and judgments must always have sound and accessible bases" (1996, 298). Then in another essay, he stated that judgment cannot be postponed indefinitely but should not be made until one has studied the other religion. However, on the same page he also noted that "there must be a willingness to make timely judgments" (2000, 127). In an even more recent work, he stated that "there can be no single judgment by which one theology is entirely affirmed and other theologies entirely negated" (2001a, 176).

5. Comparative theology is also accused of possibly being too individualistic. There is no group comparative theology; comparative theology is done typically by a single person encountering individual believers and texts from another religion. It is the practice of a small elite. Clooney, for one, is aware of this issue. He has argued that "comparative theology ought not to become yet another project carried on mainly in universities in America and Europe, with resources imported from elsewhere in the world and processed according to Western modes of thought" (1995, 546), including individual research. This is why "actual learning and actual dialogue [are needed] rather than theories about dialogue and learning" for interreligious interaction (Clooney

2003c, 321). Comparative theology must be rooted in interaction, not in individual virtuosity, even though the training it requires is so extensive.

Nonetheless, Parimal G. Patil's response to *Hindu God, Christian God* raises this issue as a problem. Patil accuses comparative theology of being "asymmetrical"—working according to the methods and language identified by "Euro-American style academics" (2001, 185). The question persists: How is this Western domination in theology to be avoided? Perhaps the only answer is to recognize that comparative theology must be a two-way street—that theorists in other traditions can and should do to Christian beliefs, texts, and practices what Christian theologians do to others' works. Comparative theologians would welcome their "mining" Christianity for insights into their own tradition.

References

Vatican Documents*

Ad Gentes. Decree on the Mission Activity of the Church. Second Vatican Council, promulgated December 7, 1965. http://www.vatican.va/archive/hist_councils/ ii_vatican_council/documents/vat-ii_decree_19651207_ad-gentes_en.html.

"Christianity and the World Religions." International Theological Commission, 1997. *Origins* 27 (1997): 149–66.

Dialogue and Proclamation. Instruction of the Pontifical Council for Interreligious Dialogue and the Congregation for the Evangelization of Peoples, 1991. *Origins* 21 (1991): 123–35. http://www.vatican.va/roman_curia/pontifical_ councils/interelg/documents/rc_pc_interelg_doc_19051991_dialogue-and- proclamatio_en.html.

Dignitatis Humanae. Declaration on Religious Freedom. Second Vatican Council, promulgated December 7, 1965. http://www.vatican.va/archive/hist_councils/ ii_vatican_council/documents/vat-ii_decl_19651207_dignitatis-humanae_en .html.

Dominus Iesus. Declaration by the Congregation for the Doctrine of the Faith, August 6, 2000. http://www.vatican.va/roman_curia/congregations/cfaith/documents/ rc_con_cfaith_doc_20000806_dominus-iesus_en.html.

Gaudium et Spes. Pastoral Constitution on the Church in the Modern World. Second Vatican Council, promulgated December 7, 1965. http://www.vatican.va/ archive/hist_councils/ii_vatican_council/documents/vat-ii_cons_ 19651207_ gaudium-et-spes_en.html.

Lumen Gentium. Dogmatic Constitution on the Church. Second Vatican Council, promulgated November 21, 1964. http://www.vatican.va/archive/hist_councils/ ii_vatican_council/documents/vat-ii_const_19641121_lumen-gentium_en .html.

Nostra Aetate. Declaration on the Relation of the Church to Non-Christians. Sec-

---

*Citations are to title and section number. The documents carry different levels of authority and are grouped together only for ease of reference. Internet citations were active when last accessed on July 25, 2006.

ond Vatican Council, promulgated October 28, 1965. http://www.vatican.va/
archive/hist_councils/ii_vatican_council/documents/vat-ii_decl_19651028_
nostra-aetate_en.html.

Redemptor Hominis. Encyclical letter of Pope John Paul II, March 4, 1979.
http://www.vatican.va/holy_father/john_paul_ii/encyclicals/index.htm.

Redemptoris Missio. Encyclical letter of Pope John Paul II, December 7, 1990.
http://www.vatican.va/holy_father/john_paul_ii/encyclicals/index.htm.

Other References

Ariarajah, S. Wesley. 2005. "Emerging New Religious Awareness and Its Challenges
to the Ecumenical Movement." In *Religions Today: Their Challenge to the Ecumenical Movement*, edited by Julio de Santa Ana, 218–32. Geneva: WCC Publications.

Barber, Benjamin. 1996. *Jihad vs. McWorld: How Globalism and Tribalism Are
Reshaping the World*. New York: Ballantine.

Bauer, Walter. 1971. *Orthodoxy and Heresy in Earliest Christianity*. Translated by
R. A. Kraft and G. Krodel. Philadelphia: Fortress Press.

Baum, Gregory. 2005. "Religion and Globalization." In *Globalization and Catholic
Social Thought*, edited by John A. Coleman and William F. Ryan, 141–56.
Maryknoll, N.Y.: Orbis Books.

Benedict XVI, Pope. 2006. "Interpreting Vatican II." *Origins* 35: 534–39.

Berne, Eric. 1964. *Games People Play: The Psychology of Human Relationships*. New
York: Grove Press.

Buckley, James L. 2000. Review of *Jesus Symbol of God*, by Roger Haight, S.J. *Modern Theology* 16 (October): 555–56.

Bush, George H. W. 1991. "Address to the Nation on the Invasion of Iraq,"
http://millercenter.virginia.edu/scripps/diglibrary/prezspeeches/ghbush/ghb_
1991_0116.html. Internet, accessed March 6, 2006.

Cavanaugh, William. 1995. "The Wars of Religion and the Rise of the State." *Modern Theology* 11 (July): 397–420.

———. 2004. "Killing for the Telephone Company: Why the Nation-State Is Not
the Keeper of the Common Good." *Modern Theology* 20 (July): 243–74.

Cheetham, David. 2000. Review of *Faith among Faiths*, by James L. Fredericks. In
Reviews in Religion and Theology 7, no. 3 (June): 358–60.

Clooney, Francis X. 1990. "Reading the World in Christ." In *Christian Uniqueness
Reconsidered*, edited by Gavin D'Costa, 63–80. Maryknoll, N.Y.: Orbis Books.

———. 1991. "The Study of Non-Christian Religions in the Post Vatican II Roman
Catholic Church." *Journal of Theological Studies* 28:3 (Summer): 482–95.

———. 1993. *Theology after Vedanta: An Experiment in Comparative Theology*.
Albany: State University of New York Press.

———. 1995. "Comparative Theology: A Review of Recent Books (1989–1995)."
Theological Studies 56: 521–50.

———. 1996. *Seeing through Texts: Doing Theology among the Srivaisnavas of South India*. Albany: State University of New York Press.

———. 1998. *Hindu Wisdom for All God's Children*. Maryknoll, N.Y.: Orbis Books.

———. 2000. "Openness and Limit in the Catholic Encounter with Other Faith Traditions." In *Examining the Catholic Intellectual Tradition*, edited by Anthony J. Cernera and Oliver J. Morgan, 103–32. Fairfield, Conn.: Sacred Heart University Press.

———. 2001a. *Hindu God, Christian God: How Reason Helps Break Down the Boundaries between Religions*. New York: Oxford University Press.

———. 2001b. Review of *The Depth of the Riches: A Trinitarian Theology of Religious Ends*, by S. Mark Heim. *International Journal of Systematic Theology* 3 (November): 329–31.

———. 2002a. "God for Us." In Cornille, ed., 2002: 44–60.

———. 2002b. "Implications for the Practice of Inter-Religious Learning." In *Sic et Non: Encountering Dominus Iesus*, edited by Stephen J. Pope and Charles Hefling, 157–68. Maryknoll, N.Y.: Orbis Books.

———. 2002c. "Reading the World Religiously: Literate Christianity in a World of Many Religions." In *Theological Literacy for the Twenty-first Century*, edited by Rodney L. Peterson, 242–56. Grand Rapids, Mich.: Eerdmans.

———. 2002d. "Theology and Sacred Scripture: Reconsidered in Light of a Hindu Text." In *Theology and Sacred Scripture*. The 47th Annual Volume of the College Theology Society, edited by Carol J. Dempsey and William P. Loewe, 211–36. Maryknoll, N.Y.: Orbis Books.

———. 2003a. "Guest Editorial." *Theological Studies* 64: 217–24.

———. 2003b. "Hindu Views of Religious Others: Implications for Christian Theology." *Theological Studies* 64: 306–33.

———. 2003c. "Theology, Dialogue, and Religious Others: Some Recent Books in the Theology of Religions and Related Fields." *Religious Studies Review* 29 (October): 319–27.

———. 2005a. "Dialogue Not Monologue: Benedict XVI and Religious Pluralism." *Commonweal* (October): 12–17.

———. 2005b. "Rahner Beyond Rahner: A Comparative Theologian's Reflections on *Theological Investigations* 18." In *Rahner Beyond Rahner: A Great Theologian Encounters the Pacific Rim*, edited by Paul G. Crowley, 3–22. Lanham, Md.: Rowman & Littlefield.

Cobb, John. 2002. *Christian Faith and Religious Diversity: Mobilization for the Human Family*. Minneapolis: Fortress Press.

Corless, Roger. 1990a. "Can Emptiness Will?" In Corless and Knitter, eds., 1990: 75–96.

———. 1990b. "Introduction." In Corless and Knitter, eds., 1990: 1–2.

———. 1994. "A Form for Buddhist-Christian Coinherent Meditation." *Buddhist-Christian Studies* 14: 139–44.

Corless, Roger, and Paul Knitter, eds. 1990. *Buddhist Emptiness and Christian Trinity: Essays and Explorations*. Mahwah, N.J.: Paulist Press.

Cornille, Catherine. 2001. Review of *Faith among Faiths*, by James L. Fredericks. In *Buddhist-Christian Studies* 21: 130–32.

———. 2002. "Introduction: The Dynamics of Multiple Belonging." In Cornille, ed., 2002: 1–6. Maryknoll, N.Y.: Orbis Books.

———. 2003. "Double Religious Belonging: Aspects and Questions." *Buddhist-Christian Studies* 23: 43–49.

Cornille, Catherine, ed. 2002. *Many Mansions? Multiple Religious Belonging and Christian Identity*. Maryknoll, N.Y.: Orbis Books.

Cunningham, Lawrence. 1987. "Crossing Over in the Late Writings of Thomas Merton." In *Toward an Integrated Humanity: Thomas Merton's Journey*, edited by M. Basil Pennington, O.C.S.O., 192–203. Kalamazoo, Mich.: Cistercian Publications.

D'Antonio, William, et al. 2001. *American Catholics: Gender, Generation and Commitment*. Walnut Creek, Ca.: Alta Mira Press.

D'Costa, Gavin. 1986. *Theology and Religious Pluralism: The Challenge of Other Religions*. Oxford: Blackwell.

———. 2000. *The Meeting of Religions and the Trinity*. Maryknoll, N.Y.: Orbis Books.

———. 2002. Review of *The Depth of the Riches: A Trinitarian Theology of Religious Ends*, by S. Mark Heim. *Modern Theology* 18 (January): 137–39.

D'Costa, Gavin, ed. 1990. *Christian Uniqueness Reconsidered: The Myth of a Pluralistic Theology of Religions*. Maryknoll, N.Y.: Orbis Books.

de Lubac, Henri. 1969. *The Church: Paradox and Mystery*. Translated by James R. Dunne. Staten Island, N.Y.: Ecclesia Press.

Di Noia, J. A. 1982. "The Universality of Salvation and the Diversity of Religious Aims." In *Mission in Dialogue: The Sedos Research Seminar on the Future of Mission, March 8–19, 1981, Rome, Italy*, edited by Mary Motte and Joseph R. Lang, 377–91. Maryknoll, N.Y.: Orbis Books.

———. 1990a. "Pluralist Theology of Religions: Pluralistic or Non-Pluralistic?" In *Christian Uniqueness Reconsidered: The Myth of a Pluralistic Theology of Religions*, edited by Gavin D'Costa, 119–34. Maryknoll, N.Y.: Orbis Books.

———. 1990b. "Varieties of Religious Aims: Beyond Exclusivism, Inclusivism, and Pluralism." In *Theology and Dialogue: Essays in Conversation with George Lindbeck*, edited by Bruce D. Marshall, 249–74. Notre Dame, Ind.: University of Notre Dame Press.

———. 1992. *The Diversity of Religions: A Christian Perspective*. Washington, D.C.: Catholic University of America Press.

———. 1993. "The Church and Dialogue with Other Religions: A Plea for the Recognition of Differences." In *A Church for All Peoples: Missionary Issues in a World Church*, edited by Eugene LaVerdiere, 75–89. Collegeville, Minn.: Liturgical Press.

——. 1995a. "Christian Universalism: The Nonexclusive Particularity of Salvation in Christ." In *Either/or: The Gospel or Neopaganism*, edited by Carl E. Braaten and Robert W. Jenson, 37–48. Grand Rapids, Mich.: Eerdmans.

——. 1995b. "Jesus and the World Religions." *First Things* (June–July): 24–28.

——. 1997. "Karl Rahner." In *The Modern Theologians*, edited by David Ford, 118–33. Oxford: Basil Blackwell.

——. 1998. "Is Jesus Christ the Unique Mediator of Salvation." In *Why Are We Here? Everyday Questions and the Christian Life*, edited by Ronald F. Thiemann and William C. Placher, 56–68. Harrisburg, Pa.: Trinity Press International.

Di Noia, Joseph A., and Jerry L. Walls. 1998. "Must the Truth Offend? An Exchange." *First Things* (June–July): 34–40.

Duffy, Stephen. 1999a. "Interreligious Dialogue: The Theological and Comparative Components." *Ecumenical Trends* 28:3 (March): 33–39.

——. 1999b. "A Theology of the Religions and/or A Comparative Theology?" *Horizons* 26 (Spring): 105–15.

——. 2000. Review of *Faith among Faiths*, by James L. Fredericks. In *Ecumenical Trends* 29: 123–26.

Dulles, Avery, S.J. 1983. *Models of Revelation*. New York: Doubleday.

Dunn, James D. G. 1980. *Christology in the Making: A New Testament Inquiry into the Origins of the Doctrine of the Incarnation*. London: SCM Press.

——. 2003. *Jesus Remembered*. Christianity in the Making, volume 1. Grand Rapids, Mich.: Eerdmans.

Dunne, John S. 1972. *The Way of All the Earth: Experiments in Truth and Religion*. Notre Dame, Ind.: University of Notre Dame Press.

Dupuis, Jacques. 1997. *Toward a Christian Theology of Religious Pluralism*. Maryknoll, N.Y.: Orbis Books.

——. 2001. *Christianity and the Religions: From Confrontation to Dialogue*. Maryknoll, N.Y.: Orbis Books.

——. 2002. "Christianity and Religions: Complementarity and Convergence." In Cornille, ed., 2002: 61–75.

——. 2003. "Inclusivist Pluralism as a Paradigm for the Theology of Religions." Typescript of an unpublished paper presented to the conference Religious Experience and Contemporary Theological Epistemology: Leuven Encounters in Systematic Theology IV. Katholicke Universteit Leuven, November 7.

Eck, Diana. 2001. *A New Religious America: How a "Christian Country" Has Now Become the Most Religiously Diverse Nation*. New York: HarperSanFrancisco.

Effross, Walter A. 2003. "Owning Enlightenment: Proprietary Spirituality in the 'New Age' Marketplace." *Buffalo Law Review* 51, no. 3: 483–678.

Elshtain, Jean Bethke, and Paul J. Griffiths. 2002. "Proselytizing for Tolerance." *First Things* (November): 30–36.

Espín, Orlando. 2002. Review of *Inventing Catholic Tradition*, by Terrence W. Tilley. *Horizons* 29, no. 2: 311–14.

Foster, A. Durwood. 1990. "Can Will Be Predicated of Emptiness? A Response to Roger Corless." In Corless and Knitter, eds., 1990: 97–102.

Fredericks, James L. 1995a. "The Incomprehensibility of God: A Buddhist Reading of Aquinas." *Theological Studies* 56, no. 3 (September): 506–20.

———. 1995b. "A Universal Religious Experience? Comparative Theology as an Alternative to a Theology of Religions." *Horizons* 22: 67–87.

———. 1997. Review of *Salvations: Truth and Difference in Religion,* by S. Mark Heim. *Journal of Religion* 77, no. 4 (October): 641–42.

———. 1998. Review of *One Earth, Many Religions: Multifaith Dialogue and Global Responsibility,* by Paul F. Knitter. *Journal of Religion* 78 (January): 133–34.

———. 1999. *Faith among Faiths: Christian Theology and Non-Christian Religions.* New York: Paulist Press.

———. 2002. "James Fredericks Interview." *Buddhist-Christian Studies* 22: 251–54.

———. 2004. *Buddhists and Christians: Through Comparative Theology to Solidarity.* Maryknoll, N.Y.: Orbis Books.

———. 2005a. "Dialogue and Solidarity: Nostra Aetate after Forty Years." September 11, 2005. Vienna (Austria). Unpublished manuscript from a lecture at the Third Official Consultation of the Pontifical Council for Interreligious Dialogue, 1–14.

———. 2005b. "Our Dialogue with Buddhism: Appreciating Nostra Aetate after Forty Years." September 25, 2005. Rome (Italy). Unpublished manuscript of a plenary address given at the Pontifical Gregorian University. 1–19.

Freud, Sigmund. 1950. *Totem and Taboo.* Translated by James Strachey. London: Routledge & Kegan Paul.

———. 1967. *Moses and Monotheism.* Translated by Katherine Jones. New York: Vintage Books.

Friedman, Thomas. 2000. *The Lexus and the Olive Tree.* London: HarperCollins.

Fukuyama, Francis. 1992. *The End of History and the Last Man.* London: Hamish Hamilton.

Gerdes, Louise I., ed. 2006. *Globalization: Opposing Viewpoints.* Detroit: Thomson Gale.

Goizueta, Roberto S. 1995. *Caminemos con Jesús: Toward a Hispanic/Latino Theology of Accompaniment.* Maryknoll, N.Y.: Orbis Books.

Griffiths, Paul J. 1994. "Why We Need Interreligious Polemics." *First Things* (June–July): 31–37.

———. 1996. "Beyond Pluralism." Review of *Salvations: Truth and Difference in Religion,* by S. Mark Heim. *First Things* 59 (January): 50–52.

———. 1997. "The Properly Christian Response to Religious Plurality." *Anglican Theological Review* 79 (Winter): 3–26.

———. 1998. "One Jesus, Many Christs." *Pro Ecclesia* 7 (Spring): 152–71.

———. 2001a. "An Evangelical Theology of Religions?" In *No Other Gods Before Me? Evangelicals and the Challenge of World Religions,* edited by John G. Stackhouse, 163–69. Grand Rapids, Mich.: Baker Book House.

———. 2001b. *Problems of Religious Diversity: Exploring the Philosophy of Religion.* Malden, Mass.: Blackwell.

———. 2003. "Complementarity Can Be Claimed." In *Learning from Other Faiths,* edited by Hermann Häring, Janet Martin Soskice, and Felix Wilfred, 22–24. London: SCM Press.

Gutiérrez, Gustavo. 1990. *The Truth Shall Make You Free: Confrontations.* Translated by Matthew J. O'Connell. Maryknoll, N.Y.: Orbis Books.

Haight, Roger, S.J. 1999. *Jesus Symbol of God.* Maryknoll, N.Y.: Orbis Books.

———. 2005. "Pluralist Christology as Orthodox." In Knitter, ed., 2005: 151–61.

Heft, James, ed. 1996. *Faith and the Intellectual Life: Marianist Award Lectures.* Notre Dame, Ind.: University of Notre Dame Press.

Heim, S. Mark. 1985. *Is Christ the Only Way? Christian Faith in a Pluralistic World.* Valley Forge, Pa.: Judson Press.

———. 1995. *Salvations: Truth and Difference in Religion.* Maryknoll, N.Y.: Orbis Books.

———. 2001. *The Depth of the Riches: A Trinitarian Theology of Religious Ends.* Grand Rapids, Mich.: Eerdmans.

Heneghan, Tom. 2005. "Laïcité Law Enjoys Wide Support, but Calls for Change Mount." *National Catholic Reporter,* 25 November: 16.

Henesy, M., and R. Gallagher. 1997. *How to Survive Being Married to a Catholic.* Liguori, Mo.: Liguori Press.

Hick, John. 1980. *God Has Many Names.* Philadelphia: Westminster Press.

———. 1989. *An Interpretation of Religion.* New Haven: Yale University Press.

———. 2001. Review of *The Depth of the Riches: A Trinitarian Theology of Religious Ends,* by S. Mark Heim. *Reviews in Religion and Theology* 8, no. 4 (September): 411–14.

Hick, John, and Paul F. Knitter, eds. 1987. *The Myth of Christian Uniqueness: Toward a Pluralistic Theology of Religions.* Maryknoll, N.Y.: Orbis Books.

Hill, Kenneth, and Rebecca Wong. 2005. "Mexico-US Migration." *Population and Development Review* 31, no. 1: 1–18.

Hill Fletcher, Jeannine. 2005. *Monopoly on Salvation? A Feminist Approach to Religious Pluralism.* New York: Continuum.

Howell, Martha. 1986. *Women, Production, and Patriarchy in Late Medieval Cities.* Chicago: University of Chicago Press.

Huntington, Samuel. 1996a. *The Clash of Civilizations and the Remaking of World Order.* New York: Simon & Schuster.

———. 1996b. "The Clash of Civilizations?" In *The Clash of Civilizations? The Debate. Foreign Affairs* (Summer): 1–25.

Jenkins, Philip. 2003. *The Next Christendom: The Coming of Global Christianity.* New York: Oxford University Press.

Justich, Robert, and Betty Ng. 2005. "The Underground Labor Force Is Rising to the Surface." New York: Bear Sterns Asset Management, Inc. Accessed March 4, 2006 at http://www.bearstearns.com/bscportal/pdfs/underground.pdf.

Kaiser, Robert Blair. 2003. "Dupuis Profile." In Kendall and O'Collins, eds., 2003: 222–29.

Keathley, Kenneth Donald. 2000. "An Examination of the Influence of Vatican II on Clark Pinnock's 'Wider Hope' for the Unevangelized." Ph.D. diss., Southeastern Baptist Theological Seminary, Wake Forest, North Carolina.

Kendall, Daniel, and Gerald O'Collins, eds. 2003. *In Many and Diverse Ways : In Honor of Jacques Dupuis*. Maryknoll, N.Y.: Orbis Books.

Kennedy, Eugene. 1979. "Quiet Mover of the Catholic Church." *New York Times Magazine*. 23 September: 66–67.

Kilby, Karen. 1997. *Karl Rahner*. London: Fount.

——. 2002. "Philosophy, Theology and Foundationalism in the Thought of Karl Rahner." *Journal of Scottish Theology* 55, no. 2 (May): 127–40.

——. 2004. *Karl Rahner: Theology and Philosophy*. London: Routledge.

King, Sallie B. 1994. "Religion as Practice: A Zen-Quaker Internal Dialogue." *Buddhist-Christian Studies* 14: 157–62.

——. 2005. "A Pluralistic View of Religious Pluralism." In Knitter, ed., 2005: 88–101.

Knitter, Paul F. 1984. Review of *God Has Many Names: Britain's New Religious Pluralism*, by John Hick. *Journal of Religion* 64 (April): 266–68.

——. 1985. *No Other Name? A Critical Survey of Christian Attitudes toward the World Religions*. Maryknoll, N.Y.: Orbis Books.

——. 1987a. "Preface." In Hick and Knitter, eds. 1987: vii–xii.

——. 1987b. "Toward a Liberation Theology of Religions." In Hick and Knitter, eds. 1987: 178–200.

——. 1995. *One Earth, Many Religions: Multifaith Dialogue and Global Responsibility*. Maryknoll, N.Y.: Orbis Books.

——. 1996. *Jesus and the Other Names: Christian Mission and Global Responsibility*. Maryknoll, N.Y.: Orbis Books.

——. 1997. "Author's Response [to reviews of *Jesus and the Other Names*]." *Horizons* 24 (Spring): 285–96.

——. 2001. Review of *Faith among Faiths*, by James L. Fredericks. *Theological Studies* 62, no. 4 (December): 874.

——. 2002. *Introducing Theologies of Religions*. Maryknoll, N.Y.: Orbis Books.

——. 2003. "Author's Response [to reviews of *Introducing Theologies of Religions*]." *Horizons* 30 (Spring): 125–35.

——. 2005a. "Introduction." In Knitter, ed., 2005: vii–xi.

——. 2005b. "Is the Pluralist Model a Western Imposition?" In Knitter, ed., 2005: 28–42.

——. 2006. "A Bridge or Boundary? Vatican II and Other Religions." In *Vatican II Forty Years Later*. The Fifty-First Annual Volume of the College Theology Society, edited by William Madges, 261–82. Maryknoll, N.Y.: Orbis Books.

Knitter, Paul F., ed. 2005. *The Myth of Religious Superiority: Multifaith Explorations of Religious Pluralism*. Maryknoll, N.Y.: Orbis Books.

Koester, Helmut. 1991. "Epilogue: Current Issues in New Testament Scholarship." In *The Future of Early Christianity: Essays in Honor of Helmut Koester*, edited by Birger A. Pearson et al., 467–76. Minneapolis: Fortress Press.

Küng, Hans. 1976. *On Being a Christian*. Translated by Edward Quinn. Garden City, N.Y.: Doubleday.

LaCugna, Catherine. 1991. *God for Us: The Trinity and Christian Life*. San Francisco: HarperSanFrancisco.

Lane, Dermot A. 2006. "Nostra Aetate: Encountering Other Religions, Enriching the Theological Imagination." In *Vatican II Facing the 21st Century: Historical and Theological Perspectives*, edited by Dermot A. Lane and Brendan Leahy, 202–36. Dublin: Veritas.

Lasch, Christopher. 1979. *The Culture of Narcissism: American Life in an Age of Diminishing Expectations*. New York: Norton.

Lefebure, Leo. 1989. *Life Transformed: Meditations on the Christian Scriptures in Light of Buddhist Perspectives*. Chicago, Ill.: ACTA Publications.

———. 1996. Review of *Salvations: Truth and Difference in Religion*, by S. Mark Heim. *Christian Century* 113, no. 7 (February 28): 236–37.

Lindbeck, George A. 1984. *The Nature of Doctrine: Religion and Theology in a Postliberal Age*. Philadelphia: Westminster Press.

Livingston, James C. 2000. *Modern Christian Thought*. Vol. 2, *The Twentieth Century*. Upper Saddle River, N.J.: Prentice Hall.

MacIntyre, Alasdair. 1984. *After Virtue: A Study in Moral Theory*. Second Edition. Notre Dame, Ind.: University of Notre Dame Press.

———. 1988. *Whose Justice? Which Rationality?* Notre Dame, Ind.: University of Notre Dame Press.

Mallon, Colleen. 2005. "Globalization at Large: Approaching the Ecclesial Question of Tradition in the Twenty-first Century." In *New Horizons in Theology*. College Theology Society Annual Volume 50, edited by Terrence W. Tilley, 135–61. Maryknoll, N.Y.: Orbis Books.

Mann, Charles. 2005. *1491: New Revelations of the Americas before Columbus*. New York: Alfred A. Knopf.

McClendon, James Wm., Jr. 1986. *Ethics*. Systematic Theology Volume I. Nashville: Abingdon.

McCool, Gerald, ed. 1975. *A Rahner Reader*. New York: Seabury Press.

McDermott, Gerald R. 2004. "Jesus and the Religions: A New Paradigm for Christian Engagement?" *Books and Culture* 10 (January–February): 9–11.

Milbank, John. 1991. *Theology and Social Theory: Beyond Secular Reason*. Oxford: Basil Blackwell.

Miller, Vincent. 2004. *Consuming Religion: Christian Faith and Practice in a Consumer Culture*. New York: Continuum.

Moltmann, Jürgen. 1993. *The Trinity and the Kingdom: The Doctrine of God*. Translated by M. Kohl. Philadelphia: Fortress Press.

Montaigne, Michel de. 1957. "We Should Meddle Soberly with Judging Divine

Ordinances." *The Complete Essays of Montaigne*, trans. D. M. Frame, 159–60. Stanford, Ca.: Stanford University Press.

Muck, Terry C. 1994. "Joint Buddhist-Christian Practice: A Critique of Corless, Habito and King." *Buddhist-Christian Studies* 14: 173–76.

O'Malley, John W., S.J. 2006. "Vatican II: Did Anything Happen?" *Theological Studies* 67 (March): 3–33.

Ong, Walter, S.J. 1996. "Realizing Catholicism: Faith, Learning and the Future." In Heft, ed., 1996: 31–42.

Orsi, Robert. 1996. *Thank You St. Jude: Women's Devotion to the Patron Saint of Hopeless Causes*. New Haven: Yale University Press.

Pannikar, Raimon (Raimundo). 1973a. "The Category of Growth in Comparative Religion: A Critical Self-Examination." *Harvard Theological Review* 66: 113–40.

———. 1973b. *The Trinity and the Religious Experience of Man: Icon-Person-Mystery*. Maryknoll, N.Y.: Orbis Books.

———. 1978. *The Intra-religious Dialogue*. New York: Paulist Press.

———. 2004. *Christophany: The Fullness of Man*, trans. Alfred DiLascia. Maryknoll, N.Y.: Orbis Books.

Parker, Laura. 2001. "USA Just Wouldn't Work without Immigrant Labor." *USA Today* July 22. Accessed 4 March 2006 at http://www.usatoday.com/news/washington/july01/2001-07-23-immigrant.htm.

Patil, Parimal G. 2001. "A Hindu Theologian's Response: A Prolegomenon to 'Christian God, Hindu God.'" In Clooney 2001a: 185.

Penelhum, Terence. 1983. *God and Skepticism: A Study in Fideism and Skepticism*. Dordrecht: D. Reidel.

Phan, Peter C. 2003a. "Jacques Dupuis and Asian Theologies of Religious Pluralism." In Kendall and O'Collins, eds., 2003: 72–85.

———. 2003b. "Multiple Religious Belonging: Opportunities and Challenges for Theology and Church." *Theological Studies* 64 (September): 495–519.

Portier, William. 2004. "Here Come the Evangelical Catholics." *Communio* 31 (Spring): 35–66.

Race, Alan. 1983. *Christians and Religious Pluralism: Patterns in the Christian Theology of Religions*. London: SCM Press.

Rahner, Karl. 1966. *Theological Investigations*. Vol. 5, *Christianity and the Non-Christian Religions*. London: Darton, Longman & Todd.

———. 1976. *Theological Investigations*. Vol. 14, *Observations on the Problem of the "Anonymous Christian."* New York: Seabury Press.

———. 1978. *Foundations of the Christian Faith*. New York: Seabury Press.

———. 1983. *Theological Investigations*. Vol. 18, *On the Importance of the Non-Christian Religions for Salvation*. New York: Crossroad.

Renard, John. 1998. "Comparative Theology: Definition and Method." *Religious Studies and Theology* 17: 3–18.

Rescher, Nicholas. 1985. *The Strife of Systems: An Essay on the Grounds and Implications of Philosophical Diversity. Pittsburgh: University of Pittsburgh Press.

Roof, Wade Clark, et al. 1993. *A Generation of Seekers: Spiritual Journeys of the Baby Boom Generation.* San Francisco: HarperSanFrancisco.

Sacks, Jonathan. 2003. *The Dignity of Difference: How to Avoid the Clash of Civilizations.* Revised edition. New York: Continuum.

Schloesser, Stephen, S.J. 2006. "Against Forgetting: Memory, History, Vatican II." *Theological Studies* 67 (June): 275–319.

Schmalz, Matthew N. 2003. "Tradition and Transgression in the Comparative Theology of Francis X. Clooney." *Religious Studies Review* 29: 131–36.

Schmidt-Leukel, Perry. 2005. "Exclusivism, Inclusivism, Pluralism: The Tripolar Typology Clarified and Reaffirmed." In Knitter, ed., 2005: 13–27.

Schreiter, Robert. 1985. *Constructing Local Theologies.* Maryknoll, N.Y.: Orbis Books.

———. 1992. "Religious Pluralism from a Postmodern Perspective: A Response to Paul F. Knitter." *Anglican Theological Review* 74, no. 4: 443–48.

———. 1997. *The New Catholicity: Theology between the Global and the Local.* Maryknoll, N.Y.: Orbis Books.

Stackhouse, John G., Jr. 2001. "What Has Jerusalem to Do with Mecca?" *Christianity Today* 45, no. 11 (September 3): 92–93.

Stetson, Brad. 1997. Review of *Salvations: Truth and Difference in Religion,* by S. Mark Heim. *Christian Scholar's Review* 26 (Spring): 358–59.

Sullivan, Francis A. 1992. *Salvation outside the Church? Tracing the History of the Catholic Response.* New York : Paulist Press.

———. 2006. "Response to Karl Becker, S.J., on the Meaning of *Subsistit in.*" *Theological Studies* 67 (June): 395–409.

Tanner, Kathryn. 1997. *Theories of Culture: A New Agenda for Theology.* Minneapolis: Fortress Press.

———. 2003. Review of *The Depth of the Riches: A Trinitarian Theology of Religious Ends,* by S. Mark Heim. *Journal of Religion* 83 (April): 289–90.

Thiel, John. 1994. *Nonfoundationalism.* Minneapolis: Fortress Press.

———. 2000. *Senses of Tradition.* New York: Oxford University Press.

Thompson, William R. 1983. "World Wars, Global Wars, and the Cool Hand Luke Syndrome: A Reply to Chase-Dunn and Sokolovsky." *International Studies Quarterly* 27, no. 3: 369–74.

Tilley, Terrence. 1991. *The Evils of Theodicy.* Washington, D.C.: Georgetown University Press.

———. 1999a. "'Christianity and the World Religions': A Recent Vatican Document." *Theological Studies* 60 (June): 318–37.

———. 1999b. "A Misreading of Haight." Letter to the Editor. *Commonweal.* November 19. Accessed April 16, 2006 at http://www.highbeam.com/library/docfree.asp?DOCID=1G1:57888974&ctrlInfo=Round19%3AMode19b%3AD ocG%3AResult&ao=.

———. 2000. *Inventing Catholic Tradition.* Maryknoll, N.Y.: Orbis Books.

————. 2004. *History, Theology, and Faith: Dissolving the Modern Problematic.* Maryknoll, N.Y.: Orbis Books.

————. 2006. "Christian Orthodoxy and Religious Pluralism." *Modern Theology* 22 (January): 51–63.

Vatican Council II. 1984. *Documents of Vatican II.* Edited by Austin P. Flannery. Grand Rapids, Mich.: Eerdmans.

von Balthasar, Hans Urs. 1966. *The Moment of Christian Witness.* Translated by Richard Beckley. New York: Newmann Press.

Wittgenstein, Ludwig. 1958. *Philosophical Investigations.* 3d ed., trans. G. E. M. Anscombe. New York: Macmillan.

Wolfe, Alan. 2003. *The Transformation of American Religion: How We Actually Live Our Faith.* New York: Free Press.

Wuthnow, Robert. 2005. *America and the Challenges of Religious Diversity.* Princeton, N.J.: Princeton University Press.

Yearley, Lee. 1990. *Mencius and Aquinas: Theories of Virtue and Conceptions of Courage.* Albany: State University of New York Press.

ZENIT (Rome). 2005. "Nonbelievers Too Can Be Saved, Says Pope Refers to St. Augustine's Commentary on Psalm 136 (137)." November 30. Accessed April 16, 2006, at http://www.zenit.org/english/visualizza.phtml?sid=80888.

Zizioulas, John. 1985. *Being as Communion: Studies in Personhood and the Church.* Crestwood, N.Y.: St. Vladimir's Seminary Press.

Index

abolitionist movement, 30
absolutes, multiple, 140
Ad Gentes: and universal salvation, 51
Africans: and forced migration, 18
aggiornamento: as correlational theology, 5, 6
Amaladoss, Michael, xiv
Americas, indigenous population of, 14-15
  and disease, 14-15
analytical philosophy: and particularists, 111
anonymous Christians, 71-78, 83, 92, 179, 180
  and faith, 74, 75
apologetics, 118, 119, 122
  and dialogue, 121
Aquinas, Thomas
  and Aristotle, 117
  and local theology, 7
Augustine
  on consequences of original sin, 52-53
  and Plato, 117
  on salvation of Jews and Gentiles, 51-52
  and universal salvation, 52, 53, 54
authority: Knitter on, 108

Barnes, Michael H., xiv
Barth, Karl: as positivist theologian, 5
believing, practice of, 8
Benedict XVI, 5, 13, 108
Berne, Eric, 2-3
Buddha, 56, 57, 113, 169

Bultmann, Rudolf: as correlationalist theologian, 4
Bush, George H. W.: and just-war criteria, 31-32
Bush, George W.: and religious conservatives, 32

capitalism, global, 39, 42, 43, 48
Catholicism, Hispanic: cultural diversity of, 22, 23
"The Challenge of Peace," 31, 32, 33
Christianity
  as the absolute religion, 66
  as hybrid religion, 162
christology
  judging the orthodoxy of, 104, 105
  of Roger Haight, 102-5
  trinitarian, 84, 86
christomonism, 86
church
  and divine communication, 107
  and French Revolution, 27
  and global culture, 72
  and grace, 71, 72, 77
  and legal system in U.S., 30-31
  and mission *ad gentes,* 58
  necessity of: for salvation, 51, 57-60, 88, 89
  and salvific will of God, 57-60
  and support of immigrants, 30
  as sacrament of salvation, 58, 89, 107
  as sacramental necessity, 59-60
Clement of Alexandria, 55

and mutualism, xiii
orientational, 129-31, 141
reflective, 18, 19, 20, 123
and theocentrism, 97, 98
pluralists
on Christ's role in salvation, 96, 104
and differences of religious beliefs, 114, 118
focus on dialogue and engagement, 94
on necessity of church for salvation, 96, 107
pneumatology, 86, 87
Pontifical Council for Interreligious Dialogue, 58
Portier, William: and sited theology, xii
practice, 10-11
    human, 47-48
    intertextual, 151
    mystical, 99, 100
    prophetic, 99, 100
    religious, 48
    and reward and punishment, 48
    rules for, 48, 49-63
    theological reflection as, 8
privatization, 13
problems, common: as ground for interreligious cooperation, 108, 109
proclamation: witness as, 58-59
proscription: and rules for practical theology of religious diversity, 50
proselytism: and tolerance, 119, 122, 123

Rabin, Yitzhak, 95
Race, Alan, xii, 123
Rahner xii, xiii, 4, 52, 64-81, 83, 85, 88, 92, 104, 110, 179, 180
    and anonymous Christians, 71, 72, 73, 74, 75, 76, 77, 78, 83, 92, 179
    and Aquinas, 65
    and Christian missionary effort, 71
    on the church, 72, 77
    and classic inclusivism, 64-73
    as correlationalist theologian, 4
    on dignity of the other, 78
    and divine revelation, 75
    on grace, 65, 66, 69, 70, 75, 76
    and Heidegger, 65

and Ignatius of Loyola, 65
and inclusivist view of salvation, xii, xiii
and Jesus as absolute savior, 81, 86
and Kant, 65
and lawful religion, 69-70
on nature and grace, 76
and particularity of salvation in Jesus, 66
on presence of Christ in other religions, 64
and religious diversity, 66
on salvation of non-Christians, 64
and the Spirit, 67, 76, 77
trinitarian theology of, 67
on universal salvation, 52
and universality of God's saving will, 66
Ratzinger, Joseph (Benedict XVI): as positivist theologian, 5
Roman Catholic Church
    diversity of: in U.S., 21, 22, 23
    geographical location of, 21-22
    nativist attacks on, 16-17
Reagan, Ronald: and conservative Christians, 31
Redemptor Hominis: and salvation through Jesus Christ, 54
religion
    absolute: Christianity as, 66
    commodification of, 10, 37-41, 180, 181
    disestablishment of, 26
    establishment, disestablishment, and nonestablishment, 13-14
    as form of life, 112
    freedom of: and immigrants, 15-16; and nonestablishment, 38
    lawful, 69-70
    nonestablishment of, 26-35, 181
    privatization of, 29-30
    wars of, 27-28
religions
    as instruments of God's grace, 104
    integration of, 133, 134
    theology of: foundationalist and nonfoundationalist positions, xii, xiv
    world: as willed by God, 79

DATE DUE

APR 24 '09			
8/4/09			
12/22			